D0907180

Five Years, Four Fronts

Five Years, Four Fronts

The War Years of Georg Grossjohann,
Major, German Army (Retired)

Georg Grossjohann
Translated by Ulrich Abele

Foreword by Theodore C. Mataxis

Historical Commentary by
Keith E. Bonn with Wolf T. Zoepf

Aegis Consulting Group
Bedford, Pennsylvania

Technical Editor: *Keith E. Bonn*
Production: *Patricia K. Bonn*
Maps: *Aegis Consulting Group*
Printer: *Mercersburg Printing*

Aegis Consulting Group, Bedford, Pennsylvania 15522
© 1999 Edeltraud Grossjohann
All rights reserved.
Printed in the United States of America
07 06 05 04 03 02 01 00 99   5 4 3 2 1

ISBN: 0-9666389-2-1 (clothbound)
         0-9666389-3-X (paperbound)

Except where otherwise noted, photos are from the personal collection of Georg Grossjohann. The photos of the Hartmannsweiler Kopf and vicinity appear by the courtesy of Lieutenant Commander Ron Wolin, US Navy (Retired), and are from his extraordinary collection of World War II militaria. Collectors may contact him in Chesapeake, Virginia at (757) 547-2764.

Contents

List of Maps   vii

A Guide to Tactical Symbols   ix

Foreword   xi

Preface   xv

1 The Polish Campaign: Stukas, Haystacks, and
   High-Ranking Generals   1

2 Interlude in the Valley of the Ahr   10

3 Through the Ardennes and into the Maginot Line   14

4 Between France and Russia   24

5 Finding the "Real War": Russia 1941   36

6 Breakout from the Mius Bridgehead   49

7 Recovery, Relaxation, and the Tedium of Reserve   55

8 Back to the Line   61

9 Disaster at Cherkassy   73

10 Uman   78

11 The 198th Leaves Russia   88

12 Back to France!   94

13 Retreat Through the Rhône Valley   115

14 Regimental Commander   131

15 Farewell to My Regiment   144

16 Intermediary   152

17 Farewell to the Front   158

18 The Last Days of the War   164

19 Discharge from the Army   169

Epilogue   176

Appendix A. The Military Curriculum Vitae of Georg Grossjohann   179

Appendix B. The Divisions in Which Georg Grossjohann Served
During WWII   187

Notes   195

Editor's Annotated Bibliography   199

Index   201

List of Maps

1-1   The German Invasion of Poland, 1–17 September 1939   4

2-1   Valley of the Ahr and Surrounding Region   11

2-2   East Prussia, *circa* 1939–40   12

3-1   Ardennes/Luxembourg/Moselle River Valley   18

3-2   The Invasion of the Low Countries and France, May–June 1940   19

3-3   Major German Attacks in the Maginot Line, 15–19 June 1940   21

3-4   Fortress Fermont   22

4-1   Germany, 1939-40   28

4-2   Northwestern France   34

5-1   Northwestern France   39

5-2   Approximate Position of German and German Allies' Forces, Late Autumn 1941   44

5-3   Defensive Positions on the Mius River Line, November 1941–June 1942   46

6-1   Attack Out of the Mius Bridgehead, July 1942   52

8-1   Successive Defensive Positions of the 198th Infantry Division, November 1943–25 January 1944   67

8-2   Attack by the Soviet *Fifth Guards Tank Army* to Create the Cherkassy Pocket, 25 January 1944   69

9-1   Withdrawal to Avoid Encirclement in the Cherkassy Pocket, 25–29 January 1944   75

9-2   198th Infantry Division in the III Panzer Corps Attack to Break Through to the Cherkassy Pocket   76

10-1   Separation of the 198th Infantry Division Headquarters and Support Units from Kampfgruppe Keiser, March–June 1944   80

11-1   Operation BAGRATION, Summer 1944   91

12-1   German Troop Dispositions, Southern France, Summer 1944   98

13-1   The Invasion of Southern France, 15 August 1944   118

13-2   Operations in Southern France, 19–28 August 1944   120

13-3   Withdrawal of the 198th Infantry Division up the Rhône Valley, 23–29 August 1944   123

14-1 The 198th Infantry Division Area of Operations,
       Late September–Mid-October 1944   134

14-2 The 198th Infantry Division Area of Operations,
       Mid-October–Early November 1944   142

15-1 Operations in the Belfort Gap, Late November, 1944   148

15-2 Situation in the High Vosges, Early December 1944   150

19-1 Post-War Germany and Austria   172

A Guide to Tactical Symbols

Types of Units

Infantry

Mountain Infantry

Volks-Grenadier

Armored Infantry/
Panzer-Grenadier

Armor/Tank/Panzer

Mechanized Cavalry/
Armored Reconnaissance

Sizes of Units

III	Regiment
X	Brigade/Group/ Combat Command
XX	Division
XXX	Corps
XXXX	Army
XXXXX	Army Group (Soviet Front)

Example

308 [X] 198

Grenadier Regiment 308, 198th Infantry Division

German Forces

Allied Forces

Prepared Defenses/
Fortifications

Foreword

The editor of this book first requested that I consider writing the foreword to this book because of my assignment just after WWII to the 7734th US Forces European Theater Military History Detachment at Garmisch, Germany, on a project gathering accounts of operations in the Soviet Union from German general officers. Initially, I was somewhat reluctant because of how little I seemed to have in common with the author, Major Georg Grossjohann. After all, we fought on opposite sides in the Second World War. I have met many of my old enemies from that war — mostly from the 6th SS-Mountain Division "Nord" against whom we fought during Operation NORDWIND in the Low Vosges Mountains—but Major Georg Grossjohann of the 198th Infantry Division and I didn't have a single battlefield in common. We did not even share the bond that sometimes connects old foes, particularly if those foes have fought honorably and well.

Neither did we have similar backgrounds as soldiers. The author was commissioned from the ranks after practically a full career as an enlisted man; I entered the military service as a second lieutenant of infantry directly from the ROTC program at the University of Washington and a brief stint as a corporal in the 41st Infantry Division of the Washington State National Guard. The author had earned the Knight's Cross of the Iron Cross before I had heard my first shot fired in anger, and he heard his last shot fired just days after my men and I had received our baptism of fire in the shrapnel-riven, snow-decked mountain forests of the Bois de Lichtenberg. Other than the fact that we had both served in some of the least-studied and unheralded battles of World War II in Europe, we seemed initially to have shared few experiences. Writing a foreword for the memoirs of such a man seemed like it might be an exercise in vagaries or generalities, at best. I have never been accused of being at a loss for words, but there didn't seem to be much that I could say about this book that anyone else could not have said just as well, and perhaps more eloquently.

However, because of my keen interest in and bias in favor of "eyeball accounts" by combat participants, I finally agreed to read the draft manuscript. At worst, I thought, it would confirm my doubts, and I would simply have to decline the opportunity to pen the requested foreword. The more I read, though, the more engrossed and intrigued I became. I found this was not just another war story of campaigns during WWII, but the author's detailed account of his experiences at small unit level during peace, mobilization, and war.

Unlike many of the memoirs of too many officers, it was not a recounting of "how we won the war," or a compendium of "should have beens/could have beens"—the latter of which are most often written by officers of the losing side of wars, whether Germans after World War II or Americans after Vietnam. Most of all, it was not a series of anecdotes designed to convince the reader that the German Army was the greatest in the history of warfare and that the lesser armies of the world would do well to emulate it in all ways. There are more than enough of those to fill the "military history" shelves of every bookstore, and they often do—especially in American military exchanges.

Instead, what I found in this combat veteran's tale was strikingly different from anything I had yet read by a German officer. Georg Grossjohann was not a member of the aristocracy, or even the scion of a proud and ancient military family. He was not born to privilege, nor did he ascend to lofty rank—or even desire to achieve one. He was an infantry soldier who did his best, and expected not only his men and his peers, but his superiors to do the same. He never shirked his duty, no matter how hazardous, and despite being given many opportunities to avoid further combat, could not stand to be away from the action so long as there was action to be had.

The increasingly heavy losses in the German Army after the loss of Sixth Army at Stalingrad and the destruction of the German field army in Africa were reflected in Grossjohann's assignments. They often caused him not only to be elevated to ever higher echelons of command in the midst of the frenzy of war, but also on short notice to join entirely new organizations with vague missions. Similarly, I assumed command of 2d Battalion, 276th Infantry in the first week of our combat. Grossjohann's units were chronically undermanned and his soldiers often exhausted. Toward the end of the war, they were often filled with replacements culled from other branches and services. Many of the men in the battalion I commanded in WWII had, until recently, been Air Corps crewmen, anti-aircraft gunners, or even students from the Army Specialized Training Program (ASTP). In his last command, many of Grossjohann's men did not even speak German. I experienced a similar phenomenon during the Korean War when my regiment, the 17th Infantry, received many Puerto Rican replacements who could not speak or understand much English; this compounded the problem we already had with our KATUSAs (Korean augmentees), who mostly could also only speak pidgin, at best. As a result of these circumstances, Grossjohann and I both understood what Clausewitz meant by the "friction" of war which so frequently resulted in "unintended consequences" in spite of well-conceived plans and orders.

As I read the flashbacks about the author's service in the post-WWI German Army, the 100,000-man Reichswehr, I remembered the predictions of my ROTC Professor of Military Science. Wounded and decorated as an infantry company commander in 1918, he recognized that the Reichswehr had been used as a cadre for Hitler's 350(+)-division Army, and foresaw that our own 190,000-soldier force would be used in much the same way. He told us that to keep step with the coming rapid mobilization, we must be prepared to assume the responsibilities of officers at least two ranks above our own. In addition, he cautioned us as young infantry officers that we must prepare our wives to be widows. They were harsh words, but also practical advice for leaders who would be out in front of units from the branch which was to endure eighty percent of the American soldiers killed in action in the looming war.

While reading accounts of his changing units during the expansion of the German Army and his subsequent turbulent assignment history, I reflected on my similar experiences during mobilization. First assigned to the US Army Reserve's 96th Infantry Division after commissioning, I volunteered for active duty and was assigned to the 6th Infantry Division. After Pearl Harbor, I was soon caught up in the expansion of the Army and "cadred" first to the 91st Infantry Division, and then to the new Army of the United States 70th Infantry Division, the unit with which I eventually went into combat in France.

The more I read, the more realized that I did, in fact, have much in common with Grossjohann, although not just from the war in which we shared only a common theater of operations. Later in my Army service, I served as executive officer for—and then commanded—an infantry regiment in the Korean War, and served four tours in Southeast Asia during the Vietnam War. Altogether, I spent about five years in combat, as did Grossjohann. Although I gradually recognized that we had a lot in common in other ways, it was in these combat tours that I acquired the "mindset" which I think is what most closely links Georg Grossjohann and me across space and time—the critical importance of "bonding" in combat, and the soldier's warrior ethos. That is what transcends our different nationalities, causes, and theaters of war. Neither of us had much time for fripperies or superficialities. The trappings of things militaristic or the transient fads of the moment—be they the transparent nonsense of National Socialism for Grossjohann, the trumped-up bodycount game of my Vietnam tours, the "Zero Defects" philosophy of my last years of service, or the "Consideration for Others" claptrap of today's Army, none of them held or would have held the slightest interest for either of us. Indeed, because such things often get in the way of more important endeavors (training, learning, fighting), we despised them and ignored them when we could. The author's unconcealed loathing of equivocation, moral cowardice, professional vanity, and selfishness among some of his fellow officers—the same kind of things scorned by Anton Myrer's archetype of the Good Officer, Sam Damon in *Once an Eagle*—struck a sympathetic chord with me. Been there, seen that—far too much of it! Take the time to perceive the author's unabashed esteem for those—of all ranks—who exhibited anything approaching the unspoken passion the author had for soldiering, and you'll discover the frank admiration of a kindred soul. All good soldiers can identify with the warrior ethos that is the basic cornerstone of esprit and high morale.

Perhaps most of all, read carefully and you will note that while Georg Grossjohann "tells it like it was" about superior and peer alike, he never has anything bad to say about his soldiers. Not once. As was pounded into me as a young officer, "there are no bad units, only bad officers." That is the mark of a military leader who shoulders responsibilities as he should, and, as General Colin Powell admonished American officers a few years back, one who "loves soldiers" with "all [his] heart, all [his] soul, and all [his] mind." In this day and age of nearly "bloodless" victories (at least for our side), wall-to-wall TV coverage of generals' briefings, and constant commentary by high-ranking "experts," all sickeningly reminiscent of the Vietnam War's "Five O'clock Follies" mentality, it is easy to forget what is most important to victory on the battlefield. That is the sacred bond between leader and led which creates the morale that enables soldiers to prevail in combat. Georg Grossjohann reminds us all that the full acceptance by the combat infantryman of this "kill or be killed" philosophy is the sine qua non for victory.

If I ever get around to writing my memoirs, although they will be mostly be about other wars and other times, I hope I can tell my story with as much honesty, class, and plain truth as this one. Perhaps then, the reader will learn as much about the real, grass roots US Army as I learned about the German Army before and during World War II from Georg Grossjohann.

THEODORE C. MATAXIS
Brigadier General, US Army (Retired)
Southern Pines, North Carolina
August 1999

Preface

I was born and raised in East Prussia, the ancient land of the pagan Pruzzens, whose inhabitants were finally converted to Christianity centuries ago by the Teutonic Order. Beginning in about 1000 A.D., our ancestors had, with varying degrees of forcefulness, rejected all attempts to bring them into the Roman fold. They maintained their own culture, language, property, and most of all, their freedom. This lasted until about 1250, when, with the blessings of the Pope and the Holy Roman Emperor of the German Nation, the Teutonic Order began the brutal subjugation of this peaceloving and hospitable people.

In the end, the Pruzzens became Christians, of course, and lost almost everything of their culture in the process. The original purpose of the Order of the Teutonic Knights, born at Acre during the Third Crusade in 1190, was the propagation of Christianity. Soon, however, this holy endeavor became of less interest to the Knights than the acquisition of as much land as possible. Centuries later, this land, eventually called East Prussia, lent its name to the whole dominion of the Imperial Electors of Brandenburg—Prussia and their successors, the kings of Prussia. Eventually, Prussia covered practically the entire area from the river Memel to the Rhine.

During its history, East Prussia suffered a fate similar to that of many border regions. It was frequently conquered, lost, and recaptured, by Poles, Swedes, Russians, and French. Nevertheless, it was, for centuries, mostly Prussian, until 1945, when it was lost to the East, perhaps forever.

Often praised as the "land of a thousand lakes and dark forests" because of its distinguished and incomparable beauty, it not only seemed unique to its inhabitants, but also to all those who spent time in my homeland for professional reasons or as guests. Sparsely populated, with about sixty-eight inhabitants per square kilometer, it was a purely agricultural land without any notable industry. Königsberg, the only major city of the region, was founded in 1255 in honor of the Bohemian King, Ottokar II. The city was protected by a castle of the Teutonic Order.

With a population of 370,000, it was a significant commercial port and gateway to the East. The amicable relations that existed for generations between traders from Königsberg and their partners in the East were resumed soon after WWI and WWII, even if the German partners may have established themselves in Hamburg after 1945.

It is well documented that my family settled and lived in the Nathanger area, near the Teutonic Order's fortress in Preußisch Eylau, since 1585. It was in the immediate proximity of the vast forests of the "Stablak," the holy region of the pagan Pruzzens. Most likely, my family had been in the country much longer, and some of my ancestors were probably of old Prussian descent.

In the middle of the nineteenth century, my grandfather took over an estate of about 1,000 acres from the counts zu Dohna. It was in the upper country, and as I once read, it was appropriately given the pretty and fitting name, "The Blond Sister of the Masurian Lakes." It was situated along the border of the formerly Polish province of Ermland, the always staunchly Catholic island in the otherwise Protestant East Prussia, and was separated from it in the south by the Passarge River. Until 1926, the beginning of the great extinction of estates in the East, this was the home of my family, beloved and unforgotten!

Because of its location at the border, East Prussia was also a land of soldiers, and its population always showed a special affection for its military men who were, after all, the guarantors of its freedom.

Children love their parents to tell them about their own childhood, and my son was no exception. Yet, he did not only want to learn everything about my time as a child, but also about my times as a soldier. Since I spent seventeen years, beginning with 1928, as a soldier, there was so much to report that I considered it best to write down as much as possible for him. This includes my twelve years of peacetime service that I almost finished, the immediately following years of war, and in the end, some stories about the times afterwards.

I was a *Zwölfender*, so called after a twelve-point buck, because under the provisions of Versailles, the minimum enlistment in the *Reichswehr* was twelve years. My enlistment began in 1928, so my time in the German Army was during a time that saw more changes than any half century had before.

At that time, we soldiers were bound by an oath only to the constitution, and thereby to the Fatherland. We were prohibited from any political activity, a regulation that was also respected to a large degree by the National Socialists . . . initially anyway. Due to this political abstinence, the armed forces were mostly kept out of the altercations before Hitler's seizure of power. Therefore, my recollections of this time derive mainly from what happened in my barracks and in my private life.

Looking back, I know that some negative memories of my time as a soldier balance out the positive. There are many cheerful, some even comical ones. The good memories exceed the others, and so it is with me as it is with millions of other old soldiers whose recollections of their active military service were always positive, in spite of occasional annoyances. I know that, unfortunately, this is no longer the case for so many young Germans whose only service has been with the *Bundeswehr* . . .

My years as a *Zwölfender* have been covered in a separate volume, aptly entitled *Der Zwölfender*, published separately by Jahn und Ernst Verlag in Hamburg. Nevertheless, I occasionally allude to some of my experiences before the war in the following pages, to add depth, color, and perspective. Very soon after 1945, more was written about the Second World War than was following the First, and these by people of different kinds and for very different reasons. By and large, there were three groups: The first group includes the historians in this country and abroad; the second includes the so-called military writers; and the last includes the numerous authors from the entertainment industry with a bias toward the political left, prevailing—at least in public exposure—in modern days.

Historians who, without sufficient distance, took it upon themselves to report about WWII and the causes for its outbreak certainly did not have an easy task. Shortly after the war's end, many important sources were, for various reasons, still closed to them. Even today, this limitation still exists in some regards, although the recent opening of some Soviet archives and other sources previously unavailable may help in this regard. In my experience, few historians made an adequate effort to delve into the period about which they were writing, to convey the naked truth as it existed at the time. Too many superimpose their *ex post facto* theories and values on the helpless characters of history, all too many of whom cannot speak for themselves. Many simply parrot what others have written before them.

The second group, military writers, were usually high-ranking officers from the German and Allied sides. They created reports with very personal views, closely connected with the personalities—and reputations—of the writers. Most of the German officers' memoirs have, in my experience, one thing in common: I rarely discover admissions of errors. They all pretend to always have known all along what to do, what was possible, what was not, etc. Afterwards, they tried to justify their participation in the wrong-doing as having always been against their better judgment.

Their Allied colleagues in that profession had problems too. After all, it took them six years to destroy the *Wehrmacht*, and at that, the Russians carried the greatest part of the load. On one hand, the Allied writers had to be careful not to pass on too much honor to Hitler's *Wehrmacht*, lest they should seem fawning or overly-magnanimous, but neither could they pass on too little, thereby denigrating their own victories. The air force writers had special difficulties—while the air raids by the Western Allies were indeed a great burden for the German civilian population, astonishingly, they had hardly any serious impact on the production of the German defense industry until 1945. The Americans, British, and French, with consistent air superiority and often even supremacy, battled against the last contingents of the shrinking, mismanaged, and fuel-poor *Luftwaffe*. Considering this, one may conclude that Allied aerial achievements may not have been quite as impressive as they are sometimes made out to be.

It is also true that many Allied military writers fail to admit their mistakes or miscalculations. In my opinion, Churchill was one of the exceptions and would stand above too much pedantry.

The third group, and financially the most successful one, was made up of the authors of the entertainment industry. For these, the lost war offered an inexhaustible supply of material to which they helped themselves even under the specter of the postwar era. I am certain that, if the victory had been ours, the same people would have found a way to use whatever material became available in some profitable way. War books, describing the war as it truly was, like many written after 1918, did not sell after 1945 . . . but those that were "Anti-" did, whether their content bore any resemblance to reality or not! All one had to do was adjust the focus.

During the course of many years, a friend from my East Prussian homeland filled a whole shelf with anti-military or, more accurately, *anti-officer* novels. The authors didn't have to worry about getting enough clientele for their books. They could bet on the resentments of all those who were once bound to obedience to others, but thought of themselves as much superior, at least by their own estimation. If this episode in their lives remained without success as far as awards, promotions, and so forth are concerned, they yearned secretly for vindication later on. The anti-authors helped them lick their wounds.

The recipe for such a book is simple. The cast of characters would typically include a brutal general, thirsty for glory at any price; stupid, incapable officers; a bunch of helpless, sensitive, and gentle soldiers; and some girls with whom the soldiers engage in a bit of sex during their home leave. That should do to fabricate such a novel.

Now for the plot. During a surprise breakthrough by the enemy, the officers naturally fail completely. After having puked the stolen French wine, the drunken general is killed by brave Red Army soldiers. Only a young sergeant keeps a clear head. He gathers the scattered *Landsers*, and leads them safely back to their own lines. Throw in a hideous war crime or two and some anti-Hitler jokes by the enlisted men, and you've got a winner every time.

After the war, I often met people, even former comrades, who told me how bitterly they struggled against their superiors' attempts to send them to officer training. Many even told me they had declined awards due them.

These almost-always specious—and easily disproven—"recollections" were only fueled by the cheap, trite, gushingly sentimental, and absolutely unrealistic trash written by the entertainers.

Of course, there *were* incompetent and even cowardly soldiers among the fifteen million who wore field gray during the war, but, for heaven's sake, not only among the officers . Such men were the exception, not the rule, no matter what those authors would like to make their readers believe. In WWII, 287 German *generals* were killed in the front lines. Between 22 June and 31 October 1941, my division lost about fifty-one percent of its officers versus thirty-eight percent of its NCOs and troops. It is obvious that relatively few of our combatant officers indulged in fanatical self-preservation. Incidentally, in the German Army, the vast majority of officers had once served as soldiers, and quite certainly, incompetence and cowardice were not qualities that were likely to get one selected for schooling and promotion to the officer ranks!

In America and England, there were, and still are, authors who produce this same type of literature, dealing with mischievous, cowardly officers and so on, maybe even at a somewhat higher literary level than on our side. This genre especially bloomed in America following their first lost war, after Vietnam.

The Russians, of course, had only heroes!

Based on the multitude of experiences I had during my seventeen years of active duty, in war and in peace, I could not have written anything like the works produced by these three categories of authors. I lack the ability to fantasize or hallucinate to the extent necessary to alter my recollections of the way it was, for better or for worse. More importantly, I do not possess the necessary flexibility of character or intellect to imagine that I saw things in, say, 1940, with the knowledge that I have today.

I also cannot bring myself to say that I opposed the Hitler regime, or that I knew it was doomed all along. I was amazed how the number of persons counting themselves as part of the German resistance reached astronomical heights after 1945. (It's still growing, apparently.)

I was not one of them. Before 1933, we career soldiers, on one hand, were blocked from participating in political events; from 1939 on, the distance between me and the enemy was often between zero and a thousand meters. In between, as an NCO, I concerned myself with policing the barracks, training soldiers, going on leave—all the stuff that one does in any peacetime army. My enlistment would have been over in 1940, but by then, I had to mostly concentrate my energy on resisting our opponents on the battlefield, and didn't have a great deal of opportunity to worry about what was going on in the political arena.

Considering how many other Germans were supposedly resisting Hitler, I often wonder nowadays about where the ninety-eight percent of the German population who voted for him came from. I wonder even more about where they went.

I cannot report anything of grand historical importance of my time as a soldier. I am not a historian, I was no commander in chief, and no chief of staff. I lived through the war with the perspective of a worm, so to speak, which basically is also true for my service in peacetime. I am certainly no entertainer.

This is simply my story. To avoid unnecessary, possibly polluting influences, I have disdained using outside sources as much as possible, and told only of my own personal memories. I do consider the possibility that my very personal memories between 1928 and 1945 may say more about the *Reichswehr* and *Wehrmacht* than some more scholarly views. Many other veterans may have different recollections of one part or another. Therefore, in their view, this book may not be quite objective, but I have done my best based on the content of my knowledge and the dictates of my conscience.

GEORG GROSSJOHANN
Major, a. D.
Altenhain, 1987

Chapter One

The Polish Campaign: Stukas, Haystacks, and High-Ranking Generals

Historical Commentary

September 1939 marked the end of bloodless victories for the Third Reich *and the beginning of general war in Europe for the second time in less than twenty-one years. After formally repudiating the military limitations of the Versailles Treaty in March 1935, Hitler supervised the vigorous reconstruction of the German Armed Forces* (Wehrmacht), *including a new Navy* (Kriegsmarine) *and Air Force* (Luftwaffe), *as well as a much larger and partially mechanized Army* (Heer). *The following four years brought immense territorial gains for Germany, without the loss of a single German soldier's life in combat. Between March 1936 and March 1939, the German Army reoccupied the Rhineland, annexed Austria, seized most of Czechoslovakia, and occupied Lithuanian Memel, all without firing a shot. As a result, when the German Army was called upon to invade Poland in September 1939, it was a hugely reinvigorated, but essentially untried organization.*

Given their defensive mission, the Polish Army seemed to have a chance against the Germans. The Germans were committing fourteen mechanized divisions, forty-four infantry and mountain divisions, and a cavalry brigade to the conquest of the twenty-three-year-old Polish state. With a standing establishment of thirty infantry divisions, a cavalry division, and eleven cavalry brigades, the Poles could effectively double that number upon mobilization. Their soldiers were generally well-trained and highly-motivated. Unfortunately for them, mobilization of their Army only began on 30 August, and the German invasion began on 1 September. Furthermore, a significant number of units had to be deployed in the east in the event of a Soviet invasion, thus diluting what was available to oppose the Germans in the west. With the conclusion of the German-Soviet Non-Aggression Pact on 23 August, the Poles had every reason to suspect trouble from the East.

To make things worse for the Poles, their Army was supported by a weak and poorly-equipped Air Force which counted fewer than four hundred combat aircraft. Overwhelmed by the 1,400 fighters and bombers of the Luftwaffe, *the Polish Air Force offered no effective resistance throughout the conflict. Tanks and antitank guns were outdated and few in number, and were deployed ineffectively in a dispersed fashion; horse cavalry was utterly anachronistic on a mid-twentieth-century battlefield, and nearly useless for anything beyond reconnaissance missions in difficult terrain. With the Polish Air Force out of the picture, the* Luftwaffe *vigorously supported the ground maneuver of the Army with, among other types, siren-equipped Stuka dive bombers which sowed not only destruction, but demoralization among the Polish defenders. To make the situation completely untenable, the Polish High Command deployed their forces well forward, with few defensive features between them and the attackers. This posture made defense not only difficult for Polish tactical commanders, but actually facilitated a massive German envelopment of a huge portion of the Polish forces, namely the Poznan Army, in western Poland.*

Basically, the German strategy was to engulf the better part of the Polish Army in a huge double envelopment, with the jaws of the pincers snapping shut on Warsaw. Further fingers would stretch out to seize Lvov in the south, and Brest in the north. To this end, the German Army High Command (Oberkommando des Heeres, *or OKH) organized their forces into two Army Groups. Army Group South, under von Rundstedt, consisted of Blaskowitz' Eighth, von Reichenau's Tenth, and List's Fourteenth Armies. Von Rundstedt's troops carried out the main effort, spearheading their assault with ten of the mechanized divisions. Army Group North, under von Bock, consisted of von Küchler's Third and von Kluge's Fourth Armies. Von Bock's units cut the Danzig/Gdansk Corridor, isolating Poland from the sea, and enveloped the Polish Modlin and Pomorze Armies from the north.*

Overall, although intending to take advantage of the superior mobility afforded by armored formations and the flexibility of the "aerial artillery" that was Luftwaffe *air support, the strategic concept and corollary course of the campaign was one more akin to the Schlieffen Plan of the First World War than to later German "Blitzkriegs." The material destruction of the Polish Army was the principal objective, rather than concentrating on the elimination of the Poles' will to fight. Indeed, although they fought valiantly and stubbornly, the outnumbered and outmaneuvered Polish Army was well on the way to destruction at the hands of the Germans even before the invasion by the Soviet Army from the east on 17 September.*

Although a few Polish horse cavalry units conducted some limited incursions into East Prussian territory, the Germans seized the strategic and operational initiative from the beginning and retained it throughout the campaign. Overall, while German panzer and Luftwaffe components performed well enough in the Polish campaign, it was the German infantry, supported by horse-drawn artillery, who fought and won the lion's share of the battles. The campaign was concluded with stunning brevity, and at a relatively "low" cost to the attackers—a little over 10,000 Germans killed.

Georg Grossjohann's part in the Polish campaign was somewhat removed from the foci of critical combat actions. On 1 September 1939, von Küchler's Third Army attacked from East Prussia against the Modlin Army and part of Group Narev. The author's unit, the 21st Infantry Division, was one of the eight infantry divisions von Küchler threw against the Poles to this end. As members of the divisional Field Reserve Battalion, Georg and his men followed in the train of the Division's combat echelons. Although the author consequently saw limited action in this campaign, his experiences were nevertheless illustrative of many of the key features of the war in Poland in 1939.

Georg Grossjohann Remembers . . .

The German populace was deeply disconcerted by the developments of 1939, as the government probably was also. We soldiers, who knew the true face of war from the stories told us by our fathers, were certainly not enthused about the prospect of an early hero's death. We were, however, prepared to do our bitter duty.

By the middle of July 1939, all of our units were at the sort of high personnel strength that we had previously only seen during mobilization exercises. Everything went along in a smooth and well-organized fashion, like a well-oiled machine. No one spoke of a looming war, and secretly, each of us hoped that the whole process would run its course as it all had before.

In the beginning of August, our 2d Battalion, Infantry Regiment 3 conducted a fortification exercise along the Polish border. We built positions for use in the event of a possible altercation with Poland. It appeared to

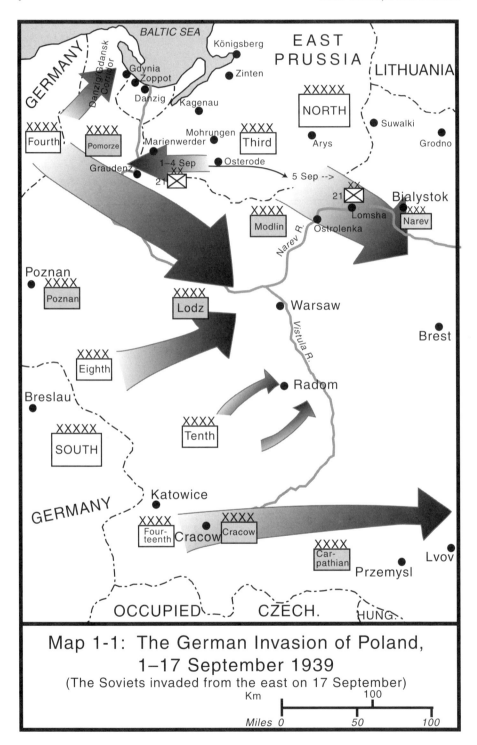

Map 1-1: The German Invasion of Poland, 1–17 September 1939
(The Soviets invaded from the east on 17 September)

me that measures were being taken to avoid leaving married soldiers, particularly those with children, in combat positions. As my company was departing our garrison, I was transferred to a newly-organized divisional replacement battalion (Field Replacement Battalion 21). The departure from my 9th Company comrades, with whom I had spent many years, was not easy. I attempted to return to my old gang as a replacement during the first days of the war in Poland, but was foiled.

The Field Replacement Battalion was stationed in the East Prussian town of Mohrungen, as was the headquarters of Third Army. I saw that the signs around the barracks simply read "Exercise Army—3d Command." The Third Army's commanding general was our old commander, *General der Artillerie* Georg von Küchler. The nucleus of this Army was composed of the three original East Prussian infantry divisions. The Third Army only had eight infantry divisions, the 4th Panzer Brigade, and the only horse cavalry brigade in the German *Wehrmacht*. The Third Army was also one of the smallest field armies to participate in the Polish campaign; the Tenth Army, in comparison, boasted eighteen divisions, including two *panzer* and two motorized divisions.

Upon arriving in Morhrungen, I reported to the *Stabsfeldwebel* of the replacement company to which I had been assigned. He was a nice, older man nearing the completion of his twenty-fourth year of service—one of the rare "twenty-four pointers!" He had only made it that far because he had been assigned to the regimental band. Now this old *Stabsfeldwebel* had been assigned as our first sergeant. Unfortunately, he would later be killed in a pointless attack in the Maginot Line.

In short order, after assembling in Mohrungen, the Field Replacement Battalion outfitted and equipped the arriving reservists. Immediately thereafter, the Battalion was entrained and transported to join the rest of the 21st Infantry Division, already in their assembly areas near the Polish border in the vicinity of Graudenz. As an older NCO, I was henceforth sent back to our East Prussian garrison town, where over a decade ago I had "endured" my recruit training.

Osterode was a town of about 16,000 inhabitants, and our adjacent garrison held about 1,000 soldiers. Despite our modest pay, our presence was always an important factor in the economy of this small city. Except for occasional unseemly incidents—and by today's standards, even these incidents were harmless affairs, such as minor fist fights—all businesses welcomed soldiers within their walls.

Businesses which provided diversions or entertainment for the troops during their free time were naturally an important part of the economic community of each garrison town. During my time there from.1928 to 1939, Osterode had two movie theaters, three dance cafés, a good dozen cozy and friendly taverns, and many excellent guest house/restaurants. There were a great many things for soldiers to do in and around Osterode. Our favorite activities included eating, drinking, dancing, taking part in different sporting activities, or traveling about the beautiful East Prussian countryside by boat or by railroad. Every weekend there were dances held in three large halls in town, although one could also choose to go to a private club, either the type to which one needed a *bona fide* invitation, or one at which one could pay to enter. Cultural activities were not especially favored by young infantrymen. Of course, the deciding factor regarding our off-duty endeavors was always the same—money!

Five marks was generally enough for an evening. To get into the mood to go to a dance hall, for example, one had to have the means to purchase the necessary potions; a little beer and maybe a shot of rye whiskey were usually enough to dispel any hesitation. The bottle of beer cost twenty-five *pfennigs* in a tavern; cognac cost twenty, and a shot of clear whiskey was ten *pfennigs*. Once fortified, we would make our way to the close combat ball.

Once at the objective—a dance hall—one had to carefully protect one's remaining resources, as the entry fees were usually about three marks. To remain in the place, one must always have a drink in front of him, so we had to use our soldierly initiative to find ways of staying. There was usually a long bar in the room adjacent to the dance hall, and this is where the poorest amongst us could be found. Grizzled veterans of the First World War made the best companions here, as they would happily refresh our drinks while regaling us with stories of their heroic deeds at Verdun or on the Somme. A truly virtuoso sponge could extend this act for hours by reacting with expressions of wonderment and astonishment as these old boys spun their tales. In the end, however, it often took equal imagination to pry oneself away from these beneficent old men; usually, conjuring the illusion of bodily needs was the answer!

It is well known that our East Prussian girls were beautiful, and the population generally also retained a positive attitude about the soldiery. In fact, among most of the girls, military service was a large part of the measure of a man, and was expected. Nevertheless, the situation in Osterode was complicated—it was not simple for the girls of a town of its size to remain respectable around a population of 1,000 predominately single young men. This was especially so for nice girls, who had to contend with many young men who were less than completely serious in their ultimate intentions. The selection of the right partner required a profound knowledge of the psyche of post-pubescent infantrymen. However, it seemed that this knowledge was passed on to the girls of every old garrison town through their mother's milk, as many of their female antecedents had confronted precisely the same challenges for generations before. Further, most girls knew that most troops were not likely to keep their mouths shut once they got back to the barracks, and that they would promptly announce the news of their successes to their barrack mates the next morning. Thus, most young infantrymen didn't stand a chance of satisfying their blooming passions with a nice girl in Osterode.

This did not mean that the citizens or girls of Osterode had anything against a long-term attachment to a career soldier . . . and we were all career soldiers in the *Reichswehr*! Indeed, quite the opposite was true. Since most twelve-pointers went on to have respectable careers in civil service, marriage to one of us was generally welcomed by the families of our garrison town.

Like many East Prussian towns, Osterode lay beside a large lake. In the lower quarter of the city, there was an esplanade which on holidays would be decorated with garlands of lanterns a kilometer long. There was also a pier with docks for small passenger ships, on which one could make excursions. Many of our East Prussian lakes were connected by canals, so travel to many destinations was easy. In the early 1930s, our battalion founded a water sports club, from which one could obtain the use of a canoe or rowboat. In the summer months, these boats were in more or less constant usage during off-duty hours, mostly to chauffeur our girlfriends around to quiet inlets or small rush-covered islands.

In the late summer of 1939, however, these idylls were rapidly becoming a thing of the seemingly distant past. It was the last days of August 1939. I had once read that the summer days before the beginning of the First World War were especially beautiful, as if Nature was presenting her greatest splendor just before the dying began. Now, twenty-five years later, one could have written the same thing. Each summer day was more magnificent than the last.

On the evening of 25 August, our company commander opined that X-Hour was imminent.[1] Only much later did we find out why the operation was delayed, and the units already on the way to their objectives pulled back. Feverish, last-minute diplomatic maneuvers to avert war were taking place. By 31 August, however, von Ribbentrop declared that he no longer had authority to negotiate. The dice had been thrown!

"Situation White" went into effect. The order to execute, which had already come down from the highest command authorities in the late afternoon, was brief: "Missions and objectives remain the same. X-Day—1 September 1939. X-Hour—0445." As I opened the window in my barracks at 0500, I heard an endless peal of thunder from the south. The artillery on the Polish border had opened fire.

I was dumbstruck. My childhood memories of the First World War were still very distinct. I hurried into the barracks square to find someone with whom to talk. There stood the former commander of our 11th Company, *Major* von T., now in the uniform of a general staff officer, and the Ia of our Division,[2] surrounded by soldiers and besieged with questions. "Yes," he said with a shrug, "this time the shooting is for real!"

It was exactly nine months before the previously longed-for conclusion of my term as a "twelve-pointer." It was well that neither the German people nor we soldiers knew how long this war would last, or how it would end almost six years later. On 1 September 1939, an epoch began that would change the face of Europe and our history. The Second World War had begun.

The Field Replacement Battalion was alerted at 0800 because Polish troops were allegedly preparing to cross the River Weichsel near the ferry at Kurzebrack, and also to the south of it. Marienwerder is situated barely four kilometers from the Weichsel, which at that point measures almost five hundred meters across. Presumably, the river bank opposite the Polish Corridor was at that time only lightly occupied by border patrols, and for some reason or other, the patrols panicked, as happens often at the beginning of a war.

First, however, we moved into position on the plateaus west of Marienwerder, and started to dig in. We dug in vain, and even refilled the holes on the same afternoon. False alarm! A few hours into the attack, the Poles already had other problems than crossing the Weichsel towards us!

From the early morning hours, almost like a shuttle, squadrons of German bombers flew back and forth over the Polish border to the south. By then, the Polish Marshal Edward Rydz-Smigly presumably understood that his march towards Berlin was not going to happen. At this hour, the bulk of the Polish Air Force had already been destroyed on the ground.[3]

On 4 September, our division had already entered the outskirts of Fortress Graudenz, which was seized on 5 September. After this we were moved to the southeast of the province and from there turned again towards Poland. The Field Reserve Battalion followed the Division across the Narev River between Lomsha and Ostrolenka, and after a few days reached Bialystok, our final objective. During the whole Polish campaign, I experienced only one combat episode. South of the Narev, while taking a rest, we were suddenly told that scattered but strong units of Polish troops were approaching from the north of the advancing division.

A so-called "battle-capable" patrol under my command mounted on bicycles was sent towards the direction from which the enemy was thought to be coming. We rode several kilometers without detecting anything until a large meadow with many haystacks aroused my curiosity. I motioned to my infantrymen to check out the haystacks, which they did by poking the straw vigorously with their bayonets. They had remarkable success, and the reason soon became obvious. After a few loud screams, many of the haystacks suddenly became *alive*. From almost every one, a few battle-weary Polish soldiers crept out, some still with their weapons, but all of whom surrendered without resistance. They had been dispersed from the fortifications on the Narev. Later during questioning, they stated that more than anything, the attacks of the Stuka dive bombers on their bunkers had undermined their will to fight.

In our advance towards Bialystok, we passed a place with numerous graves of German soldiers. They all belonged to the same company of a reconnaissance battalion that was probably ambushed right there.

On the same day, moving through sand and heath, we were passed by a long convoy. There in the first car, obviously in a radiant mood, stood the Commanding General of Army Group North, *Generaloberst* Fedor von Bock, who greeted us with his hand raised, crying "*Heil* Hitler, my dear comrades." (!)

The campaign in Poland was decided in the first eight days. The last Polish resistance, however, only collapsed on 1 October, four weeks after the beginning of the war. From a curbside vantage, I later experienced my old company's torchlight triumphant return home to a grateful populace after the conclusion of the campaign in Poland. Unfortunately, there were some dead and wounded to mourn.

Chapter Two

Interlude in the Valley of the Ahr

Historical Commentary

Excited and encouraged by the rapid and relatively cheap victory over the Poles, Hitler desired a quick reorientation of his forces and an attack on the Western Allies in November. Generaloberst *Walther von Brauchitsch, Commander-in-Chief of the Army, and* General der Artillerie *Franz Halder, Chief of the General Staff, both expressed their deep opposition to such plans knowing that the Army was not prepared to take on the Western Allies so soon. For one of the last times in the Second World War, the German General Staff successfully asserted itself to the benefit of the Army and the country. Combined with inappropriate weather, their resistance ultimately brought about twenty-nine postponements to the desired dates set by the restive Führer for the attack in the West.*

During the seven months of relatively insignificant patrol clashes in the West (dubbed the "Sitzkrieg" by reporters), the German Army stockpiled desperately needed materiel, re-equipped its armored forces with more modern tanks, trained its standing units, and mobilized even more. One formation, created from the replacement battalions of other divisions, was the 161st Infantry Division. Consisting also of East Prussians, this was the unit to which Georg Grossjohann was assigned after his brief period in Bad Neuenahr following the Polish Campaign.

Georg Grossjohann Remembers . . .

Right after the Polish campaign, the 21st Infantry Division entrained and was shipped to the western front. The destination was the beautiful valley

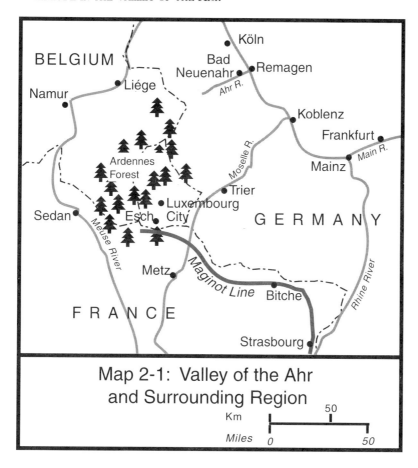

Map 2-1: Valley of the Ahr and Surrounding Region

of the Ahr River. The Field Replacement Battalion moved into the world famous spa, Bad Neuenahr, with its many elegant homes and fancy hotels. For us humble East Prussians who came from a flat and rural homeland, this was quite luxurious. Our soldiers learned rather quickly that there are pretty girls not only in East Prussia but also in the Ahr valley, although the beauty of the women here was of a different kind. The long presence of Roman legionaries and their influence on many of the tribes in this region was recognizable centuries later. One might have encountered many of these beautiful women and girls in Rome or Paris.

In the small establishment situated by the road from Bad Neuenahr to Ahrweiler, I got to know the daughter of the owner and even fell a bit in love with her. Since a close relationship was out of the question, we developed a platonic friendship. Before I had to return to East Prussia,[4] I introduced a friend of mine, a young reserve officer, to pretty Else. Soon after that, they got married, yet regrettably, this good friend and comrade fell in one of the last weeks of WWII. The young widow later on married a gastronome and turned the once modest family business into a quite elegant eatery. In the following years, whenever, by chance, I got close to Bad Neuenahr, I never missed the opportunity to pay a visit to Else and her husband.

During this time, our company commander was *Oberleutnant Graf von B.* He was an agriculturalist, and perhaps one of those who would have gone into battle with a New Testament and a volume of poems by Rainer Maria Rilke. He was a noble gentleman, yet a bit out of touch with the world. Unfortunately, he didn't live to see the end of WWII, either.

In any case, upon reaching my newly-mobilized unit in East Prussia— Infantry Regiment 371, 161st Infantry Division—I was again transferred to an infantry company, and soon thereafter was reassigned as the leader of

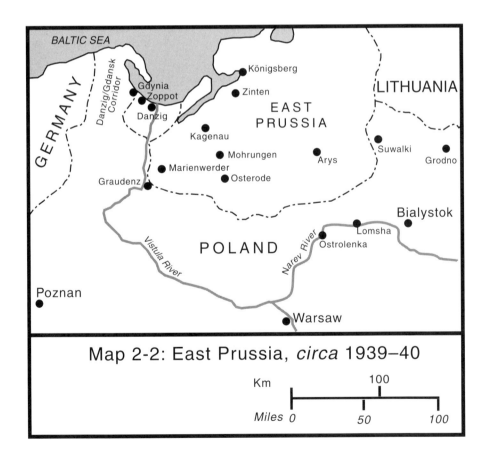

Map 2-2: East Prussia, *circa* 1939–40

the regimental pioneer platoon. The enlisted men and NCOs who were submitted by the individual companies for assignment to this newly-raised platoon were supposed to be highly physically fit, and were also supposed to be especially able with their hands. With a few exceptions, however, all that showed up were local militiamen. Protesting this state of affairs was useless. Some really bad cases were exchanged, but with the remainder, I had to be content.

Later experiences proved this to be only a temporary flaw because before long, I was no longer upset about being short-changed by the company commanders. I got embarrassed only when we had the first inspection, to almost peacetime standards, which took place under very unfavorable conditions, since the pioneer platoon was stationed in private housing. Later, during the campaign in France, during the few times the platoon was in action, our staffing worked out quite well. Even from the first skirmish, the older men with which the platoon had been furnished kept their cool and fulfilled their duties expertly, which were to clear obstacles and mines.

After only a few weeks of training for the 161st Infantry Division at the training center in Schlaga-Krug, near Arys, in East Prussia, our regiment was shipped to Zinten. There, we moved into the abandoned barracks of the East Prussian 4th Panzer Brigade.

Our regimental commander was an elderly reserve *Oberst* of cavalry, who had spent some years in China as a military advisor. Even the division commander, *Generalmajor* Hermann Wilck, was an old "Chinese." Both belonged to a team of advisors that had supported Marshall Chiang Kai Shek. This team was already active there during Seeckt's time.[5] From time to time, the members of the team would be exchanged, but all were already retired from active duty before they became advisors.

On 2 May 1940, we were once again going west, to the training center at Baumholder. This was my third trip across the *Reich* from frontier to frontier. This was not to be the last, either. During the war, I changed fronts seven times.

Chapter Three

Through the Ardennes and into the Maginot Line

Historical Commentary

Between the Non-Aggression Pact with Russia and the occupation or defeat of all of Germany's eastern neighbors, Adolf Hitler engineered a situation by which he could turn Germany's full military force against the West. After many delays, brought about by the insistence of the General Staff and by inclement weather, Germany invaded Norway and Denmark on 9 April 1944. In a masterfully conceived and conducted campaign using seaborne, airborne, mountain, and air-landed troops to overwhelm the defenders, the Wehrmacht *successfully secured Germany's northern flank and won the race for possession of the key iron ore port of Narvik. Although scattered Norwegian military operations continued until 10 June (and resistance operations continued throughout the remainder of the war), British and French forces were forced to withdraw by 3 May, marking the operational, if not tactical, victory of Germany in the campaign.*

With the northern flank and rear secure, it was not long before the Wehrmacht *unleashed its fury against France and the Low Countries. Again, on paper, the Allies should have been at least a match for the* Wehrmacht. *Overall, the number of divisions available to each side for use in France and Belgium was about equal: 122 for the Germans and 105 for the Allies (the Germans had ten more which they used against the neutral Dutch). The Allies actually possessed more and better tanks, and if their aircraft were significantly outnumbered, it must be remembered that the attacking* Luftwaffe *would be flying into the teeth of prepared Allied antiaircraft defenses.*

The combat strength of the French, and to a lesser extent, the Belgians, was significantly enhanced by extensive frontier fortifications. About half of French defense spending in the 1930s had been sunk into the construction of a 192-mile-long line of extraordinarily complex fortifications along the German and Luxembourg borders. Named after the French Defense Minister from 1929 to 1932, André Maginot, the Maginot Line's immediate purpose was to defend Alsace and Lorraine, two border provinces only wrested back from Germany in 1918. The French, who had suffered enormously from pursuit of their overwhelmingly offensively-oriented doctrine of 1914–1916, intended to avoid a reprise of the debacle of World War I by creating defenses so strong that any German attack would inevitably founder. If trenches had, at last, been found to be effective against the German attackers, then, it followed for the French, fortresses with massive steel-reinforced concrete walls, deep, gas-proof, subterranean passages (often connected by electric subways!), and disappearing armored gun turrets would halt any potential German attack at the border. The greater part of the French Army could then be used to counterattack or, if the Germans drove again through Belgium, as they had done in the First War, the Maginot defenses could serve as an economy of force measure, and allow the best units of the French Army to advance into Belgium and defeat the Germans there.

From the Führer *down, the Germans, too, wished to avoid a repeat of the horrors of the 1914–1918 Western Front. Their solution, however, was radically different, in concept and in effectiveness. In the first minutes of 9 May 1940, the* Luftwaffe *struck at Allied airfields throughout Western Europe, destroying much of the French Air Force on the ground. The* Luftwaffe *was now free to support the ground maneuver of the Army. The devastating aerial attacks were followed by airborne (parachute- and glider-borne infantry and engineers) and ground attacks into the Netherlands and Belgium. Von Küchler's Eighteenth Army overran the Netherlands in five days, while Fedor von Bock's Army Group B main attack, conducted by von Reichenau's Sixth Army, thrust into Belgium, heading due west.*

To the Allies, this appeared to resemble the "Schlieffen Plan," the stratagem used by the Germans in 1914, by which the great bulk of the German Army wheeled through Belgium and descended on Paris from the north and west. When the Allies responded by committing thirty-five of their best divisions in Belgium, they walked into a trap. Out of the Ardennes Forest burst von Rundstedt's Army Group A, forty-five divisions strong and led past the western terminus of the Maginot Line by the majority of the Army's panzer *divisions. Although their tanks generally possessed armor and firepower inferior to that of many of the Allies', the Germans employed their* panzers en masse, *using them to punch holes in the Allied line. Bypassing pockets of resistance to be engaged later by their own infantry, the* panzers *rushed into the Allied rear, wreaking havoc on supply and communications lines. The idea of this* "Blitzkrieg" *was not to conduct a decisive Clauswitzian battle of destruction, but to quickly demoralize their enemy, and destroy the Allies'* will *to fight. This was the German method to achieve victory against her ancient Gallic foe.*

With their armored forces mostly dispersed in battalion-sized units among their infantry formations, the French usually could not muster sufficient armored forces of their own to effectively combat the panzers. *As a result, the Allies were rapidly cut up, cut off, and forced to abandon defensive line after line. The British evacuated the remnants of their Expeditionary Force, without heavy equipment, from the beaches at Dunkirk, and French Army morale began large-scale collapse. The Germans were at the gates of Paris by 12 June, just thirty-three days after the commencement of the offensive, and the Maginot Line was out-flanked by the next day.*

Although the Germans' brilliant maneuver and innovative employment of armor obviated the decisiveness of the Maginot Line, attacks were nevertheless made against several sectors of the formidable fortifications. Here, French morale did not *crack, and the Maginot defenders' motto,* "On ne passe pas" *was taken seriously indeed. Witzleben's First Army broke through the* Secteur Fortifié de la Sarre, *one of the weakest portions of the Maginot Line, by 15 June. Subsequent attacks by his eleven infantry divisions were, however, but partially successful: only two significant Maginot forts (Haut Poirier and Welschoff) fell to his men's costly assaults. Even though they were conducted against the rear of the fortresses of the* Ensemble de Bitche, *in the* Secteurs Fortifié de Rohrbach *and* des Vosges, *the all-around defenses of the remaining forts enabled their garrisons to hold out, ultimately surrendering a week after the rest of French Army had capitulated. Further to the east, supported by WWI-era Krupp 420mm guns (firing anti-concrete rounds weighing over one ton) and waves of Stuka divebombers, Generalmajor Kniess' 215th Infantry Division broke through the casemates of the* Secteur Fortifié des Vosges (S. F. des Vosges) *on 19 June, between Fortress Grand Hohékirkel and Fort Lembach, but could achieve little more thereafter. Although the Germans employed artillery of up to 355mm and 420mm in caliber against Fortress* Four à Chaux (S. F. des Vosges) *and Fortresses Hochwald and Schoenenbourg* (S. F. de Haguenau) *thereafter, no further significant progress was made against the Maginot fortifications at this end of the line.*[6]

While Witzleben's men broke through in the Saar and fanned out, Busch's Sixteenth Army also tried to seize Maginot forts from the rear, at the far western end of the Line near Longuyon. Here, on 21 June 1940, Georg Grossjohann led a regimental pioneer (combat engineer) platoon against a bloc *of Fortress Fermont. Fermont was protected by outlying casemates, or pillboxes, as well as the interlocking artillery fires of Fort Chappy to the west and Fortress Latiremont to the east. From the safety of deep tunnels, thick steel-reinforced concrete walls, and thickets of barbed wire and antitank obstacles,* Capitaine *Daniel Aubert's garrison at Fermont could decimate attackers. Along with their 75mm cannon and 81mm mortars mounted in disappearing turrets—steel cupolas which could be raised to fire and lowered flush with the ground for protection—they could also use their casemate-mounted triple 75mm cannon, armored 47mm antitank guns, and turret-mounted machineguns to defend their subterranean bastion.*

Against this imposing example of the military engineer's art, Georg Grossjohann would first lead men into battle.

Georg Grossjohann Remembers . . .

On 10 May, the beginning of the campaign in the west, the 161st Infantry Division marched seemingly without end along the Hunsrück Mountains road to join the Sixteenth Army as its reserve. Although it was only May, we moved through the Moselle Valley toward Trier in glowing heat without any chance of a cooling breeze. Near Klüsserath, we had to get off the highway, and temporarily seek quarters in small villages in the wine country. Motorized columns had the right of way. When we began marching again after three days, we moved through the beautiful city of Trier, but then we turned north, because the direct road to Luxembourg City was again clogged. We crossed the border near Echternach and marched through this lovely little country up to the French border near Bad Mondorf, where the division took over security missions.

Further into the campaign, we were moved westward. It was south of Esch, approaching the Maginot Line, where for the first time we encountered the French opponent. The dark of night can be the attackers' ally, but it is also true that night combat is not one of our soldiers' greatest strengths.

A battalion of our Infantry Regiment 371 advanced toward the edge of a small wood and dug in quite close to the fortifications of the Maginot Line. The French were probably afraid we could knock out their pillboxes in the dark, so they shot harassing and interdictory fires continuously with machineguns and light artillery through the night. In the early morning hours, they must have expected an attack as they covered the woods with a furious hail of automatic weapons and artillery fire.

I had only returned to the regimental command post on the evening before, and went to sleep in the pioneer platoon area, expecting no trouble. At dawn, I was suddenly awakened by a small, heavyset, completely hysterical *Unteroffizier*, whom I remembered from my battalion in East Prussia. He yelled, "All is lost, the French are coming." Half-dressed, I ran out to at least organize the defense of our position, and to alert everyone.

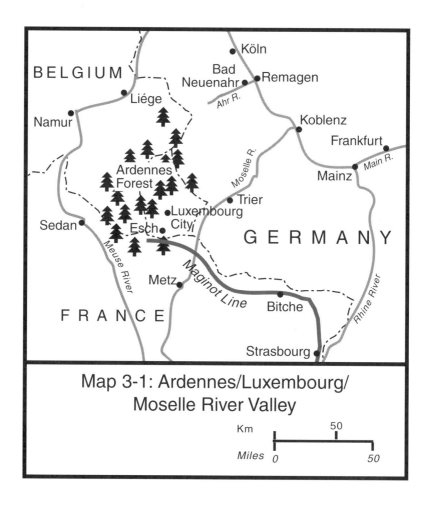

Map 3-1: Ardennes/Luxembourg/
Moselle River Valley

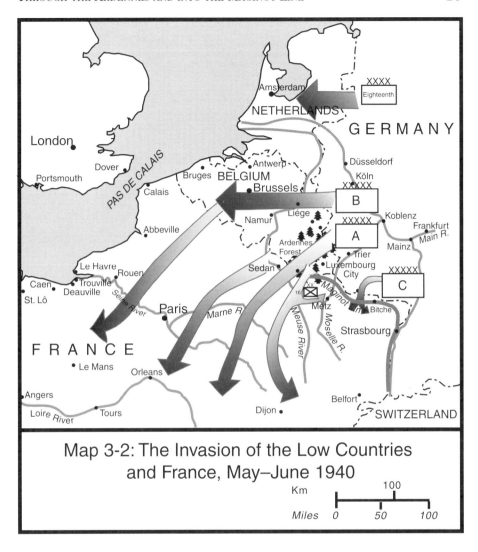

Map 3-2: The Invasion of the Low Countries
and France, May–June 1940

What I found was unearthly silence. The rising sun bathed the peaceful
border in amiable light, and far and wide, there was no sign of any advancing Frenchmen. As it turned out, the little fat guy was not the only one to
run away; the heavy barrage during the night from the Maginot fortresses
hitting the forest in which our nearest infantry battalion was deployed
made these inexperienced soldiers believe the enemy was already in our
midst. This was why several of them panicked and took off aimlessly. With
two groups of my pioneer platoon, I marched towards the enemy and a
short hour later reached the infantry battalion, which was deployed in the

woods. The attack of the French took place only in the fantasies of those who ran away. The whole thing was a quite embarrassing affair. I don't know if Division headquarters was ever informed about this, but I guessed that for a good reason, it never was. Regrettably, the barrage by the French did inflict some losses on our side. My pioneer platoon suffered one man killed.

The last serious, but also unsuccessful, action of the 161st Infantry Division in France took place against the rear and flank of the Maginot Line on 21 June 1940, along the Longuyons-Longwy road. There the division outflanked the Maginot Line, as had the armored units that had been deployed northwest of us. At 0700 we started the attack on Fortress Fermont, and some smaller fortifications which protected Fermont in the rear and flanks.

Although at the highest command echelon, there must have been precise information about even the smallest of Maginot fortifications, down at my level, certainly, there were no precise instructions available. As the regimental Pioneer Platoon Leader, I was not even asked to join the preliminary staff meeting. Therefore, I was also not asked if my men indeed had the necessary ordnance and other equipment to successfully breach pillboxes built from steel-reinforced concrete, as well as armored cupolas. I think the mission was performed in haste and without any measurable chance of success. For a division with our equipment, this task was "too big by a few hat sizes," and our nice old *Stabsfeldwebel* was not the one only who became a victim.

Later I suspected that the older reserve *Oberst* and his adjutant did not figure out how to employ the pioneer platoon effectively. They simply forgot about us. The order given to me shortly before the attack was strictly out of embarrassment for their omission.

I was ordered to send two groups of my pioneers to each of the three battalions of the regiment. After that, the Regimental Commander would ask me what I was planning to do. My answer, namely, that I would join one of these groups, seemed to satisfy him. No one ever asked what my men were really capable of doing.

Along with my group, I joined one of the battalions led by an older reserve *Hauptmann*. If I remember correctly, it was the 2d Battalion of our Infantry Regiment 371. We removed some barbed wire and cleared out a few mines. That was all we were trained and equipped to do. We stopped short before an armored turret with an excellent field of fire that was spraying the approaches with a machinegun. A berm on the edge of the woods about fifty meters from the turret provided us with some cover. Our preparatory bombardment—using Stukas, Czech Skoda 305mm howitzers,

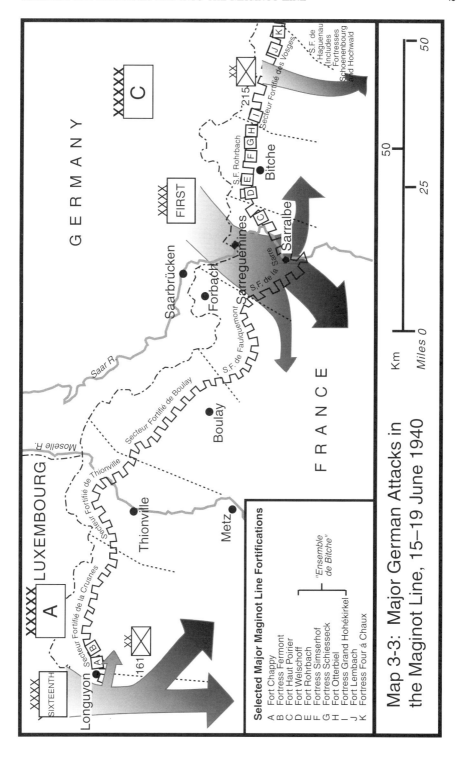

Map 3-3: Major German Attacks in the Maginot Line, 15–19 June 1940

Selected Major Maginot Line Fortifications

A Fort Chappy
B Fortress Fermont
C Fort Haut Poirier
D Fort Welschoff
E Fort Rohrbach
F Fortress Simserhof
G Fortress Schiesseck
H Fort Otterbiel
J Fortress Grand Hohékirkel
J Fort Lembach
K Fortress Four à Chaux

"Ensemble de Bitche"

S.F. de Haguenau (Includes Fortresses Schoenenbourg and Hochwald

Secteur Fortifié des Vosges

S.F. Rohrbach

"215"

Bitche

FIRST

GERMANY

Saarbrücken

Forbach

Sarreguemines

Sarralbe

S.F. de la Sarre

S.F. de Faulquemont

Secteur Fortifié de Boulay

Saar R.

Boulay

FRANCE

Moselle R.

Secteur Fortifié de Thionville

Thionville

Metz

LUXEMBOURG

A

Secteur Fortifié de la Crusnes

Longuyon

SIXTEENTH

161

C

Km

Miles 0

50   25

50

50

210mm howitzers, six *batteries* of 105mm howitzers, and even some 88mm high velocity antiaircraft guns—had accomplished nothing appreciable. Now, my pioneers were expected to make a difference. To attack the turret, we soon learned, was absolutely suicidal.

The young company commander ordered the old *Stabsfeldwebel*, our former topkick, to attack the armored turret under the cover of our fire support. For pioneers, equipped with smoke grenades, limpet mines, and, eventually, flamethrowers, it would have been quite possible to knock out the turret, but not without these implements. Nevertheless, the brave *Stabsfeldwebel* and his men sprang from cover and attacked.

Within seconds, they were all dead!

As the Regimental Commander pushed to try again, the quiet *Hauptmann* L. asked the regimental commander to personally go up front for an evaluation. After the visit, no further pressure was forthcoming.

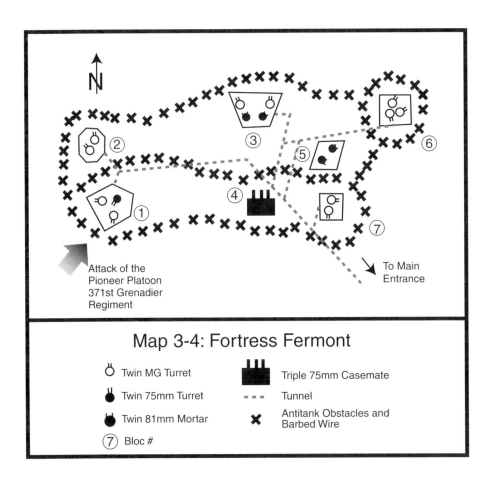

Map 3-4: Fortress Fermont

Ö Twin MG Turret	▥ Triple 75mm Casemate
Twin 75mm Turret	= = = Tunnel
Twin 81mm Mortar	✕ Antitank Obstacles and Barbed Wire
⑦ Bloc #	

In the September 1981 issue of *Alte Kameraden* magazine, I found a report about the unsuccessful attack against Fortress Fermont by a battalion of Infantry Regiment 371, which was titled, "Good Luck on Both Sides." The author wrote that on "21 June 1940, at 0700, the reinforced battalion attacked the fortress. Since there was no effective support by heavy weapons, the attack was unsuccessful, and was stopped around 1100." The reason for the author's choice of title became obvious as I read on. "On 17 June 1940, German Army 88mm guns fired against Block #4 of the fort, which had walls of 1.75 meters' thickness and in which three guns were installed. After the 88s created a one-meter-wide hole in the concrete, they ceased fire. Just one more shot would have hit the ammunition stores, creating a catastrophe." And it goes on. We, on the other hand, were very lucky, for only two days before our attack, the French infantry was completely pulled back from the trenches. They would have had great target practice when we emerged from the woods.

On the evening of 21 June, my pioneers returned to regimental control. One of the battalion commanders, *Major* Ritter, summoned me to his quarters to chew my ass. (Aha! A scapegoat!) In his opinion, it was only because of the inadequacy of the paltry sixteen pioneers under his command that Fortress Fermont had not been taken by his battalion. One can only hope that not even he would have believed such nonsense.

The attack was, to use common parlance, as useless as a goiter. On the next day, 22 June, the guns were silent. A few days later, our little *Oberst* accepted the surrender of the Fortress Fermont, from its commandant, Capitaine Daniel Aubert.

Together with my colleagues from the cavalry and communications units, I visited the barracks where the defenders of Fermont were being held temporarily. They all seemed in good spirits, but in reality, it was only gallows humor. Quite rightfully, they tried to convince us that we should not feel like the victors! After all, Fermont only surrendered when the rest of France capitulated.

In spite of considerable losses, we did not contribute a great deal toward the victory in France. Nevertheless, good intentions and brave actions, even if not very successful, were recognized and rewarded. For my service with my pioneer platoon, I was awarded the Iron Cross, Second Class . . . but the campaign in the west would have been won even if we had stayed in Zinten.

Chapter Four

Between France and Russia

Historical Commentary

France officially surrendered to Germany on 22 June, and, although they had in no way been defeated by her, to Italy on 25 June. With suffi-cient ammunition, food, and water to sustain resistance through a pro-tracted siege, several of the garrisons of the Maginot Line held out until 30 June or even into the first days of July, but in the end, they, too, sur-rendered. France was partitioned into an occupied zone (Roughly, the northern two-thirds of the country, and the entire Atlantic coastline) and a pro-German "rump state" controlled by a puppet French govern-ment seated at the spa town of Vichy.

Less than a month after the capitulation of France, in a speech made before the Reichstag, *Hitler offered a peace settlement, in unspecified terms, to Churchill and the British people. Even before the Prime Minister could publicly offer his rebuff, the British Press declared its rejection of the idea. From airfields in the occupied zone, the* Luftwaffe *then launched what would become known as "The Battle of Britain," Hermann Göring's attempt to destroy the Royal Air Force (RAF) and pave the way for the invasion of the British Isles. Due to her declaration of war on Germany in the wake of the invasion of Poland, Great Britain had already been attacked by* Luftwaffe *bombers since as early as the autumn of 1939. The attacks which began in July, however, were far more extensive and much more intense.*

In anticipation of the establishment of air superiority over Great Britain, the Wehrmacht *began preparations for launching Operation* SEELÖWE *(SEALION), the amphibious invasion of the British Isles. Had the* Luftwaffe *wrested control of the British skies from the RAF, it would have been in this, the first invasion of Great Britain since that of the Normans led by William the Conqueror in 1066, in which Georg Grossjohann would have next seen action.*

He was spared that ordeal, however, due to the failure of Göring's Luftwaffe *to destroy the RAF. By the middle of November 1940, it was apparent to OKW and, more importantly, to Hitler, that the Battle of Britain had been lost. Although Georg Grossjohann could not have known it, Hitler began turning his attention east, toward the Soviet Union.*

Even as the Battle of Britain reached a crescendo, events unfolded in the Balkans and in Africa which ultimately required significant German military exertion. In September, the Italian Army invaded Egypt, only to be routed completely in December by counterattacking British Commonwealth forces. Within a few months, the Italians were ejected from East Africa by the British, and pushed further west into Libya as well, with huge numbers of Italian soldiers surrendering to miniscule British units. Meanwhile, as Rumania's territory was systematically "diplomatically" dismembered—and her population stolen— by Hungary, the Soviet Union, and Bulgaria through the summer of 1940, Italy invaded Greece from Albania during the last days of October. Here, too, the "new Roman Legions" of Il Duce *suffered a humiliating defeat, this time at the hands of General Metaxas' Greek forces. With Hungary and Rumania firmly in the Axis fold by November, the Germans struck in the late winter and spring of 1941 to restore their Italian allies' political-military position on several fronts, and to prepare for operations against the Soviets.*

In March 1941, the Serbians engineered a coup d'etat *in Yugoslavia and repudiated the recently-concluded agreement to join the Axis. Germany invaded Yugoslavia from Hungary on 6 April and conquered her in twelve days . . . although brutal partisan warfare would continue there for the rest of the war. Simultaneously,* Wehrmacht *forces invaded Greece from Bulgaria, and defeated Metaxas' Army—and its British Commonwealth reinforcements—by the end of April. In May, the* Luftwaffe *launched the largest airborne assault in history against Commonwealth forces on Crete, and in fewer than twelve days of fighting, this strategically-placed key to the Aegean was in German hands.*

German mechanized forces under one of Hitler's favorite officers, Erwin Rommel, began arriving in North Africa in February, and by mid-April, the Afrika Korps had driven the British back to the Egyptian frontier.

Thus, by the spring of 1941, Germany occupied or otherwise controlled every bit of territory in Europe which bordered on the Soviet Union and the western territories of her recently-expanded Empire, that is eastern Poland, Lithuania, and Bessarabia. The invasion of the Soviet Union, Operation BARBAROSSA, *however, had been delayed at least a month by the military diversions necessitated by Mussolini's ambitions and Italian military failures.*

Georg Grossjohann Remembers . . .

Immediately after the conclusion of the campaign in France, the 161st Infantry Division was moved again, this time from west to east, and assembled in and around Suwalki, close to the new German/Soviet border. (See Map 2-2.) Suwalki bordered immediately on our East Prussian homeland, and penetrated the once Polish territory like a small wedge. Even though barely ten months had passed since the end of the war with Poland, the town had already changed significantly. The townspeople made a friendly, organized impression. There had already been established a large, well-stocked hotel-restaurant, called the "German House." The German inn-keeper seemed to advertise the quality of his cuisine with his corpulence.

Our Regimental Commander, *Oberst* Newiger, who often used quite subtle expressions, stated that if this gastronome "closed his eyes, he would explode."

Although *Oberst* Newiger's frequent sarcasm was indeed biting, it paled in comparison to the methods of an old company commander of mine from my days as an enlisted man. *Hauptmann* Erwin M., or "Erwin the Only," as he was known (behind his back!) to his soldiers, was one of the most unforgettable men I ever met in the Army. I served under him from 1932 to 1936.

He was of medium build and slim, not unpleasant in appearance, with small, cold eyes and thin lips. His pallor and exceptionally thin physique led me to suspect that he might suffer from a stomach ailment, which, as I later found out, was indeed the case. He seemed to suppress the resulting pain by consuming an enormous number of cigarettes but, of course, he thereby achieved exactly the opposite. His illness may have already been chronic and certainly was one of the causes for his grumpy, icy demeanor.

A Great War veteran of the Eastern Front, Erwin was happiest when he had just finished chewing someone out. He always referred to us, his soldiers, in the third person, a strange and annoying anachronism from the days of serfdom in East Prussia. For instance, Erwin would never order a soldier to run by saying, "Run, Schmidt!" but rather by barking, "He is to run!"

My introduction to Erwin the Only was memorable. After a brief stint in the guardhouse for a minor infraction of regulations (it was my fourth—and last—tour in the clink since I had enlisted), I found that my company had a new commander. The *Stabsfeldwebel* approached the door to the commander's office, waited a moment, stretched his stately body, cleared his throat, and only then, with bowed posture, knocked modestly at the entrance. After a quick "*Ja!*," I was pushed into the small room, and stood at attention while the *Stabsfeldwebel* identified me to the *Hauptmann* as a bum just out of the stockade.

The room was filled with blue smoke, and a haggard, pale human with thin, ash-blond hair, who first did not even take notice of the sergeant's report, sat there, motionless, behind his desk. His eyes almost closed, he seemed to mobilize all his strength, like a guru, to be prepared for my appearance. He only got up a while later and stood before me, seething.

In a boiling rage, the *Hauptmann* proclaimed through clenched teeth exactly what I could look forward to if I caused him to punish me just one more time. Calming as quickly as he had become enraged, he then sat down behind his desk, seemingly sated. Later on I realized that he was always content and at ease after thoroughly chewing out someone. For almost four years, he would hover above me like the sword of Dionysus hung over the unfortunate Damocles.

Although possessed of a similarly sharp tongue, *Oberst* Newiger was infinitely more cultured and also more insightful than Erwin the Only. After the campaign in France, he had spoken to all the officers and officer aspirants. "Gentlemen," he said at that time, "You may in all confidence tighten the straps on your helmets. We have no reason to celebrate. The skirmishing in the outposts is fortunately behind us. But the war will actually begin when the big powers come into the arena." Few of us could have known how prophetic his words truly were.

In civilian clothes or dressed as border officials, officers from the Division continuously observed whatever happened on the Russian side of the border. It didn't take long to find out that there, too, was a well-camouflaged deployment in process.

Later, during the Russian campaign, the 161st Infantry Division from East Prussia experienced all the merciless cruelty of war against an equal opponent from which it was spared during the French campaign. In

August–September 1944, after the defection of the Rumanian Army, the 161st was destroyed like so many other German divisions. In 1964, my fraternity brother, *Generalmajor* Hans Kissel, came out with a book published by Wehr und Wissen Verlag entitled *The Catastrophe in Rumania*. In the notes of this book, I found the story of *Oberleutnant* Steinmeyer, commander of the 4th Battalion of the Artillery Regiment 241 of the 161st Infantry Division, written 5 January 1945. *Oberleutnant* Steinmeyer marched 750 kilometers in thirty-two days, continuously being chased by Russian partisans; on 23 September, he and his men reached our own lines. Steinmeyer was killed in action on 21 April 1945, in Müden an der Aller! Thus was the swan song of the brave men of this East Prussian division.

Late in the summer of 1940, after we had been in Suwalki for several weeks, many personnel of the 161st were sent back to the *Reich* to provide

Map 4-1: Germany, 1939–40

Km 100

Miles 0 50 100

the cadre for other units. I remember that from the regimental staff of Infantry Regiment 371, only some of the cavalry officers and the Regimental Adjutant remained—in the latter case, probably to break in the new commander. The Adjutant was an *Oberleutnant* from an old Silesian noble family, who later took his own life upon discovery of his homosexual relationship with a subordinate. I learned about this only years later, through one of his cousins who went with me on a trip to Rumania. *Oberst* Newiger, who always showed special appreciation toward his former adjutant—which was certainly justified—never mentioned anything about this to us, even though he most likely knew of it. Probably, the whole affair was highly distressing to him because he had often enough presented this officer as a singularly fine model for the rest of us.

After leaving the 161st, we traveled once more through the *Reich*, from east to west, and ended up in Ludwigslust, in Mecklenburg. Here, we joined the newly-formed Infantry Regiment 677 of the 332d Infantry Division. Ludwigslust was the residence of the former grand duke of Mecklenburg, who retired in 1918. Like our East Prussia, Mecklenburg was mostly thinly populated farmland, in which sixty prcent of the land was owned by one percent of the farmers—mainly, the nobility. Ludwigslust had about 14,000 inhabitants. Before WWII, it was the garrison of Cavalry Regiment 14. The commander then was *Oberst* (later *Generalmajor*) Friedemund von Arnim. By the time we got to Ludwigslust, a reserve cavalry unit was stationed there, under the command of *Oberst Freiherr* von Rodde, with his adjutant, *Leutnant Graf* von Bernsdorff.

A career officer once told me about a little episode that supposedly happened in the officers' mess of the riding academy of Hannover. To receive higher education in the art of equitation, an artillery officer was once sent there, but his name lacked the "von" of the noble class. When at the table, he took the liberty to say a few words, he was instantly rebuked by one of the cavalry officers, "If someone is from the artillery and is bourgeois, one should keep his mouth shut and be ashamed of himself!" Given this sort of attitude, it is understandable that at Ludwigslust, we East Prussian grenadiers were only met with the greatest suspicion!

When our new humble, commoner regimental adjutant timidly asked his noble colleague if our officers could use the officers' mess of the cavalry regiment for a social event, he was turned down out of hand. The excuse was that the cavalry mess was home to so many valuables, including gifts from the former reigning houses of Mecklenburg, that we could not be allowed entry. Our little *Oberst* had been born a cavalryman, had formerly served with Ulan (Lancer) Regiment 8, had married into the nobility, and was only assigned to the infantry through a misfortune. He was greatly hurt by this biased treatment by a comrade of his own branch of the Army. Our *Oberst* called the baronly cavalier and asked him if, by chance, all these valuables couldn't be secured so that we might be allowed to temporarily use the officers' club.

The cavalry adjutant responded at once with extreme annoyance, since this question was sheer sarcasm. To reply in this fashion to our *Oberst* was a mistake, as *Oberst* Newiger was at any time prepared for a quick, acerbic, and often outright biting remark. For example, we were once moved by train through a certain town. Our regimental veterinarian turned to the commander and said, "*Herr Oberst*, it was here in Landsberg that I earned my spurs as a vet." *Oberst* Newiger's quick response was, "and in the meantime, you took them off again," meaning that the vet was no longer a particularly good horseman. On another occasion, his aide-de-camp, a cavalryman like the *Oberst*, apologized for being late for dinner, explaining that he was just coming back from riding. Without looking up from his plate, the Regimental Commander responded, "Well, if you want to call what you do riding."

A few days after the gentleman from the cavalry refused us the use of their mess, *Oberst* Newiger met the fellow, *Leutnant Graf* von Bernsdorff in the street, and confronted him. The subject of the confrontation was not, however, the despicable way he had denied us the use of the mess, but for being out of uniform and for rendering a sloppy salute. "Would you mind buttoning up the collar of your coat, *Graf* von Bernsdorff?" snapped the *Oberst* in his best Berlin accent. "You are neither a general nor do you wear a medal around your neck! And, if you have a chance, get an education from a professional officer on how a *Leutnant* should salute an *Oberst*!" Having said this, he left the dumbstruck young nobleman perplexed. *Oberst* Newiger left him alone and contentedly went his way.

We celebrated our social event in a nearby town, in a modern club of a *Luftwaffe* bomber squadron that was stationed there. They had immediately offered to help us out. Most of the female population had already been impressed by the young, highly decorated pilots of the squadron to the disadvantage of the arrogant, old, and stuffy comrades of the reserve cavalry regiment. It was obvious that even the ladies of the local nobility, including the royal highnesses, preferred the aviators to the cavalrymen. Unfortunately, our party, which was celebrated in combination with the pilots, did not pass without some hard feelings. One of our battalion commanders, an older major, got riled up during a disagreement with our *Luftwaffe* hosts. He attempted to win the argument by pulling rank, which was, of course, resented by the other pilots. We younger ones spontaneously took sides with the young *Luftwaffe Hauptmann*, and I probably went too far. The *Major* later paid me back in a malicious way.

The people of Mecklenburg and their grand duke are known to be descendants of the Slavic Obotrites, who settled in the area between Trawe and Warnow rivers after the Germans had left, in about 500 A.D. In the twelfth century, the prince of the Obotrites became sovereign of the German *Reich*, and his people embraced Christianity. In 1815, Mecklenburg became a grand duchy.

After living in the valley of the Ahr among descendants of Roman legionaries and western European peoples, we East Prussians became acquainted with a different sect of our German population. Unlike the lively, talkative Rhinelanders, people here seemed calmer and more circumspect. They were especially concerned with good manners, which may have been due to the presence of the grand duke and numerous noble court officials.

Our infantrymen naturally showed special interest in the female part of the population. One could easily modify the saying about Polish women that Slavic women (in reference to the origins of the ladies of Mecklenburg) have charm beyond compare.[7] While the girls of the Ahr valley were dark-haired or of dark complexion, here they were mainly blond with blue or gray eyes. If the women of the Rhineland, because of their membership in the Catholic Church, may lean toward being reserved in their conduct with men, here, in this respect, one could see joyful unconcern. To a great extent, our soldiers succumbed to the charms of these beautiful girls.

Even I could not help being tempted. This temptation ultimately provided the opportunity for the old major to avenge himself in an underhanded way for my having taken sides in the *Luftwaffe* pilots' club.

After the French campaign, the national ban on dancing was lifted. One evening, the officers of the regimental staff proceeded to the ballroom of their favorite hangout, "Prince Blücher" (during the occupation by the Soviets, it was renamed "Ernst Thälmann," after the Communist writer!). Overcoming some hesitation, even the Regimental Commander had joined us. Among those many girls in attendance, there were some beauties that even provoked honest compliments from our usually dour commander. He asked an especially beautiful girl several times for a dance, and it was just the one who, a few weeks later, would oversleep in my apartment. After heavy drinking, I did not succeed in getting her back on her rather nice legs!

Quite miffed, her boss, who was the manager of the local post office, called up the regimental staff, and reported that one of his girls was missing. He further stated that she had last been seen with an officer of our infantry regiment. Fortunately, the Regimental Commander was on leave, and I hoped that grass would grow over the affair by the time he returned. Of course, in farm country such as Mecklenburg, where there is grass, there are cows, and one came along to graze, just as the grass began to grow. . . .

It was known in this little town that the *Major* who had assumed command in the *Oberst*'s absence was not without sin himself, so his dressing down to me was more for my stupidity than my morality. Instead of broadcasting the matter too much, he reported every detail to *Oberst* Newiger when he returned. I had to report to the Regimental Commander!

In the eyes of the *Oberst*, I was a unconscionable roué, a ladies' man, who frivolously seduced the prettiest girl in the town. Even after I assured him that everything was harmless, and almost all the officers of the staff had been witnesses to the fact that, indeed, the beautiful one had been terribly drunk, the Old Man didn't believe me and—as I have to admit today— from his point of view, he was right.

The young post office girl was transferred immediately to Schwerin which, at least officially, settled the matter for her manager and for my *Oberst*. Shortly before the end of the War, I met her once again. She had married a physician who was at the Kurland front. I could only wish for her from the bottom of my heart that she might see him again in good health.

Months before this incident, a rumor went around saying that I had been recommended for commissioning. In preparation, I had a pair of officer's riding boots made, and riding pants to go with them. One morning I was awakened by my orderly with the words, "Good morning, *Leutnant!*" My unsettled past prevented me from immediately being promoted to *Oberleutnant*, as would have been in keeping with my seniority, dating to 1935. According to this, I was the most senior *Leutnant* in the entire army!

At lunch, in his usual way, the *Oberst* Newiger remarked, "You look so conspicuous!" From the corner of my eye, I noticed that he was carefully watching, probably to find out if I scratched the plate with my fork or even would eat peas with my knife! The Regimental Commander and his adjutant, by the way, in accordance with their rank, were quartered in the elegant villa of the *Gräfin* (Baroness) Voss. She was born in America and, years later, very kindly assisted my first wife and then eight-year-old daughter when they were refugees from East Prussia.

Of course, in the months following the activation of the new 332d Infantry Division, we worked eagerly to complete the training of our soldiers, officers, and NCOs. There I noticed that our Regimental Commander regarded the National Socialist regime in a negative way. Shortly after the French campaign, Goebbels publicly declared Hitler the "*Grössten*

Feldherrn aller Zeiten," ("Greatest field commander of all time") which in common parlance became shortened to "Gröfaz." One evening when this was discussed in our temporary mess, *Oberst* Newiger said in his thick Berlin accent, "Greatest commander of all times? Well, I don't know. Something like this must be learned," implying that Hitler's military education left much to be desired.

I noticed his laxity about Party protocols again during the sandtable exercise in which all the officers of our newly established division took part, and which was directed by our *Oberst*. At this training event, the Regimental Commander had to report to the Commanding General that all officers were present. According to regulations, because he was not wearing his cap, this was to be accompanied by the "German Greeting."[8] Yet *Oberst* Newiger simply reported with a brief bow to the General.

Whether the *Oberst*'s lack of political enthusiasm irked the Commanding General, or whether it was simply a payback for his acerbic style, I cannot say, but at the sandtable exercise, our *Oberst* took a shot in his Achilles heel! When he inaccurately quoted some excerpts from the "Holy Script" of the art of command from HDV 300/1, *Die Truppenführung* (the operational doctrine manual), he was condescendingly corrected by the Commanding General. *Oberst* Newiger blushed like a virgin after an unseemly proposition.

I have mentioned that I was embarrassed in the first inspection of my pioneer platoon, because of unfavorable circumstances. Here, in Ludwigslust, I presented the Regimental Commander with a picture-book inspection, which impressed all the guests enormously. Yet, this inspection had not the least to do with our mission as pioneers; rather, it was a parade-ground-style exhibition of spit and polish.

In spring 1941, the 332d Infantry Division moved from Ludwigslust to one of the most beautiful places in France, on the Atlantic coast near Deauville. Here, our Regimental Commander got much more classy quarters than the ones in Ludwigslust, namely a villa of the famous perfume manufacturer, Madame Coty. The villa was situated in a magnificent park, high above the city, with a magical view of the Atlantic Ocean. To be fair, it was not only our *Oberst*, but all of our soldiers who had the sort of quarters in Deauville that most of us had only seen in movies. Every well-to-do Frenchman seemed to have his summer residence there.

There was then no sign of the fortifications that were later were built in that area because, at that time, everyone still dreamt of "going to Eng-e-land."[9] Of course, we did take great notice of the preparations that were being made for such an endeavor. There was a single, insignificant ship-loading exercise . . . and that was all. The loading exercise was for

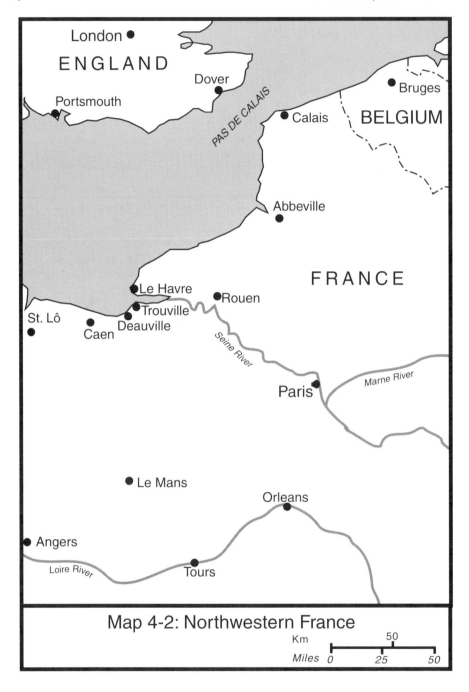

Map 4-2: Northwestern France

Operation SEALION, the codename for the invasion of England. It took place for us in the delta of a little river between Deauville and Trouville-sur-Mer. The small ship on which we were loaded induced strong suspicion regarding its seaworthiness. Additionally, one could only load at high tide because very soon afterwards, the water level in the small port would drop again . . . almost down to mud at low tide. I think the difference between high and low tide was around ten meters, more or less. I was probably not the only one who was so concerned; *Grossadmiral* Raeder evidently shared my misgivings and those of myriad others about the practicality of this operation. With what there was for transports and warships for their protection, the German armed forces could not risk an invasion of England.

The view of *Oberkommando der Wehrmacht* (OKW)[10] at that point was probably already directed east, which was unfortunately confirmed by a radio bulletin we all heard on the morning of 22 June 1941.

Chapter Five

Finding the "Real War": Russia 1941

Historical Commentary

German, Rumanian, Hungarian, and Slovakian troops launched Operation BARBAROSSA *against the Soviets on the morning of 22 June 1941. On 1 July, German and Finnish units attacked the Soviets in north Karelia, to make complete the conflagration along the western border of the Soviet Empire. After years of uneasy peace and decades of wary cooperation, the two great European continental land powers collided in a cataclysm that would ultimately change the map of Europe for the next half century.*

The collision was truly of colossal proportions. The German force consisted of 119 infantry and mountain divisions, nineteen panzer divisions, and fifteen motorized divisions attacked in concert with twelve Rumanian divisions and some Slovakian and Hungarian formations. It ran along a 995-mile front (exclusive of the additional 620 miles on the Finnish front, on which eighteen Finnish divisions and a further four German mountain and infantry divisions were engaged), which rapidly grew to almost 1,500 miles as the great offensive progressed. The Axis forces initially took on a Soviet military juggernaut which included 150 infantry divisions, eighteen motorized rifle divisions, eight cavalry divisions, and thirty-six tank brigades in the Western Military Regions.[11] Using about 2,800 combat aircraft, the Luftwaffe smashed the Soviet Air Force, destroying about 1,200 planes on the first day alone.

Although there is strong evidence that Stalin knew of the approaching German invasion—since the opening of Soviet archives, there are even indications that he may have been planning an attack of his own later in the year—for some reason, his operational commanders were ignorant of the impending German offensive. With air superiority rapidly established, the German invaders pressed their tactical surprise and quickly overwhelmed forward elements of the Soviet Army, inflicting devastating losses on their foes. "Blitzkrieg" seemed to be working its magic again, as thousands of Soviet units collapsed in the opening days. Just five days after the commencement of hostilities, the Germans encircled and eventually captured 290,000 men in a great envelopment by Field Marshal von Bock's Army Group Center in Belorussia; by 5 August, von Bock's panzer-tipped Army Group captured 300,000 more. The Soviets fought with varying degrees of tenacity against the assaults of the other German army groups. This inconsistency was probably indicative of the chaos borne at higher levels by Stalin's officer purges of the late 1930s. Nevertheless, by the onset of winter in late 1941, the Germans and their allies had gained over 2,300,000 square kilometers of territory, captured about 3,500,000 Soviet soldiers, and killed about 4,000,000 more. Army Group North besieged Leningrad; Army Group Center's advanced elements reached Moscow's western suburbs; and Army Group South had overrun the Ukraine, nearly all of the Crimea, and was threatening to break out to seize or cut off the Caucasus oilfields.

Yet, despite these almost inconceivable losses, "Blitzkrieg" failed to destroy the Soviet will to fight. Although two panzer armies had enabled Army Group Center to rapidly maneuver and achieve decisive encirclements, the single panzer army assigned to Army Groups North and South, respectively, did not allow their commanders to maneuver at the tempos attained by the main attack in Belorussia. When Germany unleashed BARBAROSSA, she sent her sons to war with as many horses for transport as she did motor vehicles—about 600,000 of each. The tempo of operations across the vast Ukrainian steppes and through the forests and swamps of Lithuania, Latvia, Estonia, and north Karelia was limited by the pace of dismounted infantrymen and plodding draft animals. Dissipated over an area many times greater than France and Belgium, and slowed to a pace with which the enemy soon learned to cope, the overwhelming psychological impact of the Wehrmacht's well-coordinated maneuver did not have the same effect on the Soviets of 1941 as it had had on the French of 1940. The Soviet Army bent and stretched, but it did not break. By the time the winter arrived, the Germans had yet to take Leningrad or Moscow, and the woefully unprepared German Army had to halt its drive east. Even as the Landsers[12] huddled and stamped about for warmth in the bitter Russian cold, the Soviets brought in troops from the Chinese border, called up huge numbers of fresh recruits, and were rallying for a savage counter-offensive.

While the Germans inflicted immense casualties on the Soviets, the German Army and its allies—which by the late summer included 60,000 Italian infantrymen and cavalrymen—also suffered heavy losses in men and materiel. By the end of September, when Georg Grossjohann was transferred to Army Group South as a replacement officer, German losses amounted to about 535,000 officers and men—roughly fifteen percent of the 3.4 million men the Wehrmacht *had on the Eastern Front. By the time he reached the 198th Infantry Division, it had nearly reached the zenith of its advance for the year, and was already engaged in repelling spirited counterattacks by the enemy.*

Georg Grossjohann Remembers . . .

In the late spring of 1941, my regimental commander was sent to a unit which was to be involved in the operations on the Eastern front. For his farewell, I held a formation of my pioneer platoon as an honor guard in front of his quarters. The *Oberst* appreciated this with surprising friendliness, and shook my hand, which he rarely did.

Once, in my presence, a company commander extended his hand toward the *Oberst*, which elicited the remark, "Do me a favor and wait until I extend my hand to you, before you extend your fin to me!" Most likely, the departure from beautiful France and maybe the departure from us made him more mellow!

A few times during the war, I wrote to him and always received nice, gracious replies. At the end of 1944, he was a *Generalmajor* commanding a security division. He was retired in January 1945, and after the war he lived in Berlin.

In spite of all of his abrasive idiosyncrasies, I kind of liked the cynical old dwarf; somehow he always reminded me a little of my eccentric old company commander from my enlisted days in East Prussia, Erwin M.

For a period while still in France, I was ordered to Tours to attend a course of instruction for company commanders. At this time, I had the opportunity to visit the world-famous *chateaux* in the Loire Valley. During my last weeks in France, I also visited Paris, Rouen, Angers, and Le Mans. Being an East Prussian who in the past hardly ever crossed the borders of his home province, this meant an abundance of new impressions.

Our regiment was moved for a few weeks from the channel coast into the hinterland. The regimental staff was quartered in the *chateau* of the

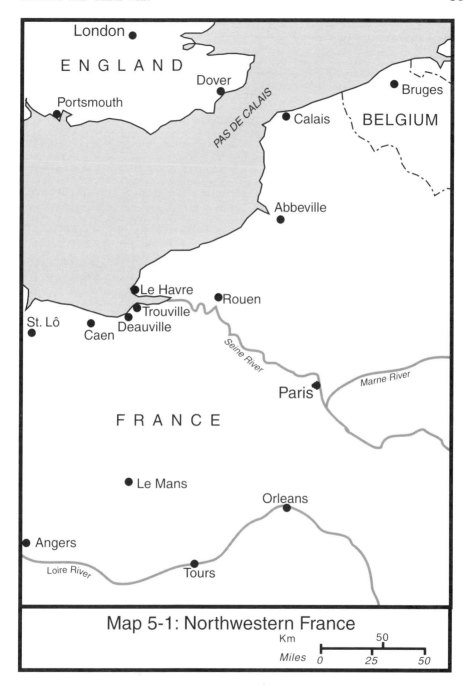

Map 5-1: Northwestern France

manufacturer of fine liqueurs whose products are world-famous. The relationship between the owner of the *chateau* and his family and our soldiers was friendly and congenial, and I mean that for both sides. This was the case almost all over France, but was especially evident in Normandy; for historical reasons, the people there were not very fond of the English, so we had a common antagonist.

After the campaign in Russia started, the daughter of the *chateau* owner told me that now we Germans would surely lose the war. Officially, of course, I could not agree with her.

In late summer, I was notified of my transfer to the officer replacement pool of Army Group South on the Eastern Front. This was my final farewell from a unit whose men were mostly from my East Prussian homeland.

My first station in Russia was Kirovograd where the officer replacement pool of the Army Group was located. The changeover from green, beautiful France to cheerless, gray Russia was so severe that it took a long time to get used to it. Quarters for officers in the pool were in the former local headquarters of the Soviet secret police, a subdued brick building. This building clearly showed marks from bullet strikes in the basement walls, solitary confinement cells, and so on. In short, the facility had everything that a secret police headquarters would need for its occupants to be effective in their trade.

At that time in Kirovograd, there was also a giant camp with thousands of Russian prisoners of war (PWs) who, after the commencement of the so-called "mud period," were standing around, knee-deep in mud. Even if these were our enemies, I still felt the situation of these people was shocking and unspeakably depressing.

Most certainly, the Army Group headquarters could not be blamed for their misery. We simply lacked the capabilities of sheltering them, and especially lacked the equipment necessary to transport the PWs quickly to better facilities. But I don't want to conceal that in some places, the treatment of Russian PWs proceeded incompetently! Atrocities and mutilations committed on some German soldiers elsewhere presumably contributed to the maltreatment of many Russian PWs.

When I was moved to the east, I was actually convinced that I would be too late to see action. *Reichspressechef* Dr. Dietrich declared on the radio that all that was needed in Russia from that point in late summer would be "police actions."

Well, I was taught differently when I arrived there.

After a few days in Kirovograd, I got orders assigning me to the unit to which I would see almost all of my combat in the war, namely, the 198th Infantry Division, a Württemburg-Baden outfit. I reported to the commander of Grenadier Regiment 308, an older man whom I at once noticed was extremely well-liked by his men. This *Oberst*, "Papa" Schultz, told me in his thick Swabian accent, "You cannot give my Swabians the same run around as you give to your Prussians!" He explained his reservations as soon as I reported. As I later established, I was indeed almost the only non-Swabian in the officer corps of his regiment.

There was tremendous bitterness amongst the infantry soldiers at the front over the misinterpretation and misunderstanding of the realities of their situation. There was not much time for me to get used to the Eastern Front. A few hours after reporting, I was on top of a treeless hill, across from a mine that was occupied by the Russians. My strongpoint (!) was called the "Linsemeyer Heights," named after a *Leutnant* of that name whom I had been sent to replace. The occupants of the position consisted of only a few NCOs and enlisted men from our 1st Battalion. To the left and right there were big holes in the line. The only support for the defenders of the lonely hill was a platoon of heavy infantry guns, which had been shooting interdictory fire on the terrain in front of the Linsemeyer Heights and the mine beyond. For me, the *real* war began only now, on top of the Linsemeyer Heights.

During my trip to the front, I met *Feldwebel* Reiff, the platoon leader of the infantry howitzer platoon. He was an officer aspirant and later served consecutively as my temporary adjutant and then commander of the 13th Company of Grenadier Regiment 308. He was a very congenial and spirited gentleman with a good sense of humor and excellent manners. After the war, he enjoyed a very successful career as a government official. He became the highest official in his home county and remained as ministerial director, chief of the state chancellery of Baden-Württemberg until his retirement. After the war, I visited him often. A few years ago he retired in Switzerland.

I only remained on the Linsemeyer Heights for a few days, but it was enough to get acquainted with the mentality of my future comrades. For the Swabians, the war was a extremely unpleasant, senseless business, but a reality that could not be avoided.

Sober, orderly, and practical, they dealt with this business with the same strength and energy as in their peacetime endeavors in their Swabian homeland, which, in their view, would have made much more sense. With few exceptions, these Swabian *Landsers* were tough, enduring, reliable, brave, loyal, and good comrades. A few days later I was again transferred, this time from the 1st to the 2d Battalion of Grenadier Regiment 308. At dusk, I went up with the troops carrying the dinner meal to my new unit, where I would remain for the next eight difficult months.

First, I reported to the battalion commander, a reactivated reservist who, as a civilian, had been a school dean and who had a hard time hiding his evident helplessness regarding the demands of this war. After a brief interview, I moved on to the command post (CP) of the 7th Company.

When I arrived, the company was heavily engaged in the process of driving off a Russian attack. I dropped my few belongings in the shabby shelter that housed the CP, then I hurried with a messenger a few hundred meters further to the front. The air contained "a lot of iron" because we were being greeted from the opposite side with tracers that zipped by our ears. Out of breath, as we were taking cover behind the corner of a house, the messenger pointed towards a haggard form, standing upright and without any cover. A cigarette in the corner of his mouth, the wraith was firing shot after shot towards the attacking Russians, and seemed to be providing a running commentary in a thick Swabian accent. "That one's had it!" "That was nothing, no wait, that one's had it too!" and so on.

This was clearly not the time to report to my new commander; rather, I thought the proper form was to take part in the defense against this attack, until the haggard commander declared "OK, then, I think that's it." Only then could I report.

As bullets zipped by, I said, "For God's sake, *Herr Hauptmann*, why don't you take cover?" He responded, "Dear young friend, I am suffering from a kidney problem. The ground is too cold for me to lie down."

This was my introduction to my new company commander. In thirteen years of military service, I had never met anyone remotely like him. Along with the messenger, a few soldiers, and me, he sauntered back to his CP with his rifle under his arm like a hunter, the cold cigarette butt still in the corner of his mouth. Grinning, he sat down in his shabby camp.

Only afterwards, he came up with a few questions, including whether I had already reported to the battalion commander. After I confirmed that I had, he brooded for a few moments. Finally, very pensively, he said, "You know, the one thing I want to tell you is that the battalion commander is a very big asshole." Such a dire and candid appraisal of a commander by one of his subordinates was something completely new to me. Of course, any soldier may *think* things like this at one time or another, but can he say them out loud? Of course, criticism of superiors—behind their backs—was nothing new in my Army experience. . . .

From my enlisted days, I remember the wisecracks of *Leutnant* von St., who gave "Erwin the Only" his nickname. He was definitely not a fan of our harsh and strange company commander, and in fact, I think he had been assigned to our company to be "indoctrinated" by Erwin. Bismarck once stated that the world may be able to copy Germans in many ways, but one could never copy the Prussian *Leutnant*. Perhaps *Leutnant* von St., was one of those officers. What Bismarck said was an understatement, however, because that type of officer existed throughout the German lands! *Leutnant* von St. descended from Moravian nobility and afterwards, as a Silesian, was actually only a "booty" Prussian. He came up with numerous funny lines, but, of course, never when Erwin was nearby! And that was hard to do, since Erwin had agents who informed him about everything, not to blow the whistle on others, *of course*, but naturally *only* out of concern for the company's well-being and esteem! *Jawohl!*

I remember well a lesson *Leutnant* von St. particularly enjoyed teaching. It was definitely not a subject of which Erwin would have approved. It was about the decorations on the inside of wall locker doors. Like their counterparts all over the world, German soldiers embellished the insides of these doors with photos, not only family snapshots, but photos of women . . . often quite sexy ones. These pin-ups were the subject of the *Leutnant's* favorite speech. He would lash out against "tasteless" arrangements of photos. "When Private Przybilsky hangs up Uncle August on the right, and Aunt Berta on the left, it is just not right that a naked woman lewdly sticking out her _____ should be in between!" *Leutnant* von St. would sternly counsel. Then, with blue eyes twinkling, he would order, "Rearrange them in a more tasteful fashion—like this," and, upon demonstrating a more "acceptable" arrangement, he would go on to the next locker. Never did he make a man take them down.

Leutnant von St.'s independent character registered in many ways. Several times, he showed up for duty not in black riding boots, but in mountain boots and leggings, adorned with tassels. He justified this by his love for the mountain infantry. Later on, he succeeded and was transferred to the *Gebirgsjäger* . . . with whom he was killed in action shortly after the start of the war.

True to his personality, he left everything he owned to his soldiers.

My new, acerbic company commander had, in civilian life, been a teacher of modern languages in a girl's high school in Konstanz, and he stated that he had applied for transfer to the Afrika Korps because of his kidney problem. As far as the "cold ground" was concerned, it made me think that the nights in Africa would also be quite cold. . . .

In the following days and weeks, we had to turn back enemy attacks almost every day. By the end of November and early December, we

Map 5-2: Approximate Position of German and German Allies' Forces, Late Autumn 1941

- - - Approximate trace
of frontline positions

Km   100 200 300

Miles 0   100   200

received orders to clear all our bridgeheads east of the Mius River. Afterwards, our position was mostly along the western bank of the river. By late November, the frost had not yet completely set in, so all necessary movements had to be accomplished in mud up to our knees.

Shortly after we cleared the bridgehead over the Mius, our cold-sensitive *Hauptmann* left us, but not to reinforce the Afrika Korps, as he conveyed to me. I assumed command of the company. From now until the summer offensive began on 11 July 1942, our division held its position steadfastly against continuous attacks by the Russians.

The first Russian winter for us came in the early weeks of December, which made it incredibly difficult to construct a continuous front. Instead of using shovels, we had to use explosives to excavate bunkers and trenches. Since the Mius positions were way up front, we could only work on improving them at night. Almost every evening, we had to retake the positions under construction from the Russians, who settled in them as soon as the pioneers stopped working at dawn.

We did not possess a continuous front throughout almost the whole winter of 1941–42. The abundant snowfalls which meanwhile had come also made it impossible for the Russians to penetrate between the geographically disparate villages. My company was deployed in Gribovka, one of those solitary Russian villages directly on the west bank of the Mius. In this icy cold we had the saying, "He who is thrown out of his village is lost."

On 11 December 1941, Germany declared war on the United States. When I heard this on my *Volksempfänger* radio receiver[13] in my cottage in Gribovka, I immediately thought of our little *Oberst* Newiger and his somber prognosis after the campaign in the west. Indeed, all the world powers had entered the war and, with the exception of Japan, unfortunately all were against us!

Shortly after Christmas 1941, the 2d Battalion of Grenadier Regiment 308, of which my 7th Company was an integral part, was pulled out of the foremost front lines to Pelakeyevka, the location of the Regimental CP, to enjoy some urgently needed days of rest combined with an also badly needed delousing. During these days, and all further rare days of rest, I always had quarters in a cottage, situated directly next to the company orderly room. My first sergeant was an older *Oberfeldwebel* named Sickerle, from Pfüllingen. He was a notary in civilian life. A Swabian notary definitely at that time did not have to be a licensed lawyer, but simply some sort of paralegal professional.

My Russian, or more precisely, Ukrainian hosts, were as nice and friendly as the French had been during my time in Normandy. I was always given a sofa covered with black wax-coated sheet cloth to sleep on, while the whole family retired to sleep on the giant stove. Unfortunately, my sofa

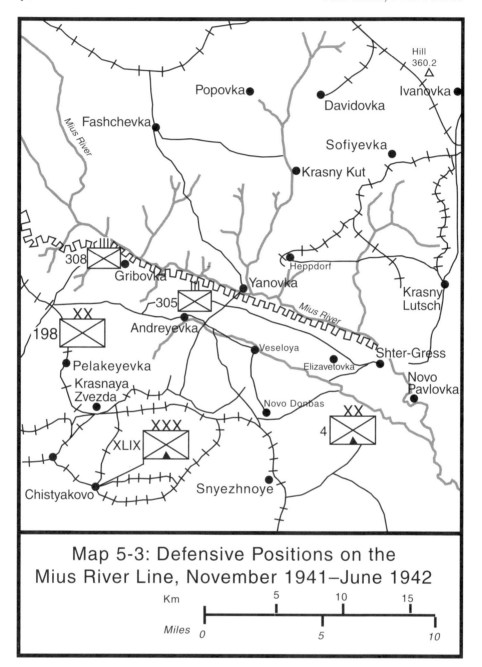

Map 5-3: Defensive Positions on the Mius River Line, November 1941–June 1942

was so full of bugs that in the morning I always looked as if I had the measles. My hosts, who seemed to be completely immune to bedbugs, were always greatly amused when I got up in the morning swollen from stings and bites. But their harmless glee in my misfortune was certainly not ill-intended.

During the war, I learned to appreciate and admire what a Swabian unit can offer besides its soldiers' military qualities, organizational talent, and diligence. I found the Swabians also to be quite inventive. For example, to ensure that the roads were trafficable during the upcoming period of thaw, the village streets in the division area were filled with anthracite coal instead of rubble because the coal was abundantly available from the nearby mines.

As this work progressed into spring, the pioneers and their Russian helpers made a surprising discovery which mainly was absorbed with incredulity by the younger members of the population. After half a meter of mud was removed from the road, which was then supposed to be filled with coal, there appeared a well-conserved cobblestone surface. Only very old villagers admitted that they remembered its existence.

The Division's pioneers, supported by nondivisional engineers, began the construction of a railroad for the division's use, which later benefited the whole corps. The supervisor was *Oberleutnant* Dr. Angelberger. A total of sixty-five kilometers of track were moved and numerous blown bridges were repaired. Two locomotives were built from parts picked up from different places. An iron foundry was also constructed to produce the miscellaneous parts needed for these projects. Almost a thousand paid Russian auxiliary workers were employed for these projects.

This railroad was vital for our logistical support because motorized vehicles, even if available, could not be used in the mud, and horses were moved far behind the lines due to a lack of stables and fodder.

At the regimental CP, even a festival hall with a stage was built, which could be used for cultural events.

On Christmas Eve, my company was again moved to a rest area. Unfortunately, I could only spend one night on my vermin-infested sofa because the next day, the Russians zealously renewed their attacks on Gribovka. The attacks were made by the Soviet *197th Rifle Regiment*, which lost half its soldiers in two days of attacks during the Christmas holidays. Gribovka remained securely in our hands.

By the end of 1941, our division had lost 203 officers and 5,426 enlisted men killed, wounded, and missing. At the beginning of 1942, *General der Gebirgs Truppen* Rudolf Konrad, Commanding General of the XLIX Mountain Corps, after a visit to the division, made an entry in his diary on

4 January 1942, "Protection from cold leaves much to be desired. Many cold casualties, including two dead; lacking winter clothing; horses heavily weakened, hardly any fodder left, raw (hay or straw) was gone completely. The Russian winter is our enemy." He concluded with this summary of our Division and its situation, "[I have] generally the best impression of the men's worth, but [the situation] is a shocking reality."[14]

Chapter Six

Breakout from the Mius Bridgehead

Historical Commentary

The heavy casualties in the 198th Infantry Division mirrored those of the German Army in the East overall. By mid-December, losses amounted to 775,000, or about twenty-five percent of the total of Axis troops committed against the Soviets. Vigorous Soviet attacks continued throughout January and February 1942, all along the front with the Germans. Like the German offensive of 1941, however, the force of the operations was insufficient for the magnitude of the missions, and by March, the Soviet counteroffensive had lost its potency. Nevertheless, the winter combat inflicted over 200,000 more battle casualties on the Germans, and nearly another 500,000 cold-weather casualties on the unprepared invaders. An indication of the horrors endured by the soldiers who survived that first winter in Russia can be gained from the nickname the Landsers *gave to the campaign medal the German Army issued for the winter campaign of 1941–42, "Frozen Meat Medal."*

In the summer of 1942, the Germans launched an offensive designed to end the war with the Soviet Union. Even though the German economy and society had been elevated to a full-war footing—exactly what Hitler had been trying to avoid by using "Blitzkrieg" operational techniques— the attackers were fewer in number than they had been during the initial invasion of the Soviet Union in the previous summer. Unlike the Soviet Army, the German Army was never able to replace the human losses sustained in the winter of 1941–42, and though the materiel losses had been made up and quality improved, even the quantities of tanks did not exceed the numbers present at the launch of BARBAROSSA.

Army Group South—of which Georg Grossjohann's 198th Infantry Division was a part—was to make the main attack of the 1942 offensive. While Army Group North continued the siege of Leningrad, von Bock and his men were to seize the strategically-critical Caucasus oilfields. To reach them, the Soviets would first have to be dislodged from their positions near Izyum on the Donets, and the left/northern flank would have to be anchored on the Volga, near Stalingrad. Although the German divisions of Army Group South were brought up to about eighty-five percent strength (the units of Army Groups Center and North were only brought to fifty percent strength), they faced a daunting task, both from a tenacious enemy and from the difficulties implicit to an ever-lengthening supply line. To make matters worse for the invaders, the Soviets launched a spoiling attack in mid-May, forcing the Germans to fight before they were completely prepared. Ultimately, this attack redounded to the Soviets' disadvantage, as Generaloberst *Ewald von Kleist and the First Panzer Army enveloped the attackers and took over 214,000 prisoners near Izyum.*

As the offensive began, Army Group South was reorganized into two new commands. Army Group A, with the Seventeenth and First Panzer Armies, was to seize the Caucasus oilfields, while Army Group B drove to the Volga and protected its rear with the Second, Sixth, and Fourth Panzer Armies, as well as the Third and Fourth Rumanian, Eighth Italian, and Second Hungarian Armies.

Georg Grossjohann Remembers . . .

With the waning winter, our situation improved from day to day. Gradually, a continuous front was created, even connecting us in the north with our Italian brothers-in-arms from the Celere Division.

The construction of the positions pushed on, and especially precarious positions were strengthened with barbed wire. The gradually improving beautiful spring weather caused us to feel quite at home in our position. My company was alternately deployed on the *Burg* ("Fortress") or *Schanze* ("Lair") positions, two areas in the regimental sector that were especially exposed.

Other than some local actions on both sides, the division sector was relatively quiet for weeks if not months. At that time I received a guest, an aspiring general staff officer from the artillery who was spending the usual apprenticeship with another branch of the Army under my supervision. I knew how often such an apprenticeship ended in a military cemetery at the front, which is why I told my action-starved guest at once that he was here to learn, and not to be a hero. He survived, and after the end of his term, thanked me warmly, both for the experience, and for his survival.

On 28 June 1942, Army Group B to the north started the big summer offensive. Our division, which belonged to Army Group A, remained still in its position on the Mius. Beginning 28 June, the Russians probed our front more and more with reconnaissance and raid patrols, which were turned back. On the morning of 30 June, the Russians attacked my company's position in the "Fortress" with the *3d Battalion, 694th Rifle Regiment*, reinforced by a machinegun company.

On this morning, almost all our officers, including me, were participating in a wargame in the rear, when a motorcycle dispatch rider brought the absent general the message, "Extremely strong enemy attack in the sector of the 2d Battalion, Grenadier Regiment 308, on the "Fortress" and "Lair" positions!" From the distant sounds of combat, I had suspected that already, even before the messenger arrived. My commander and I were at once taken in the motorcycle sidecar to the battalion CP. I hurried to my bunker and from there, rushed forward in short bounds under strong enemy artillery fire, up to the "Fortress," where my *Leutnant* Jutersonke was the platoon leader. I only got there at the finale. The young officer, who looked like a Viking -- and fought like one -- had not only held on to the position, but had, with his handful of excellent soldiers, even taken thirty-four prisoners and captured twenty-five weapons. About sixty dead Russians were left behind.

A few words about my young company officer are in order. Our off-duty relationship was like that between an elder and younger brother. Often we conversed in his or in my bunker and forged plans for post-war life. Unfortunately, on this day, *Leutnant* Jutersonke had only thirteen more days to go in his short life. On the afternoon of 13 July, only a few steps from me, he was killed in action.

I was promoted to *Oberleutnant* in the spring of 1942, retroactive from 1 November 1941. I was finally starting to catch up with my seniority.

Before we left Gribovka during the beginning of the German summer offensive in 1942, I reflected once more on how amiably and without enmity the Ukrainian population presented itself. This was especially true for my occasional hosts in Pelakayevka. They always willingly gave me what they had—sometimes a couple of fresh eggs or a few slices of their exquisite homemade bread. I reciprocated now and then, with a little bottle of cologne or a bar of good soap, things we soldiers from time to time received from the Army canteen. Both were highly appreciated, especially by the daughter of the house. It was pitiful how this nice relationship was

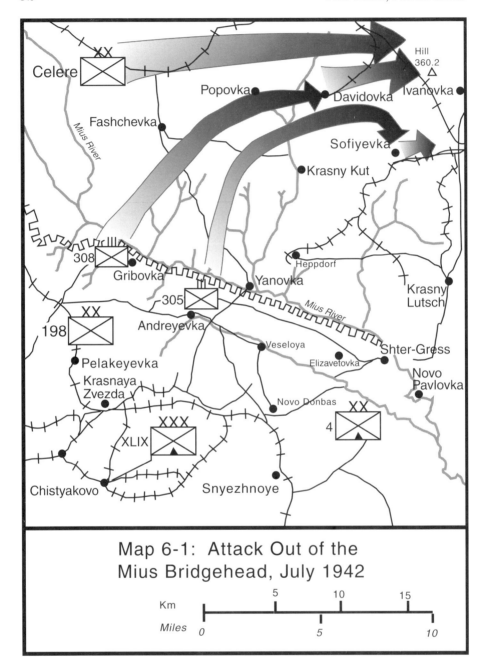

Map 6-1: Attack Out of the Mius Bridgehead, July 1942

later changed due to bad mistakes in the political realm. Surely it was not only those mistakes, but also the fact that we were stuck at the Mius. This probably made those that were especially friendly towards us give second thoughts to their attitude. Of course, nobody wanted to be called a collaborator, in case the Germans eventually pulled back. In the Union of Soviet Socialist Republics, as elsewhere, that could cost dearly.

Early on the morning of 12 July, we initiated an attack from Gribovka across the Mius. For us, this was the beginning of the last big offensive, driving more deeply into almost endless Russia. On the first day, we advanced almost twenty kilometers against heavy resistance by enemy rear guards. Yet we remained near Davidovka, as dusk settled in. Again and again, the artillery of the Russian rear guard would hit us hard in the evening and during the night with heavy artillery concentrations. The commander of the 1st Battalion, Grenadier Regiment 308, the former regimental adjutant, *Hauptmann* Gross, was killed by a direct hit on his CP.

The next morning, our Regiment moved up to a railroad embankment, because on this 13th day of July, we were near the attack's center of gravity. All the roads were muddy due to a cloudburst on the evening of 12 July, which also had the unfortunate effect of preventing our artillery from displacing in time to support the attack. I, therefore, had to execute the directed attack on an *ad hoc* basis, without an artillery preparation. Our losses were accordingly high. "At 1600, 2d Battalion, Grenadier Regiment 308 stormed Hill 360.2, which had been strengthened with bunkers and barbed wire. The 7th Company under *Oberleutnant* Grossjohann and part of an Italian motorcycle rifle company of the Celere Division which voluntarily joined the attack, especially distinguished themselves."[15]

The Italians, by the way, proved themselves to be quite worthy battle partners during this attack on the strongly fortified Russian position. Offensive operations probably better suited the Italians better than defensive ones, however. My roughly two hundred-man group lost about 25%, even though the operation was over in a little more than thirty minutes. The necessary artillery preparation was sorely missed.

I have already mentioned that among the numerous soldiers killed in action in this attack was my *Leutnant* Jutersonke; additionally, my right hand was smashed by a bullet, although I didn't notice at all at the time. Seeing that blood was seeping out of my sleeve, one of my men brought it to my attention after we had reached our objective. The bullet that had gone through my hand ricocheted off the bolt of my submachinegun. Otherwise, it would have entered my torso. I was extremely lucky. That both of our officers were put out of action was once more proof of the good training of the Russian snipers, who always finished off the most important targets first.

I had one major realization from this attack. In a "man-on-man" battle, one senses absolutely no fear, presumably because one finds oneself in a situation absolutely without mental distraction. I was not especially afraid of fire from infantry weapons, because in my experience, if one is hit, chances are that one will either recover or will die quickly. My Achilles heel was artillery fire, because I had seen the effects of shrapnel often enough to know that it could tear off a limb. I could only imagine how awful it would be to live without arms, legs, or with other cruel mutilations. In late evening, my company was pulled out and I had to report personally to the regimental CP. Given the magnitude of my wound, which had in the meantime caused my smashed hand to swell thickly, I went to the aid station first. When I appeared at the regimental CP, I was awarded the Iron Cross, 1st Class. *Oberleutnant* Leitner, the regimental adjutant, used his own medal in the ceremony.

Later on, our battalion adjutant, *Oberleutnant* Dr. Rittmannsberger, told me that there had been strong consideration whether it might not have been more fitting to recommend me for the Knight's Cross.

Only two days later, the division was relieved by the Italians and was sent towards the Caucasus. In these three days the Division suffered the following casualties:

> KIA: 9 officers, 16 NCOs and 58 soldiers;
> WIA: 15 officers, 55 NCOs and 359 soldiers;
> MIA: 1 NCO and 9 soldiers.

Chapter Seven

Recovery, Relaxation, and the Tedium of Reserve

Historical Commentary

After the breakout from the Mius bridgehead, the 198th Infantry Division and Army Group A drove on across the Don River and into the Caucasus Mountains. The immediate goal of the offensive was to seize the Caucasus oilfields near Maikop, Grozny, and Baku; the ultimate goal of the German offensive in the Caucasus was to break through to Iran and eventually link up in the Middle East with Axis forces from North Africa.

Elements of Army Group A penetrated as far south as Mount Elbrus, where, on 21 August, mountain troops briefly raised the Swastika. There, in late summer, with supply stretched to the breaking point, low on fuel, and with casualties rapidly mounting, the German attack faltered and ground to a halt. The 198th Infantry Division established and occupied positions in the western Caucasus, near Krasnodar and Tuapsa.

Throughout the late summer and autumn of 1942, the lines remained relatively stable. To the north, Army Group B was stopped at the Don River line, while the German Sixth Army battered its way into Stalingrad. Here, some of the few German troops across the Don fought throughout the autumn to seize this ruined industrial city on the Volga River. They never quite succeeded in taking the town named after the Soviet dictator, but the battle did seriously weaken the Germans, who could not replace the enormous losses they were sustaining . . . while their Soviet enemies could.

The Soviets launched their winter offensive in late 1942, and cut off the Sixth Army around Stalingrad, while driving the rest of Army Group B back from the Don. Simultaneously, they attacked to drive the Germans out of the Caucasus entirely. By the end of January 1943, the quarter million German and Axis soldiers who were encircled at Stalingrad had been reduced to 90,000—all of whom were captured by the beginning of February. Within a few weeks, over three hundred miles to the south, the 198th Infantry Division retreated across the Kuban Peninsula and crossed the Kerch Straits to the Crimea during several months of fierce, costly fighting.

With the loss of the Sixth Army, the German chances of defeating the Soviets disappeared. At best, they could hope for a draw and negotiated settlement.

Georg Grossjohann Remembers . . .

In the following days, I was passed on from one base to the next because field hospitals near the front had to be kept available for more serious casualties. So, after some time, I ended up being billeted in a small hospital in Vienna; the treatment of my hand took place in the very renowned Billroth Hospital in the same city. My injury was precisely what infantrymen called a "homebound shot." It was serious enough to get one sent back to the *Reich*, but not life-threatening. To make matters even more comfortable, while a patient in the hospital, one could move around freely and did not have to stay in bed.

Coming from Gribovka to Vienna was like being transferred from filthy icewater into a perfumed bath. A wounded warrior was, at least as long as the war lasted, always the object of gifts and favors of all sorts, and the Viennese were especially good at that.

My little auxiliary hospital was situated in the 19th District, a part of the city that was not exactly populated by the poorest of the poor, as I was informed by the people who knew the locality!

There were invitations of all sorts. My hospital was, amongst others, administered by a well-to-do, as well as attractive, business lady who invited us, from time to time, to her house or the local restaurants. To be sure, the French cognac which she offered us in the restaurants had to be drunk from small Mocha cups, but, *c'est la guerre!* I also got to know other nice people, like a young student-actress from the Reinhardt Institute. She invited me right from a public swimming pool to her home. Her mother owned a small millinery and was a native Viennese. Her father, whom I never met, was Bulgarian.

The seventeen-year-old was a little beauty, as were most of her fellow students from the Institute. Her mother was a little jealous of the pretty daughter, but obviously very concerned about her purity, which, as far as I was concerned, was absolutely sacrosanct. We did indeed like each other a lot, but I always remained as steady as a "Tin Soldier."[16]

After my time in Vienna, when traveling through the area, I visited her and her mother two more times. During my last visit she announced, almost triumphantly, that another man took that which I, during my time with her, had disdained! This proved, she said, that I was a real gentleman. This was indeed honorable, but only a small consolation, considering what I had missed.

After Vienna, I was transferred to Ulm and soon after that to a reserve unit (Reserve Grenadier Battalion 470) in Dijon. The regimental commander was an extremely snappy soldier, an *Oberstleutnant* who, in civilian life had been a school teacher. He required us to perform duties and services, many quite insignificant, which a regular army commander would not have asked.

His adjutant was an older, rather arrogant, reserve *Leutnant*, who tried in vain to give instructions to us company leaders. Collisions between those two inexperienced soldiers and me were clearly in the cards. There was definitely a huge difference between leadership styles—and priorities—at the front, and those that were practiced in non-combat situations. . . .

Erwin the Only didn't think much of us, his soldiers. He thought of us as a bunch of lazy bums and semi-sissies, who were in the *Reichswehr* to have a continuous fire lit under them. This adversarial attitude even pervaded his off-duty time. Clad in civilian clothes and a strange green hat with a brown ribbon—of which he was inordinately proud and wore all the time after duty hours—Erwin would stride across the market square in our garrison town of Osterode with stiff and formal steps. Erwin possessed some of the abilities of a chameleon, mainly that he could see anything from unbelievable angles. The news of his approach always caused all of us from his company to dart indoors immediately, or to speed away furtively in the opposite direction, so that he would find the square completely empty of any of his men.

We similarly avoided him in garrison whenever we could. I understood the dangers and the trouble I could get into, so I avoided crossing his path. Whoever happened to meet him had to count on being berated. The soldiers left the company's quarters through the back door if the signals said that Erwin was approaching the main entrance. Once, when I was in a hurry going to the latrine, I fortunately saw him in time to run back into the building without him noticing me! A little discomfort was better than a lot of military distress.

Anyone who suffered the misfortune of running into the Only by mistake would offer him the kind of snappy salute that would almost knock his cap off his head. Erwin's salutes to his subordinates, however, were perfunctory and rude—he answered every salute by raising his hat barely above his almost bald head without turning the latter by even a millimeter to the side. However, he registered the smallest imperfection in the attire or salute of the soldier involved.

This procedure gave Erwin a sense of grim satisfaction. Woe to him who would overlook Erwin! In a lesser case, he could make his victim feel miserable for the remainder of the evening, barking a few sour words. But usually, he saved the reprimand for the next morning, when he could stand in front of the formation and publicly humiliate the guilty parties. These were the times when he would really open fire!

There was no doubt that in peacetime he could drill a company to a high standard, but he achieved this by using ways and means that were available even to the most stupid of "leaders." I never heard anyone accuse him of trying to influence one of his soldiers, as an educator would, in a calm, objective dialogue. His work as a teacher consisted of either yelling at people or putting them in jail. I learned a lot from him, though—about how to avoid undue attention from superiors and, even more, about how *not* to lead soldiers.

Although the regimental commander and his martinet adjutant were disagreeable, the battalion commander was a very nice older major of the reserve, with whom it was easy to deal. I personally only dealt with collective combat training, as did my former company chiefs. All the other stuff I left to the NCOs and very efficient NCO in charge.

On one particular occasion, about one hour after the start of the duty day, because I had no plans for the moment, I went to inspect the individual skills training being conducted in our small training area. There I found the Regimental Commander and his Adjutant, in an obviously ungracious mood. When I was asked why I only now appeared for duty, I answered, with excruciating correctness, "If the *Herr Oberstleutnant* had read the training schedule, then the *Herr Oberstleutnant* would have learned that not I, but *Oberfeldwebel* Eisele is in charge of this training event at the moment." Besides, I reminded them, I had fourteen years of active duty already, and I knew quite well how to distinguish between training events where my attendance was needed, and those at which it was not! Although the adjutant tried to make this a three-way discussion, I at once refused to tolerate any criticism by him. After both marched away, furious, I returned to our company area.

A few days after my arrival at Dijon, I was surprised in a socially pleasant way. On this day, an officer's meeting was scheduled and to my delight, I discovered my "kidney-ailing" former company commander from Russia in the crowd. He had not been sent to the Afrika Korps, as he had hoped, but he came for his own good to this peaceful reserve outfit. I soon realized that his opinion of the present commander was absolutely identical with the one he had uttered about our commander in Russia, except for the fact that here he had much more justification, as I learned better each day.

For this *Hauptmann*, most people seemed to be *"Armleuchter,"* for almost always when I talked with him about anybody, I got the same answer, "You know, one thing I will tell you, he is a *very* big asshole!"[17]

For the Swabians, this strong expression is not especially coarse or even malicious. The traditional request by the medieval knight Götz von Berlichingen, for example, could mean the expression of joyful surprise, that is, "Hey, now kiss my ass, you too are in the Ukraine?" I often heard this from my Swabians.

But back to my *Hauptmann*. He was not at all unfriendly, but a cynic who treated superiors with indolence, and peers and subordinates with sometimes great condescension. Even if I was never quite sure whether he thought that I, too, was an *Armleuchter*, I did like him a lot for his high impertinence, as well as for his cold-blooded bravery which I witnessed in Russia. Sometimes he even invited me to his apartment in Dijon and later in Auxerre. He always had as company a more or less attractive French woman with him (usually "less," but sometimes "more!"). When I once stated that his present choice was not especially attractive, he said, "Dear young friend, you don't yet understand about this, but this woman has wonderful skin!" Of course, I could not have known.

On another occasion, I asked him why he had to have women around him so often anyway. He replied in his Swabian dialect, "That I can tell you right away. It's nice and it feels good!" Of course, I could not object to or disagree with this, but I sometimes wondered how a fellow like him could have been a professor at a girls' high school before the war. . . .

He spoke French perfectly. In civilian clothes, and maybe wearing a beret, he could surely have been taken for a younger *beneficiaire du rentes* who always have been around in France in great numbers. Years later, I visited him in his house in Konstanz. He seemed to be somewhat less aggressive and cynical than in the past. The reason for that was probably the presence of a lady, quite a vigorous one at that, who was his wife! My wife, who accompanied me, mentioned after the visit that this old boy still looked over any passable woman in his distinct and unmistakable manner.

Like every company leader, I, too, was allotted a small apartment. For my personal assistance, our first sergeant selected as my orderly. He was a pleasant, older infantryman, who was a farmer from Emetsheim near Weissenburg in Franconia. Until my return to Russia, he took care of me with great devotion and dedication. I paid him back by secretly getting him two weeks of furlough for harvesting, in spite of a ban on taking leave.

Later, when my transfer to Russia was confirmed, I asked him if he would like to accompany me. Only after pondering for quite some time, he replied, "*Herr Oberleutnant*, I have five children!" With this, my question was answered. Needless to say, he stayed back, but later died in the fields of France anyway. Years after the war, I once went to see his family in Franconia.

In January 1943, we Germans experienced a horrific shock—Stalingrad. From then on, I did not want to stay in France, but to return to my division on the Russian Front. I was surprised to learn that it was almost as difficult to return to the front as it was to get away from it!

Chapter Eight

Back to the Line

Historical Commentary

*While Georg Grossjohann trained troops for commitment to combat else-
where, the initiative changed hands on the Eastern Front for the final
time. Not only had the Germans suffered a devastating defeat at
Stalingrad, but their attempt to score a major victory in July 1943 actually resulted in a shocking disaster for German arms . . . one from which
they would never recover.*

*In early May, the plan, dubbed Operation ZITADELLE (CITADEL)
had been agreed upon by the commanders of Army Group Center (von
Kluge) and Army Group South (von Manstein), and the OKH Chief of
Staff, Zeitzler. The only dissenting opinion of those present at Hitler's
meeting in Munich was voiced by Guderian who, in his new post as
Inspector of Panzer Troops, wanted to build up a panzer reserve in the
event the Allies opened a second front.*

*Guderian had good cause to fear a second front, too, as only ten days
after the meeting in Munich, frika surrendered in Tunisia, representing
the loss of another 240,000 German and Italian soldiers and their equipment. This loss, however, only fortified Hitler in his desire to strike a
major blow against the Soviets, and so the preparations for ZITADELLE
went forward. On 4 July, Army Groups Center and South launched their
massive attempt to encircle and destroy eight full Soviet armies of the
Central and Voronezh Fronts using eleven German corps, six of them
panzer corps.*

*When the smoke cleared on the steppes two weeks later, the overall
results were clear. The attack on the heavily-fortified salient had failed.
Worse (for the Germans), in fighting which had involved the largest tank*

battle to that time, the Germans lost roughly 70,000 dead, and probably three times as many wounded. These irreplaceable manpower losses were complemented by an even more egregious (operationally speaking) loss of tanks and combat aircraft. Although the numbers are still difficult to precisely assess—thanks to wartime propaganda and inflated claims—the simple fact is that the Germans lost the great reserve of armored forces which they could have used for the conduct of an elastic, mobile defense in the East. Even though the Soviets unquestionably lost even more of everything—men, tanks, planes, and guns—than the Germans, their burgeoning industrial and military personnel capacity, supplemented by American Lend-Lease materiel coming in through Murmansk and Iran, combined to ensure that they would possess the initiative for the rest of the War. To add to the calamity, the losses came even as the British Eighth Army *and the US* Seventh Army *were invading Sicily, the stepping stone to Italy, requiring the diversion of German forces, such as the battered II SS Panzer Corps, to the Mediterranean Theater.*

The Soviets followed up their victory in the Kursk salient by quickly launching a massive summer offensive nearly all along the line with the Germans. Their main effort came in the agriculturally—and industrially—important Ukraine, occupied by the Germans' Army Group South— the command to which the 198th Infantry Division was now assigned. Although the Germans belatedly began preparing two lines of defense— the so-called "Panther" and "Wotan" lines—it was too late to forestall the Soviet juggernaut. The best that the Germans of Army Groups South and Center could do, in many cases, was race the Russians to the Dniepr, and establish defensive positions on the west bank. Other than the Pripet Marshes, the Dniepr was the last major natural defensive feature in the western Soviet Union.

In the middle of October, the Soviets renewed their drive in the Ukraine, and two full Soviet army groups, namely the Steppe and Voronezh Fronts, attacked the armor-poor Army Group South, driving them back across the Dniepr

Georg Grossjohann Remembers . . .

Only in the late summer of 1943, after having quite an argument with the Regimental Commander and his adjutant, did I succeed in securing reassignment to Russia. By then, both of them finally had enough of me and they let me go. From an officer at our personnel branch, I learned that the two had attempted to put one over on me. The young major from the General's staff, to whom I had to report, explained to me after reviewing my personal records that, suddenly, I was not going to be reassigned to my old division in the south, but to another division in the central section of the Eastern Front! I watched him when he studied a piece of paper that was attached to my personal documents, and at once I smelled a rat. By the way, I knew about the reputation of the division mentioned by him, as well as that of their Commanding General. This was an outfit in a situation where an old-timer like me could be shipped out to take part in some target practice—as a target! I got up and asked to be allowed to speak to the Commanding General. The major acted terribly upset—why and what for? I told him that I volunteered for the front, knowing how things were there. But, I said, it was incomprehensible to me why one would make the life of a front soldier unnecessarily difficult by refusing him the opportunity to return to the environment to which he was accustomed, namely, to the circle of his old comrades at the front. After this, it suddenly worked and I didn't have to bother the Commanding General anymore.

At the railroad station in Stuttgart, I said good-bye to my loyal Franconian who accompanied me until then, and whom I also never saw again. Until the final marching orders came for Russia, I was put on hold for several days in Tübingen. One thing I learned while being with the reserve unit was that the urge to go to the front was quite underdeveloped for those who were established in that unit. So it seemed that anybody who voluntarily reported back to the front became a silent provocation, an admonition, for them to follow suit, and soon. During an inspection of my reserve company, in the presence of the (appropriate) commanding general, I happened to overhear him say to our smart *Oberstleutnant* during the final talks, "This one (meaning me) you hold on to, one can see he is a fighting soldier." The answer to my repeated request for transfer, therefore, was always, "A soldier will do his duty wherever he is assigned!" This clearly was a very good alibi for those who wanted to hold down the fort right at home.

The soldiers at the front were always surprised if a face known to them from the past reappeared amongst them. They somehow felt betrayed and abandoned if someone left and did not return.

The waiting time in Tübingen was bleak, boring, and depressing. There were several other officers waiting for their marching orders with me, but each was absorbed in his own thoughts, which were probably not very joyful. To be honest, I, too, had doubts. Was it wise to intervene in one's destiny during wartime? But, *"Alea iacta est!"*[18] But at least I could take a few nice memories with me on this second trip to Russia. . . .

During my second tour of duty in France, I took home leave. While in East Prussia, I ran into a small, bull-necked *Stabsfeldwebel* who passed by me while rendering a perfect salute. It was the Brazilian Coffee Bean!

During my advanced individual training in late 1928, in the last months before I was assigned to my permanent regiment, I was stationed in Marienwerder. Like almost all barracks in Prussia in those days, the barracks there were huge, square blocks of brick buildings. But the main building with its impressive facade looked like a medieval fortress. Slightly renovated inside, they were nevertheless spotlessly clean and exquisitely austere in their furnishings. I came to know them well during my tenure at Marienwerder because I rarely received a weekend pass—thanks to my new drill sergeant.

The sergeant was small and bullish, with a neck like an ox. He was also the most terrible superior I ever had. He was forever sneaking around us, growling like a bad-tempered pit bull. The dangerous thing about him was that he never yelled, but simply reported even the smallest infraction of regulations to the first sergeant.

He was worse than a simple martinet, though. He formulated cunning devices by which he could determine if we were fully concentrating during drill. After the command, "Attention," for example, he sneaked behind the formation and randomly poked his thumb against our rumps. Woe to the man whose cheeks were not taut and hard as iron, but relaxed and flaccid. Furiously, the sergeant would grumble, "Why don't you tighten up your Brazilian coffee bean?" This amazingly distinctive expression became even more unforgettable because it was uttered in the unmistakable drawl of those who came from the regions hard by the Polish border.

He had anther trick, too. After he made us stand at attention for a long period of time, he would unexpectedly whack the back of someone's knee with the edge of his hand, so that the man concerned would collapse as if he was hit by lightning—unless he had his legs tightly locked. This presented us with a dilemma, because of course, to lock the knees for long periods of time was a sure way to pass out. . . .

For a while, the Brazilian Coffee Bean and I had a nice conversation, while he looked again and again at my shoulder straps. Apparently, he had never imagined that I would amount to anything. At that time, he was platoon leader in a training unit. Based on my experiences, I could see him there in my mind precisely. We parted in peace and never met again.

I also used this assignment for opportunities to again visit famous wine-producing regions, among them Beaune and Chablis; I had gone to Paris, and traveled once more to Deauville, where I had been stationed prior to my assignment in Russia. The situation in the coastal area had changed completely. Deauville looked like a fortress, and I was not allowed to enter certain districts on the coast, even wearing my uniform. While in Deauville, I remembered an episode that took place during the spring of 1941. On a trip back from Paris to Deauville, in a crowded train, I stood next to a young lady, a secretary with the German Embassy in Paris, who liked to spend the weekends in Deauville. During our conversation I found out that she was not only from Berlin, but startlingly enough, was also a neighbor of our little *Oberst*, whose villa was next to the one of her parents in Schlachtensee. I, poor soul, at that time called the *Oberst* at his villa Coty to tell him about this pleasant surprise. For myself, I most likely ruined a beautiful weekend, because after her visit to the villa, my travel acquaintance was rather changed. Then I understood immediately that the "old man," remembering the Post Office girl from Ludwigslust, must have warned her about me . . . "Roué!" It was now almost two years later, so I decided on my return trip to ask about her at the Embassy. It was my good fortune that from then until my transfer to Russia, she and her girlfriend were my guests several times in Auxerre, where I had a little house available, embedded idyllically between a prison and an insane asylum!

But enough of idylls. Finally the day came, and after an almost endless, oft-interrupted train trip, I reached the forward command post of the Field Army to which the 198th Infantry Division was assigned. I wanted to get information about the location of the current command post of our division, but on my way there, I discovered a truck with the tactical insignia of the 198th Infantry Division—a white cross on a swallowtail red background. (Our Swabians chose this after the Danish National flag, having occupied Denmark in April 1940.)

After hours of driving on completely worn-out roads, I spied our division flag. We arrived in Solotarevka, about twenty kilometers southwest of Kremenchug, on the bank of the Dniepr River, which was our present main line of resistance. Within eight months after the Stalingrad catastrophe, the German forces had been thrown back five hundred kilometers. That was shocking!

The first old acquaintance I met was our former battalion adjutant, *Oberleutnant* Dr. Rittmannsberger, who now, evidently for reasons of age, had been reassigned as the aide-de-camp to the Division Commander.

After very heartfelt greetings, Rittmannsberger asked me with amazement why I would still walk around as an *Oberleutnant*, since some time ago I was to have been promoted to *Hauptmann*. In the regimental personnel office, the chief orderly, also an old acquaintance, procured for me the additional two pips needed for wear on my epaulets from now on.

At that time, the Commanding General was out front with a regiment at a section where the Russians had tried all day to reach the west bank of the Dniepr—which they did shortly before my arrival. And then it happened exactly as it happened during my first deployment in Russia. The Commanding General had left word that I should immediately be moved up front to replace a battalion commander who had just become a casualty. I did not like that at all. As a commander myself, I always avoided dispatching men just returned from home-leave directly to the front. Even an experienced front soldier needs a few days to orient himself on the conditions in his new position, to be able to dodge at least some menacing situations. After all, it was not even my old regiment, and under those conditions I could also have gone to the division in the central section of the Eastern front, as my former nemeses had conspired to send me. The amiable Dr. Rittmannsberger promised to put a word in for me with the Commanding General. A messenger drove me to the front where I reported to the Division Commander, who was unknown to me, and to the corresponding Regimental Commander. Meanwhile, darkness fell and there was no time for further orientation, so I spent the night in a foxhole near the regimental command post.

The next morning I got the happy news that I would be transferred to my original regiment, Grenadier Regiment 308. This was made possible because there, too, another suitable replacement had arrived at about the same time. Since this gentleman was a newcomer to the division, it was decided that it would make no difference if he started freshly here or there.

During my absence, *Oberst* "Papa" Schultz, our well-liked Regimental Commander, had been relieved of his post. He declared that this was due to the intrigues of one of the general's staff officers, who was a scoundrel, and who, because of irregularities with supplies, shot himself, as well as an *Oberst* who had temporarily commanded the Division. This officer looked like a nutcracker, and apparently was one, too. Despite the relief, Papa Schultz was awarded the Oakleaves to the Knight's Cross, and went on to be promoted to *Generalmajor*.[19]

First, I reported to the Regimental Commander. *Oberstleutnant* Ludwig Gümbel was a friendly, congenial Bavarian who was a Regular Army officer. Well educated, he fortunately was the exact opposite of what I had just left behind in France. Later on, he became my Division

Commander after I took over the Regiment from him. We have remained in friendly contact since the war. I assumed command of the same battalion in which I had commanded a company. To my pleasant surprise, the battalion adjutant was the former leader of the infantry howitzer platoon which, way back in 1941, had covered me so splendidly during a Russian attack on the "Linsemeyer Heights." The aide-de-camp was also a casual acquaintance, whom I met several times after the war when he was the technical director of the casino in Konstanz.

There was not much action on the Dniepr during my first few weeks in command of the 2d Battalion, Grenadier Regiment 308. It was only the calm before the storm, however, because the entire division would be engaged in extremely severe combat during the winter of 1943–44 and the following spring. We only avoided complete annihilation by a hair's breadth.

Beginning in November 1943, we were pulled back from the Dniepr position and moved by rail to Byelaya Zerkov, about one hundred kilometers south of Kiev. Near Kiev, the Russians established a bridgehead across

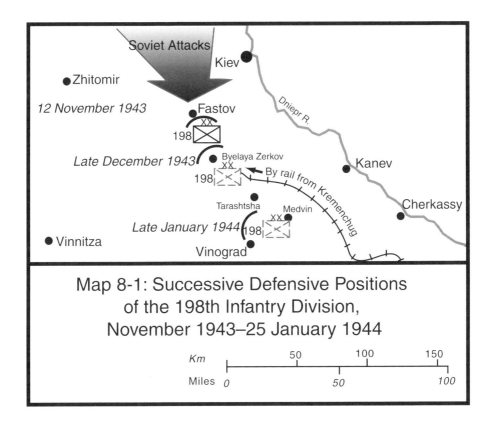

Map 8-1: Successive Defensive Positions
of the 198th Infantry Division,
November 1943–25 January 1944

the Dniepr which bulged ominously about one hundred kilometers to the west. Fastov, an important railroad junction in the sector Kiev-Zhitomir, Kiev-Vinnitza, was lost.

As of 12 November, our division was deployed in a defensive posture south and southwest of Fastov. Originally, the Russian bridgehead to the south had been much deeper and reached beyond Byelaya-Zerkov. There it was halted by the 2d SS Panzer Division _Das Reich,_ and pushed back almost twenty kilometers to the north in a counterattack. Only because of this was it actually possible for us to detrain in Byelaya-Zerkov. On 15 November, our XLVIII Panzer Corps attempted to break into the Russian bridgehead. Zhitomir was recaptured and numerous enemy tank units were destroyed. The enemy suffered heavy losses, but seemed to have inexhaustible reserves available. For all that, the Russians still needed several weeks thereafter to realign and reconstitute their assault units in the bridgehead. On 24 December, the Russian attack started again towards the west and on 29 December, also towards the south and southwest.

The Russian attack did not hit us until late evening on 29 December. The Russians apparently realized that the best time to attack the sparsely manned opposite line was during the hours of darkness.

A superior, confident attacker, supported by strong tank units, needed only to move forward to roll over us. At night the defender, most of all his artillery, is blind against an opponent who constantly moves.

It would take too much for me to describe in great detail the dramatic and depressing events of the ensuing weeks' winter battles. Our completely overextended infantrymen, far inferior in numerical strength, still did the almost humanly impossible.

When the Russians tried to break through towards the Uman with a spearhead of tanks, they were driven back again and hundreds of their tanks were destroyed. The 198th Infantry Division took part in this, too. One evening, when I wanted to rest my badly-bruised battalion in a village for a couple of hours, I was summoned by the commander of a division who had emplaced his command post nearby for just a few hours. He wanted to rescue one of his subordinate units, which was encircled in Luka, a village southeast of Byelaya-Zerkov. To this end, he intended to employ two dozen assault guns available to him, and he was careful to request—not _order_—my infantrymen to lend a hand. To get my people back on their feet from the deep sleep of exhaustion would have been almost impossible, were it not for the prospect of being able to ride on the assault guns to the assault positions just shy of the objective. I agreed to support his relief attempt with my battalion.

We drove with the assault guns through a forest that ended just before Luka. The guns then moved into position and opened fire on the moonlit

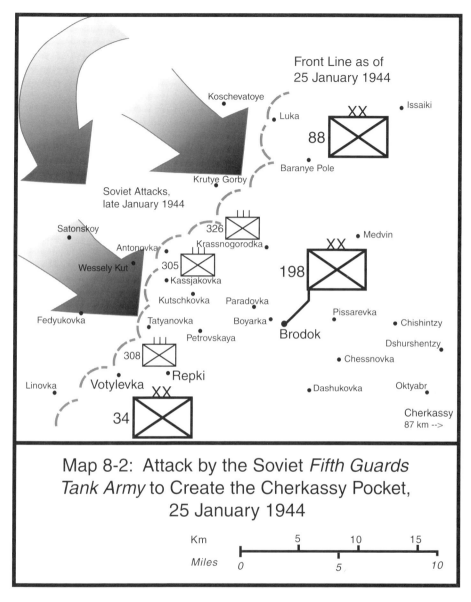

Front Line as of
25 January 1944

Koschevatoye

Luka

Issaiki

88

Baranye Pole

Krutye Gorby

Soviet Attacks,
late January 1944

Satonskoy

Antonovka

Krassnogorodka

326

Medvin

198

305

Wessely Kut

Kassjakovka

Kutschkovka   Paradovka

Pissarevka

Fedyukovka   Tatyanovka   Boyarka

Chishintzy

Petrovskaya

Brodok

Dshurshentzy

308

Chessnovka

Repki

Linovka   Votylevka

Dashukovka

Oktyabr

34

Cherkassy
87 km -->

Map 8-2: Attack by the Soviet *Fifth Guards Tank Army* to Create the Cherkassy Pocket, 25 January 1944

Km	5	10	15

Miles	0	5	10

village with tracers, which soon set the buildings afire. With the objective thus illuminated, the assault guns then opened fire with their 75mm cannon, and we stormed towards the village. The Russians were completely surprised. Our soldiers pulled them from sheds and foxholes, some only scantily dressed. Unfortunately, we could only free a few of our comrades. The next morning we saw why—only a few infantrymen had survived the vicious combat that had taken place during the encirclement.

Our only booty was an American Willys jeep that stood with running engine in front of a cottage. Maybe some high-ranking Russian officer intended to use the it to escape; instead, I used it for many weeks as my staff car.

On 25 January, the 198th Infantry Division was deployed in a defensive posture facing *west*, not east. The extension of the badly decimated division stretched for more than twenty-five kilometers! Our regiment had to take over the southernmost sector, which was about ten kilometers wide, loosely connected to a regiment from the adjacent 34th Infantry Division to the south.

We defended the northwest rim of Votylevka and the open area on both ends of the town. As Graser described it, "The 198th Division was situated at the NW tip of the advanced front, exactly at the point from which, according to prior experiences, an attacker would set out to complete an encirclement. Its lines were sparsely manned and thin, without any depth, without sufficient reserves of its own, without antitank defenses, without alternate (fall back) positions."[20] That about sums it up—our mission was critical, but our position was tenuous indeed.

Late in the evening of 25 January, I visited the soldiers of the 6th Company, who were hunkered down in foxholes they had hastily scratched out in the open field. The company commander, *Leutnant* Ottowitz, a young officer with the congenial manners of a well-educated Austrian, reported brisk action by the opponent right after dusk.

Together, we listened to the typical clanking noise of tank tracks, and even isolated voices from the opponent's side. They were surprisingly close, too. At about midnight, I returned to my command post. Since I had not been out of my clothes for weeks, I decided to at least take off my boots, as well as my jacket and trousers. I fell asleep right away.

At 4:40 AM, on 26 January, a tremendous barrage came down on Votylevka, not only in our area, but on a sector more than thirty kilometers in width. The Russians must have employed hundreds of batteries in the artillery preparation for their attack. Artillery shells of all calibers crashed into our positions. Waves of 122mm rockets added their howling cacophony, too, before slamming into the earth around us. The enemy paid particular attention to the coordinating point where our division's lines joined those of our neighbor to the north, the 88th Infantry Division. It was a major attack!

We had only seconds to grab our weapons and clothes and to dive into a deep, narrow ditch which, as a precaution, we had dug out behind our house and covered with wood beams, dirt, and a thick layer of straw. A few minutes later, our cottage was already broken into pathetic pieces. From now on we could do nothing but crouch in our trench and hope. Just before leaping into the shelter, my *Leutnant* Armbruster got his hands on a bottle of cognac which, after the first seconds of shock were over, was soon passed around. Its contents helped deaden the terrific, pounding shock that went on and on and on. . . .

At 6:00 AM sharp, exactly eighty minutes later, the devastating barrage stopped suddenly. . . . Dead silence prevailed!

Knowing that the soldiers of the Red Army started their attack—with tactical correctness—right after the end of their preparatory barrage, we broke out into the open and saw that everything in Votylevka, with a very few exceptions, was razed to the ground. Even the few trees had become stripped skeletons. Only the remains of a couple of chimneys still stood in the smoking, greyish-black moonscape of huge craters. As we fortunately found out afterwards, my battalion, as well as our Regiment's 1st Battalion, defending the outer perimeter of the town, did not suffer substantial losses. But my 6th Company, deployed outside of the town, was totally overrun. According to statements from the few infantrymen who escaped, the young company commander and his messengers were taken prisoner. These surviving *Landsers* of the 6th Company also reported that the Russian infantry and tanks broke through in great numbers between Votylevka and the 34th Infantry Division to the southeast.

There was only some minor battle noise to hear from the outskirts of the town. Apparently, after all the fireworks they had expended on the village, the Russians thought an attack on them was a waste of time and resources. From the Regiment's command post, which was about five kilometers behind us in Repki, our regimental physician appeared to establish communications. Dr. Stochdorph seemed relaxed, grinned amiably, and asked nosy questions. He reported that Repki, too, had been hit heavily by the Russian artillery, with about the same results as the barrage on us.

After I informed him that we did not yet have a clear picture of the situation, he had his *Kübelwagen*[21] turned around and drove back to report to the Regimental Commander. Dr. Stochdorph was typical in my experience—during the whole war, I never personally witnessed any physician or clergyman who was not exemplary in the practice of his duties. The Roman Catholic chaplain of our division even took part—naturally unarmed—in dangerous assaults. Our physicians, often enough, were surprisingly good at soldiers' tactical tasks, and our staff physician was no exception. Without any special preparations, he would have been fully capable of leading a battalion or even a regiment. These qualities not only helped greatly in the command and control of our units, but also naturally earned the even greater respect of us combat infantrymen.

Next, we marched towards the enemy, to the command post of the 1st Battalion, commanded by *Hauptmann* Dr. Majer. We were perplexed beyond all limits (and full of joy) to find his cottage completely unharmed in the midst of this lunar landscape. We entered and found the commander, his officers, and messengers still a little pale, but again composed, conducting a command and staff meeting. Unlike us, these lazy guys had not even bothered to dig foxholes, but survived the barrage by prostrating themselves on the floor of their cottage, covered by woolen blankets, which we still puzzled about afterwards. They could not establish a clear picture about the situation on the outskirts of the town either. As it was established later on, the tremendous barrage didn't do much damage where they were. But the horses and vehicles left in the town were a complete loss. As Graser describes,

> Some battalions and companies of the division held on to their strongpoints and repelled the attacks of the enemy infantry during the late morning in heavy fighting. Yet, the enemy tanks, in their first approach, protected by the fog, had already broken through the weak front between the towns and penetrated the artillery positions. Votylevka was retained, involving the 1st and 2d Battalions of Regiment 308 in heavy battles. The Regimental staff of Regiment 308, together with the 7th, 8th, and 10th Batteries of the Artillery Regiment 235, repelled a tank attack on Repki.[22]

I have to say that the Russians most likely could have taken Votylevka before noon, if they had seriously attempted to do so. But, they reasonably decided that it was smarter to avoid assaulting an objective which would fall in due course without a fight.

Chapter Nine

Disaster at Cherkassy

Historical Commentary

The winter of 1943–44 was grim for the German Army practically every-where. With the exception of the units of the Twentieth Mountain Army in northern Karelia, every German unit in contact with the Soviets had been pushed back significantly by winter's end. In Italy, since the Allied invasion in early September had knocked the Italian government (and most of its Army) out of the war, the Germans had had to commit more than twenty divisions—including six from the Eastern Front—to the defense of the Italian Peninsula. Even then, it was not enough to prevent the Allies from establishing further air bases from which to bomb the Reich from a new direction. Although they had contained the Allied beachhead near Anzio, the battles there and on the Gustav Line further south were fierce, and in no case afforded the initiative to the German Army.

As the Soviets' First Ukrainian Front (as the Voronezh Front was redesignated in late October 1943) charged across the steppes in late December 1943, they threatened to encircle Army Group South's Fourth Panzer Army. Forbidden by Hitler to withdraw, two German corps—the XI and the XLII—were surrounded south of Cherkassy.

The Soviets now turned the tables on their German nemeses. Just as the Germans had done during their sweeping advances in the summer and autumn of 1941, the Soviets quickly hemmed in the cut-off XI and XLII Corps with the Twenty-Seventh *and* Fourth Guards Armies. *Simul-taneously, the Soviets established an outer defensive ring with the* Sixth Tank *and* Fifth Guards Tank Armies, *to prevent a German relief of the trapped units.*

Georg Grossjohann Remembers . . .

As a result of these massive attacks, on 28 January 1944, the Russians closed their encirclement of our XI and LXII Corps in a pocket around Cherkassy. The 88th Infantry Division, until then our neighbor to the right, was pushed back to the north, and our 198th Infantry Division was pushed back to the south and southeast. A huge gap resulted in the middle. To face the new challenge, we executed an almost exact turn by 180 degrees, so that our front was again facing east. It now ran between Risino and Vinograd, with the Grenadier Regiment 308 defending on the right flank of the Division. This "slide" southward occurred during the night of 26–27 January, in the teeth of bitter resistance from many Russian units. Only on 11 February did the costly attack to break through to the encircled units begin.

Our Grenadier Regiment 308 was supported by many tanks from the III Panzer Corps. After a fifteen-minute barrage by artillery and heavy-*Nebelwerfers*, as well as repeated sorties against enemy positions near Zhubenny Stav by a squadron of *Stukas*, we started to move forward. Subsequently, we seized Zhubenny Stav and drove to the edge of the town of Yablonovka. There, because of some crisis in Vinograd, we relieved one of our sister regiments, Grenadier Regiment 326, that had already pene-trated that area, and now had to push on to Vinograd itself.

On the night of 11–12 February, our regiment received orders to attack beyond Yablonovka toward Tichonovka because during the previous after-noon, enemy elements there had destroyed the support convoy of one of our *panzer* divisions. My colleague from the 1st Battalion and I shared the opinion that our completely exhausted men could just not physically accomplish this mission, which would have to be performed at night in knee-deep mud. This estimate was fortuitous on our part, as it turned out, because the regimental and division commander insisted unbendingly on the execution of this order, and they, therefore, were forthcoming in the provision of significant armored support for the operation.

For my men and I, the attack on Tichonovka was an exact repeat of the night attack on Luka. We directed the tanks through deep mud and stifling darkness with green-lensed flashlights. Then it began. Pulling up on line before Tichonovka, the *Panthers* first poured machinegun fire into the town, igniting many buildings with tracers. Again, these burning buildings illuminated the objective for us. As targets became visible, the long 75mm cannon of the *Panthers* sowed havoc among the stunned Russian defend-ers. By the time we, the infantry, surged forward into the town, the Russians hardly put up a fight at all. Casualties among our men were

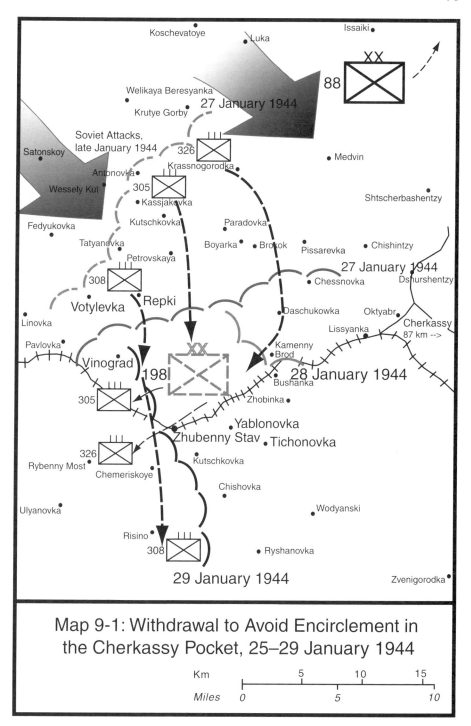

Map 9-1: Withdrawal to Avoid Encirclement in the Cherkassy Pocket, 25–29 January 1944

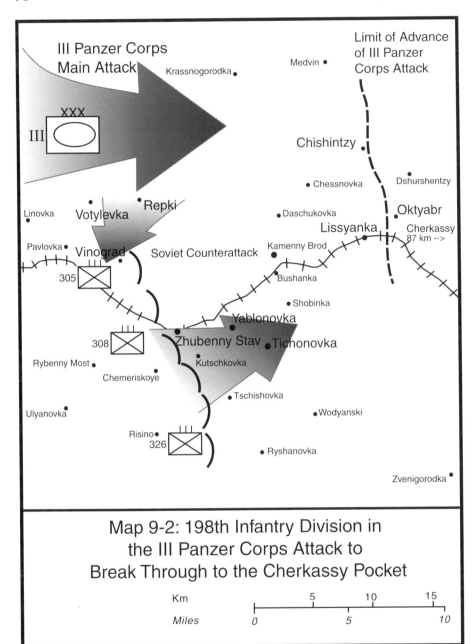

III Panzer Corps
Main Attack

Limit of Advance
of III Panzer
Corps Attack

Krassnogorodka

Medvin

XXX

III

Chishintzy

Dshurshentzy

Chessnovka

Linovka

Votylevka

Repki

Daschukovka

Oktyabr

Lissyanka

Cherkassy
87 km -->

Pavlovka

Vinograd

Soviet Counterattack

Kamenny Brod

305

Bushanka

Shobinka

Yablonovka

308

Zhubenny Stav

Tichonovka

Rybenny Most

Kutschkovka

Chemeriskoye

Tschishovka

Ulyanovka

Wodyanski

Risino

326

Ryshanovka

Zvenigorodka

Map 9-2: 198th Infantry Division in
the III Panzer Corps Attack to
Break Through to the Cherkassy Pocket

Km   5   10   15

Miles   0   5   10

practically non-existent, and we took numerous prisoners before the night gave way to daylight.

This attack might not have been possible to execute during daytime. The III Panzer Corps had advanced about thirty kilometers and stood only about thirteen kilometers from the encirclement, on the general line Lissyanka-Oktyabre-Chishintzy, but the energy of its attack faded.

Therefore, on the night of February 16–17, the encircled corps got orders to break out. This was ultimately accomplished only with the sustainment of painful losses of men, as well as the total forfeiture of heavy materiel. Some 20,000 to 25,000 of our soldiers were finally saved behind the thin security lines we formed. Once again, one of these stupid orders to halt, this time for two army corps to stick to the Dniepr, led to a catastrophe . . . which Cherkassy was, in spite of spectacular breakouts. It was unimaginable and simply irreplaceable, considering the men and materiel we lost by stubbornly sustaining positions and so-called "strongholds" since Stalingrad. The Russians could have avoided their big losses in 1941 also, had they always withdrawn in time into the enormous depth of their land. By 1942, they often did this quite well. We had lost any initiative. The Manstein-Masterwork, to deliver devastating blows even during a retreat, was now, in 1944, no longer possible due to the absence of the strength essential for this sort of counterpunching.

Chapter Ten

Uman

Historical Commentary

In early March 1944, the Soviets continued their winter offensive, attacking in the far north in Karelia, from around Leningrad against the Germans' Army Group North toward the Baltic nations, as well as further into the Ukraine in the south. Having been forced to defend and withdraw, then defend and withdraw again throughout the winter of 1943–44, the Germans were nearing exhaustion. With the siege of Leningrad lifted after over nine hundred days of encirclement, Soviet morale was conversely raised to new heights.

The Soviet attacks were successful almost everywhere, although they were again stymied in the Arctic north. Their attacks in the south, in which the First, Second, *and* Third Ukrainian Fronts *and* Eighth Guards Army *battered the First and Fourth Panzer Armies, very nearly succeeded in destroying the latter, and ultimately drove Army Group South completely out of the Ukraine.*

After its near-annihilation in the Cherkassy pocket, the 198th Infantry Division was again cut off near Uman. Many elements only finally got out with what their men could carry. Until it was pulled out of the line and sent to France to be reconstituted, the 198th was only a shadow of its former self . . . like many German units in the East at this time.

Georg Grossjohann Remembers . . .

Even though the Russians had failed to destroy all the German forces in the pocket at Cherkassy, they attacked our division on 5 March in large

78

scale, similar to the attack on Votylevka. This time our division was pushed back into the position from which it had started in 1941. My battalion was deployed in Chemeriskoye and repulsed all attacks for several days, even those involving tanks, until that early morning of 5 March. The Russians now declined to bypass towns or villages. When the artillery bombardment ceased, they moved south along both sides of my command post. For the time being, we remained crouched in our cottage, and when my adjutant asked me, "*Herr Hauptmann*, what are we going to do now?" I answered, "The commander-in-chief [Hitler] is trembling [with anticipation]!" At least we had kept a bit of grim humor.

In the dense fog and smoke, we were able to withdraw continuously in consonance with the Russians' attacks. The division parried strong Russian thrusts with its weak forces during the daytime, and at night withdrew to the next defensible positions, ultimately reaching the vicinity of Uman on 9 March. This was where we then experienced the *grand finale*.

By this time, the Russians had already physically cut off the regiments of the 198th Infantry Division from the division command post. Consequently, the Division commander radioed an order placing all fighting units of the division under the control of *Oberst* Keiser, Commander of Grenadier Regiment 326. Just when I turned up to meet the *Oberst* to establish contact, the following radio message arrived from the division: "There are forty Russian tanks on the highway from Novo Archangelsk to Uman. Attention!" *Oberst* Keiser sarcastically replied, "What do you mean, 'attention!'? Do we have to stand at attention when those things get here?"

The *Oberst* was well known for his dry sense of humor and for his unflinching bravery. It was determined that we should break out during the night towards the south, which could be possible because, until now, the enemy had only tanks with relatively few infantry units in place. We could exfiltrate between tanks much more easily than through the lines of dug-in infantry.

During the late morning, I had, as a precaution, ordered reconnaissance to find possible points for crossing a small river behind us, the Umanka. The leader of the recon patrol reported everything to be in order. The little river could be crossed by moving over an embankment with a small bridge. But late that afternoon, the Russians attacked directly with many tanks and, regrettably, we had nothing with which to counterattack. So I ordered my battalion to withdraw across the river in small units and to reassemble in the woods to the southwest.

When we gathered at the bank for the crossing, we were hit by a wicked surprise. What we found was not a little river anymore. The water of the Umanka had risen by at least two meters and also flooded the

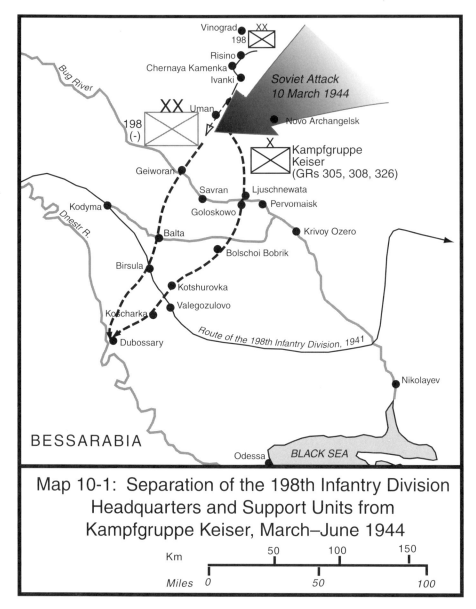

Map 10-1: Separation of the 198th Infantry Division
Headquarters and Support Units from
Kampfgruppe Keiser, March–June 1944

embankment by almost a meter in height. The current was so powerful that a man by himself could hardly get a foothold on the embankment. But we had no choice. If the reinforced battalion of Russian tanks reached the hills near the Umanka's banks, they would finish us off in a few minutes. I was first to enter the water, up to my hips, and ordered every other man to grab the hand of the one ahead of him, without closing up too much, to prevent the upstream water from building up pressure against this wall of men. This technique occurred to me from my peacetime pioneer training. To put it mildly, I had to summon every gram of authority I had to convince my men to do this. There was quite some panic among many of the infantrymen, because of the torrential waters and the danger of being pulled off the embankment and swept away to drown. One had to keep a meter's distance, and nobody in the chain could let the hand go of the man in front of him, at whatever the cost. Even Susi, my beautiful riding horse, was actively involved in this crossing. When, in spite of all the warnings, one of my soldiers was pulled from the levee and got carried away by the river, I chased Susi into the water and fished out the unfortunate man by yelling for him to hold onto the horse's tail. Some horsedrawn carriages were out of luck. One was pulled from the embankment and sank immediately in the water's vortex. Regrettably, it was loaded with wounded soldiers, for whom there was no salvation. Another one tipped over towards the oncoming river and was also pulled by the torrents, only to be caught under a bridge a long way downstream.

The draught horses could, in their agony, only keep their heads above water and I had to shoot them, which was very hard for me. Yet, it spared the dear animals a far more tortuous death. This was one of the darkest days of my life. As my battalion, or more precisely, what was left of it, reached the south bank, I gave orders to the senior company commander to gather the men in the woods behind us and wait. In the manner described, I personally, along with my Susi, picked up several non-swimmers from the north bank, among them also a couple of our *Hiwis*.[23]

Afterwards, when I reached the woods, the battalion had already marched on in daylight, contrary to my explicit order, and suffered heavy losses from fire from Soviet tanks. The battalion had become dispersed and was decimated; the remnants were later absorbed by other units. Later, I took no measures regarding this stupid disobedience. What would have been accomplished? What was done was done, and it would not have helped anyone. Later the same year, the company commander responsible for this, a *Hauptmann*, was badly wounded during an attack in the Vosges Mountains. He died a few weeks later in a hospital in his Swabian homeland.

Down to this day, I am unable to explain what could have caused the sudden surge of the Umanka's waters. Someone must have blown up a dam or opened a sluice of some sort. Whether it was done by the Russians to hamper our withdrawal, or by a German commander, in hopes of impeding the Russian pursuit, could not be determined.

A few infantrymen reached the woods together with me and we waited for dusk, because between our little forest and the nearest woodland was an open field of at least five hundred meters' width, which slightly ascended from the riverbed of the Umanka. On the upper rim of this open space, a few Russian tanks were already in position. Any attempt to cross the field in daylight would have been suicide. We avoided any unnecessary movement that could have drawn the attention of the Russians upon us.

I will never forget one sad and painful experience while we were waiting. Over and over again, in short intervals, we heard agonizing calls for help from badly hurt infantrymen, whom we unfortunately could not help. If we had tried, the Russians would have shot us to pieces across a veritable shooting gallery. After some time, we watched Russian tanks with infantry mounted on them moving in the direction of the calls for help. For us, condemned to observed this without the ability to help, this was also a terrible ordeal!

At the onset of darkness, we walked out of the woods. I impressed on my men the importance of ignoring any challenges by the Russians, and the criticality of simply pressing on. I led my Susi by her rein. First, nothing happened, but shortly before the edge of the opposite forest came the first Russian call—none of us made a sound. After the second, more energetic challenge, our small group opened wild, random fire into the woods just in front of us, directly into the midst of the Russians, who dispersed and fled into the forest.

As it developed, my little group broke through the encirclement without the loss of one man. Even my faithful Susi, who once before saved my life and freedom, was safe. A few weeks earlier, I had ridden toward what I thought was a German unit, to make contact with its commander. I was mistaken. The mass of soldiers in white snow-camouflage marching towards me made me suspicious. The moment I stopped, the first bullet buzzed by my ear. The distance to the leading Russian was only about 150 meters. With lightning speed, I turned around, without having to direct Susi, for she seemed to know what it was all about! In a few seconds, we were safe behind the nearest cover.

After the lucky breakout by the remnants of my battalion, and after almost an hour of laborious trudging through dense brush, we reached the southern end of the forest. There was complete silence, and one could only hear the yelping of dogs in the distance. That meant that there must be a village out there somewhere nearby! We moved toward the barking until we could make out the silhouette of a village in the dark. We moved on, very carefully, up to the first cottages. Not a soul stirred, and there was no sign at all of the presence of Russian or German soldiers. We moved into the village until we saw an older man standing in front of one of the little wooden houses. We asked the elderly gent about "*Russki Soldat*," and he shook his head in the negative. Then I asked him about *"Germanski Soldat,"* and he nodded, and said *"Da, Da,"* and pointed to a small hut.

Who can describe our joy when, after knocking, an older *Hauptmann* from our regimental staff appeared in the doorway? Completely exhausted, he had seemingly accepted his fate, and was now relieved and happy to confront not the expected Russians, but comrades from his own regiment!

We knew that we could not trust the civilians anymore because they were threatened with draconian punishment for assisting the Germans in any way. They would undoubtedly report our presence to the nearest Russian command at the first opportunity—and they could not be far away. We moved on and came to a halt only near the last cottages at the southwest end of the village. We placed sentries there. The others crept into two little huts and got rid of their water-soaked winter clothes to dry them out on the giant stoves in the peasant huts. An old Russian couple, without any sign of interest in what was suddenly happened around them, sat at the table and occasionally exchanged a few softly spoken words.

Incidentally, we made the surprising discovery that our winter battle dress, quilted with man-made fibers, was almost waterproof. I found that my uniform and undergarments remained quite dry. Suddenly, one of the sentries came in and reported engine noise from the nearby village street. A patrol was sent out immediately and returned shortly, accompanied by a liaison officer from our division! There was great joy and surprise on both sides. The *Leutnant* informed us that the commanding general had been sending out motorized and dismounted patrols continuously since afternoon to try and locate the scattered and isolated fragments of his division.

On 12 March, the 34th "Moselland," the 4th Mountain, and the 198th Württemberg-Badener Infantry Divisions were mentioned in the daily *Wehrmacht* report. It was a swansong, really, because not much was left of these three divisions. The next morning I reported to the division staff. Since I literally did not have a unit to command, I became, as of now, a duty soldier at the disposal of our division commander who, for the time being, took over the provisional Corps headquarters, called "Korpsgruppe von Horn." Divisions, corps, or armies were now fairly meaningless titles. In reality, they were totally burned-out shells without any significant fighting power.

During the ensuing days, if we had a chance for a rest, it was only when the enemy regrouped his units, or waited to move up his heavy weapons, or halted to conduct mechanical maintenance for his tanks.

Since I was without a command, *Generalleutnant* von Horn used me as a sort of utility player, performing various tasks requiring an officer with a fair amount of combat experience.

First, I had to supervise an advanced command post with a couple of messengers. The main command post had already displaced further south. Since during daytime one could quite clearly survey the terrain ahead, we were practically safe from surprises. But in the late afternoon, the Russians appeared in large numbers on the horizon, including a horse cavalry unit. They were moving directly toward us with alarming speed! By field telephone, I informed the command posts of each of the "divisions" of our provisional corps that I was compelled to pull the plug on my connection, and withdraw to the new command post of the corps. *General* Hermann Bernhard Ramcke personally came on the line when I spoke with the headquarters of the 2d Parachute Division. He ordered me to stay and to pick up the fight against the attacking enemy. I could not change his mind by telling him that I was alone with only a few messengers and telephones, and probably could not offer any real resistance. He said, "You will stay and you will fight! Understand? I am going to stay and fight here, too!" Since the Russians had come dangerously close in the meantime, and had even had bypassed us to the west, I ignored Ramcke's directive, and ordered the phone disconnected, after which we rapidly withdrew.

After this, by the way, I heard no more from *General* Ramcke. However, he must have changed his mind about conducting a fanatical defense. Otherwise, he could not have appeared as the commander of the coastal fortress of Brest, France, in the summer of 1944.[24]

I proceeded to the corps group's main command post to report the displacement of my forward CP to the Ia. I explained that the Russians had simply come too close for comfort. I advised him that, based on my observations of the speed of the Russian advance, I believed that the enemy could not be far from the main command post either. In fact, I said, one should be able to observe his advanced elements already, from the end of town. . . .

We beat a rather speedy departure!

Ultimately, my suggestion to emplace a machinegun at the command post was not discussed any further.

My next job was that of a crossing site commander at a pontoon bridge crossing the Ukrainian river Bug, between Savran and Pervomaisk. (See Map 10-1)

A bridge commander's mission is to regulate the progress of traffic over the bridge and, if necessary, to destroy it when the time is right. In this mission, I was supported by a unit of field gendarmes, who actually controlled the traffic across the span, checked passes and orders, and so on. This meant sometimes assigning priority to a unit if it is justified and necessary; an example would be a fighting unit which was moving towards the enemy and therefore needed right of way. I was never confronted with such a case. During the campaign in France in 1940, this was almost the rule, because everybody feared to be too late.

When it comes to withdrawals, much less to retreats, it would be best to appoint a field marshal as bridge commander instead of a *Hauptmann*! Nothing is more difficult than to make a superior officer understand that here at the bridge, the bridge commander has to make decisions in the name of *his* respective superior. In my entire career, I had never drawn so many chewings-out from colonels, majors, staff officers, and so on—in one case even from a major general—as during these two days on my bridge! The field gendarmes, the so-called "Chain dogs,"[25] were absolutely deaf when it came to chastisement or upbraiding by superior officers not in their chain of command, including massive threats with courts martial and so forth. I decided I could learn quite a bit from them.

The most critical task of a bridge commander is to destroy the bridge at the precise moment. To ensure safe passage of every possible friendly unit, bridges must not be destroyed one second too soon; to ensure that the enemy cannot pursue withdrawing friendly forces across the bridge, for God's sake don't blow the damn thing one second too late! The ideal moment to push the plunger on the firing mechanism is when the last friendly soldier who needs to cross steps off the bridge, and the first "bad guy" starts to get on it. Unfortunately, it rarely works out this way.

Some of us may remember that Hitler ordered *Major* Scheller, the site commander at the Ludendorff Bridge at Remagen in March 1945, to be shot because the fuse for the explosive charge failed as a result of enemy fire, thus the bridge fell into the hands of the Americans rather undamaged.[26] It is unfortunate that no superior officer dared to prevent that brutal, senseless execution!

In those two days, I did not once close an eye. During daytime, I continuously watched the bridge and kept contact by sight with the pioneer sergeant who had to handle the plunger connected to the electric fuse. At night, I stood at the north bank and listened into the darkness. In addition, there were listening posts in front of the bridge at all times; enemy units could show up at the bridge ahead of the last rear guard, or even ahead of dispersed groups of our own.

After two days, the retreating listening posts reported that the Russians were concentrically approaching our bridge. We cleared off from the bridge and I then gave the signal for the detonation. In many instances the detonation of a bridge is of questionable importance. Troops with modern equipment can hardly be stopped, even by a blown-up bridge. After the detonation, the middle spans of our bridge floated slowly down river.

The northern and southern parts of the bridge washed up on the corresponding banks. From a small hill, we saw Russians at the river and then returned to the corps command post, where we found that we were only protected by a thin line of patrols. None of us could know if any of our own people were left behind on the north bank of the river. Considerable doubt remains in my mind to this day.

My last, somewhat out-of-context, job in Russia was that of a town commander. I believe the name of the town was Sekretaria, or something similar. It was spaced out like all the towns in that part of the Soviet Empire, where a few square kilometers more or less don't matter. In the evening hours, when I entered one of the few bigger, sturdier, buildings to find out who and what was in it, I found it stuffed full of German *Landsers*. Even though some were badly wounded, it seemed apparent that nobody cared about them. I was so perplexed that I literally could not utter a word! When I found my tongue, I promised the wounded that I would do everything I could to get them moved out of there.

I walked briskly to a radio position and asked if they could make contact with any higher staff, maybe the army staff. The operators answered in the affirmative. Then, I asked them to send a radio message to the army that, "There are many heavily wounded in Sekretaria and it is no longer possible to transport them by land. Could transport via air be carried out? Signed Battle Commander Sekretaria."

The answer from Army headquarters was, "Yes, tomorrow after daybreak! Mark landing strip, keep wounded ready in immediate proximity!"

When I returned to the town command post, I found a very good looking Russian woman there, of German descent, who was probably dropped off here by some supply unit before it left Russia. In tears, she begged me to help her. The next morning I arranged for the selection and marking of a landing strip for the transport plane, which was so ardently awaited. The only possible place we could find was a totally soaked meadow, and I had most serious qualms about having a transport plane land there. I did not have any other choice, since the wounded were already waiting, full of hope, next to the selected landing strip.

When the JU 52 appeared at low altitude on the horizon, we could only keep our fingers crossed! Thank God, the landing went well, but the undercarriage sank at least ten centimeters into the soggy ground. After disembarking, the crew members walked around their bird, shaking their heads. The pilot, a young sergeant, said, "I don't know if I can take off from here, even with the plane being empty." But we loaded anyway, at least all those who could, with all certainty, not survive ground transportation. The young aviator resigned to God's will, stood by, and maybe counted the possibility that he might have to return to his squadron on foot. We who stayed behind promised him that we would push with all our strength, which he acknowledged with a tired smile. But the miracle happened!

Almost at the end of the meadow, the plane climbed sluggishly aloft, stalled shortly, but finally flew away, while heavy clumps of clay fell off the undercarriage to the ground. When I returned to the town command center, I was again greeted by my Russian woman from the night before, and I assured her again that I would take care of further transportation for her. Just when I put my arm around her shoulder to console her (!), the general appeared in the door! I reported, "Town command center without any special occurrences!" which he accepted in view of the facts, with a smirk. Then he wanted to know about the cargo plane he just saw. When I informed him about what I discovered last night and consequently set in motion, he was highly amazed that I succeeded, in these days, to organize, practically unaided, aerial evacuation for wounded soldiers. It seemed to him almost like a miracle.

It seemed like one to me, too.

Chapter Eleven

The 198th Leaves Russia

Historical Commentary

In November 1943, Stalin, Churchill, and Roosevelt met in Tehran to forge a common strategy for the conduct of the remainder of the war. Among other agreements, Britain's Prime Minister and the American President promised to pressure the Finns to accept a separate peace, thus freeing even more Soviet troops for operations aimed at Germany herself. They also promised an invasion of France in the spring of 1944, and in return, Stalin guaranteed a Soviet offensive in parallel.

The Soviet offensive, intended to coincide with the Allied landings in France (which were originally scheduled for May 1944), was Operation BAGRATION. Starting in the early summer of 1944, the Soviets hurled at least 5.5 million men and hordes of tanks against no more than 2.5 million German and Rumanian soldiers, from Bessarabia in the south to the Arctic Circle. In the - far north, although they had no appreciable success against the German Twentieth Mountain Army, the Soviets succeeded in inflicting sufficient damage on the Finns to convince them to agree to the American and British entreaties to pursue a separate peace. By September, Finland was out of the war.

By August, this massive push brought the Soviets into Estonia, Latvia, and Lithuania in the north; East Prussia and Poland in the center; and Hungary and Rumania in the south. In Italy, the Allies broke through the Gustav Line in May and began the final drive on Rome. On 6 June, the Allies invaded Normandy, and forced still more German forces to be diverted from the East.

Operation BAGRATION had succeeded in bleeding the German Army and their allies white, and now their soldiers were desperately fighting

*on three "conventional" fronts, as well as the massive anti-partisan cam-
paign in the Balkans. Fortunately for the 198th Infantry Division, after
three hellish years of fighting in the East, none of the three great enemy
offensives of the spring of 1944 directly involved them—they were withdrawn first to Rumania, then to the still quiet south of France for reconstitution as a full infantry division.*

Georg Grossjohann Remembers . . .

During our next required withdrawal towards the Rumanian border, I
almost fell from my horse due to weakness. My temperature was almost 41
degrees Centigrade (about 106 degrees Fahrenheit). Somewhere I was put
on a hospital train on which I left Russia for good. It was almost at the
same spot where, in 1941, our division had started its advance towards
Russia crossing the border river Pruth. Now in April 1944, almost three
hard years of war, full of deprivation, were behind the gallant 198th
Infantry Division, yet all the sacrifices were in vain!

Little by little, the hospital train took me to Galatz, Rumania, and during this time I recovered enough to make me want to return to the troops.
In Galatz, I had the opportunity to fly to Bacau on a dispatch plane. If I
remember well, beginning in April 1944, this was the location of the Eighth
Army staff. In any event, I had gone from a saddle onto a train during wet
and cold weather, just the way I was, carrying nothing with me. No under-
wear, no socks, nothing -- just my uniform and those heavy felt winter
boots. In the meantime, beautiful spring weather had arrived in Rumania.
I almost felt like a bum among the well-clad Rumanians and the sharply
dressed soldiers of our rear echelon elements. This became very clear to
me when I tried to get information about the current location of the 198th
Infantry Division from the Eighth Army staff.

The "chain dog" at the main entrance of the impressive building serving as residence of the staff wouldn't even let me enter. That's how
shocked he was by my sad appearance. He then relented and at least
allowed me into the lobby. It had an aura of noble calmness. With curiosity, I read the signs on those huge French doors. Demi-gods all, they included the Army commander, Chief of Staff, Ia, Ib, Ic, first aide-de-camp, and
so on. Sometimes one of the doors opened quietly and an elegantly-clad
military gentleman strode across the hall and disappeared behind another
door. Sharply creased trousers, mostly with red stripes,[27] and highly pol-
ished shoes seemed to be the rule here. I looked down at myself and began
to be ashamed! Nobody noticed me anyway, until one of the "chain dogs"

had pity on me and offered to find out where the command post of my division was supposed to be at this time. Once I got the information, I promptly proceeded to the army motor pool and there I found a truck that was going in the corresponding direction. In the second half of April, I reached the division or, more accurately, what was left of it. It was in Roman, some sixty kilometers west of the Pruth, the border river between Russia and Rumania.

In the imagination of our highest Commander-in-Chief, Roman, too, was apparently supposed to become a "stronghold" or even a fortress! In any case, right after my return, I was entrusted with the management of the construction of fortifications around Roman. If I was informed correctly at that time, an agreement with the Rumanian head of state, Marshal Ion Antonescu, stated that no measures could be taken against the Jewish part of the Rumanian population. But the Jews came by the thousands, probably under duress, to work on the bulwarks. They were mostly deployed where they lived and so I set up a two-hour break at noontime every day to enable these people to eat at home.

At some time or another, I was appointed liaison officer with the Rumanians. My impression of the plain soldiers was positive, but regrettably it was not so of their officers. Most of the soldiers were unpretentious sons of farmers, since Rumania was, as it is to this day, a fertile agrarian country. The officer corps came almost exclusively from the large cities and was heavily Francophiliac. These officers seemed none too anxious to get near the fighting. When I mentioned to the Rumanian officers that their staffs were much too far removed from the front, they responded that there was "sufficient telephone wire" available. . . .

There were other indications of problems with their leadership. Several times I was invited to dine at a Rumanian division command post. Each time it was a big dinner of several courses, and the affairs could go on for hours. Yet I never saw the regular soldiers eat anything else but one-pot meals, consisting mostly of big beans.

The German officer corps had a different attitude in that matter. The German company commander was last in line at the field kitchen. This was tradition!

On 11 May 1944, the 198th Infantry Division was reassigned from Eighth Army, and *General der Infanterie* Otto Wöhler, its commanding general, gave them a heartfelt farewell. In 1984, I had the pleasure of a telephone conversation with the ninety-year-old general, who was spending his golden years in his home and birthplace, Gross Burgwedel.

The division was to be reconstituted in a training camp in the "Protectorate of Bohemia and Moravia."[28] I had asked for home leave, which I was

Map 11-1: Operation BAGRATION, Summer 1944

— — — Approximate trace of
frontline pcsitions before the
commencement of BAGRATION

Km   100 200 300

Miles 0   100   200

granted. It was one of the few I had during the war and it also became my last one. Barely ten months later, the Red Army swamped my East Prussian homeland. I spent my short leave in a convalescent home for officers in the once so elegant Zoppot, which was well known to me since my childhood. (See Map 2-2) When my leave was over, I had to report to the replacement center in Dresden (See Map 4-1). There I learned, as a great surprise to me, that my destination would not be the Protectorate, but southern France!

I had to ask twice to be sure that the sergeant behind the desk had not made a mistake. It would take a few days for the transportation officer to be able to give me precise information. Before that, they said the exact position of the division was still unknown. So I could stay a few days in beautiful "Florence on the Elbe" (Dresden), which at this point in time was still without any sign of destruction. It had been declared an open city.

One day I visited the world-famous Semper Opera, the builder of which also had created the Burg theater in Vienna. Another time, I went to see the Volks Opera. Out of respect for the many wounded in the hospitals of the city, the repertories preferred light works. Eight months later, of course, Dresden was extinct, totally destroyed in a firestorm caused by Royal Air Force bombing. . . .

Russia was now behind me. What we soldiers on the River Mius in 1941 had perceived would happen had come to pass. In our guts we had known, even then, that for us the war was lost. Later, many different versions about losing the war circulated. For example, *Generalmajor* Karl Wagener, onetime Chief of Staff of Army Group South, felt that Hitler's "Orders, #45," issued on 23 July 1942, after the successful conclusion of the spring campaign and the battle of Kharkov, were probably the decisive cause for the loss of the Russian campaign. The objectives contained in these orders caused an expansion of the front line of the Eastern Front to a total of 4,000 kilometers, including the drive into the Caucasus. It was just too much for an army that had yet to make good its losses of the previous autumn and winter.

General Wagener also felt that the OKW always made "Step 2" before "Step 1," meaning, going directly after geographic and economic targets, instead of considering them a gift of a military accomplishment.

In another vein, von Manstein believed that the irreversible loss occurred at Stalingrad, and that it came about as a result of a combination of mistakes. He thought that covering the whole northern flank of the Sixth Army fighting around Stalingrad with almost exclusively non-German units—Hungarian, Italian, but mostly Rumanian—was an unusually high risk. This enticed the Russians, who were always exceptionally well-informed, to start their penetration of the front lines right there, and ultimately to destroy the Sixth Army as well in the huge encirclement that was our debacle at Stalingrad.

We valued the Rumanian units as the best of our allies, but based on my observations of their leadership, I feel that leadership in the field should have been given to their field marshal and chief of state, Antonescu. He was an effective soldier and expressed his willingness to take over the command. Looking over the strategic map of our Army Group South in the fall of 1942, one did not have to be a field marshal to understand what an enormous, immeasurable risk our highest leadership had taken at Stalingrad.

There are many other explanations for our loss in the East. To those of us at the front, it seemed as if the decisionmakers in the higher command had lost their senses. In the presence of my division commander and his staff, I once stated, "Our highest leadership at this time only knows two principles, 'Comb out the rear echelons,' and 'hold positions.' We seem to have forgotten everything else."

Whatever the problems were, though, it is difficult to comprehend that all our experienced, talented, and trained generals, as well as general staff officers, did not succeed in forcing their convictions upon the OKW and Hitler—for once! In my opinion, this was truly the real reason for, and greatest failure of, our Army in the Russian gambit.

Chapter Twelve

Back to France!

Historical Commentary

The Allied landings in Normandy rapidly drew German forces from northern and central France into the seething cauldron of the bocage. Nevertheless, Operation FORTITUDE, the Allied deception activities designed to convince Hitler that the main invasion effort was coming in the Pas de Calais, succeeded in tying down more than seventeen divisions in Belgium and the Netherlands for several critical months after the 6th of June.

The Germans' Army Group G also remained in southern France, engaged in anti-partisan activities and arrayed in defensive postures from just south of St. Nazaire on the Bay of Biscay to Nice on the Italian frontier. Under the command of Generaloberst *Johannes Blaskowitz, one of Hitler's least favorite commanders, this Army Group consisted of thirteen infantry or coastal defense divisions and, after mid-June, a lone* panzer *division, the 11th. While Rommel's Army Group B fought desperately to keep the Allies boxed into the hedgerows, the forces of Army Group G prepared for other possible Allied landings, from the French Riviera to the Spanish border, and along the virtually unfortified Bordeaux region.*

General der Infanterie Friedrich Wiese's Nineteenth Army *was specifically responsible for defending the southern coast of France. Wiese's three corps controlled the better part of eight divisions dedicated to coastal defense, including Georg Grossjohann's 198th, deployed on the French coast close to the Spanish frontier. The other divisions committed to the defense of the southern French coastline included the 189th Infantry and Nineteenth Volks-Grenadier, also west of the Rhône River;*

most of the 338th Infantry, around the mouth of the Rhône; the 242d and 244th Infantry along the Côte d'Azur; and the 148th between Agay and the Maritime Alps. The 11th Panzer Division remained in reserve near Toulouse, a significant distance from the beaches, and the 157th Reserve Mountain Division was fighting partisans in the Vercors Massif, too far away to participate in attempts to repel the invasion.

Starting belatedly in May 1944, Generaloberst *Blaskowitz employed about 14,000 laborers of the Organization Todt to significantly strengthen his units' defenses between Nice and Marseilles, the most likely landing sites for Allied troops. These laborers and their supervisors built almost six hundred steel-reinforced concrete casemates; installed hundreds of field and coastal guns of up to 340mm caliber in revetted positions; fortified hundreds of existing beach-front hotels and other buildings; and laid hundreds of miles of barbed wire and other obstacles. Nevertheless, it was a matter of much too little, much too late, over a frontage that was much too broad. In the sector of the 198th Infantry Division in the west, there were practically no defenses at all by the time of the Allied landings far to the east.*

Worse for the Germans of Army Group G, as a result of constant aerial photo reconnaissance and reports by French resistance spies, the Allies knew almost everything there was to know about the locations of what defenses did exist. This intelligence coup was only partially offset by the Germans' knowledge, supplied by ultra-high altitude Luftwaffe *reconnaissance and stay-behind agents in Italy, of the impending Allied invasion of southern France. Even so, although the invasion fleet carrying Allied units from Italy and other Mediterranean ports of origin was detected by the* Luftwaffe *enroute, a late course change by the invasion fleet under cover of darkness and other deception measures still managed to allow landing the greatest proportion of the Allied invaders where they were not expected.*

Georg Grossjohann Remembers . . .

During my trip to southern France, I stopped over once more in Paris and found it to be almost unchanged, in spite of the invasion being in full swing. But the train I took two days later through the Rhône Valley further south was overcrowded. It seemed as if every Frenchman who could afford it was traveling south to escape the expected battles in northern France.

After arriving in Narbonne and reporting to the division staff, I learned about the awards that had been assigned to my colleague, Dr. Majer, and me for the last difficult weeks and months in Russia.

Byelaya Zerkov, Luka, Votylevka, Tichonovka, Chemeriskoye, Uman—those had only been the climaxes of these trying times. As of 1 April 1944, we were both promoted to major and reconfirmed as commanders of our battalions. Some time later, I also received the German Cross in Gold for actions in Russia in early 1944.

Although I had no way of knowing it at the time, the promotion to major would be my last.

I remember well the consequences of my first promotion to a leadership position. On 1 June 1934, I was promoted to *Obergefreiter*, thereby joining the ranks of the "old men" who could get away with calling five an even number. Shortly thereafter I was sent, unexpectedly, for NCO training in Arys (See Map 2-2). The course lasted three months and had almost five hundred students. The fact, however, that I graduated fifth in the class of these five hundred—the highest-ranking graduate from my company—apparently did not impress Erwin the Only in the least. From that point forward, he did not trust me. My quick transformation from Saul to Paul was obviously too much for him.

To Erwin the Only, I was now ambitious and career oriented. After our return from the course, he had a few words for us and—as a side remark—stated that he did not appreciate ambitious people! I did not expect to hear any words of acknowledgment, let alone praise, as they were reserved strictly for his favorites. For me, it was only important that at least he could not bawl me out for my especially good grades.

Soon after that, I escaped from him for another three months because I was invited to be an instructor for the very next course at the NCO school. When I returned this time, there was a big surprise waiting. One of the *Hauptmann*'s favorite sergeants—I suspected him of also being a "listening post"—requested me as a squad leader in his platoon. I wasn't sure if he wanted me for my good evaluation or if Erwin thought I would be well "taken care of" under the nurturing wing of one of his intimates. . . .

There was a well-known motto amongst we infantrymen, "Enjoy the war, peace will be terrible." Thus, we spent the few weeks that remained in radiant sunshine of the Mediterranean coast until the beginning of the invasion on the French Riviera. But all of us, especially those from the eastern part of the *Reich*, were concerned about what the future would bring!

On 20 August, following an intense barrage, ninety Russian divisions and forty tank brigades crossed the River Pruth and flooded Rumania. Then, on 24 August, Rumania broke off relations with the *Reich* and the following day declared war on Germany! The break-off of Rumania created a desperate situation for the German Sixth and Eighth Armies. The new Sixth Army, re-established after Stalingrad, was completely annihilated, as was about half of the Eighth Army. Sixteen German divisions were lost, and the fate of 80,000 missing in action remained forever unaccountable! This made us realize what unimaginable good fortune our division was granted when we were shipped out of Rumania!

The 198th Infantry Division took over a huge section of the Mediterranean coast, reaching from the peak of the Pyrenees almost to the delta of the Rhône river. My regiment was assigned the southernmost part, the right wing of which ended directly at the Spanish border.

My colleague Majer resided in "Chateau Valmy" near Perpignan, situated picturesquely against the impressive backdrop of the Pyrenees. My slightly more modest residence was "Maison Rouge," near the road from Perpignan to Canet-Plage. In addition to the highly-touted "Atlantic Wall," the Propaganda Ministry occasionally talked about a "Mediterranean Wall." My little *Oberst* Newiger would probably have commented on that with "Well, if you want to call that a 'Wall'!" I am not aware of anything that was built that could legitimately could have been called "fortification" in the sector of my regiment! Our predecessors had built dug-outs of the most primitive type, which would not even survive shelling from the lightest artillery. Personally, if I were under fire, I would rather have dug into the flat sand, instead of looking for shelter in such a dug-out. Some of them were constructed of brick, believe it or not, and plastered with cement, somewhat like a stucco house.

The *Organisation Todt (OT)* did actually exist in Perpignan and occasionally could be seen surveying something somewhere, but with that, their activity was exhausted. Sometimes I visited the *OT*-Bureau in Perpignan to discuss problems with the construction of positions. The only result was that I once invited a very attractive secretary for an excursion to Port-Bou on the Spanish side of the Pyrenees. As Spain remained neutral, it could happen that one was seated at the same table with English or Americans in a restaurant. We Germans in our uniforms were always treated especially nicely by the Spaniards. In any case, I could not spend one single *peseta* during my visit to Port Bou. Whatever my companion and I consumed was paid for by a nice Spaniard. Had I then known that at that time, a cousin of mine by marriage was the German Consul-General in

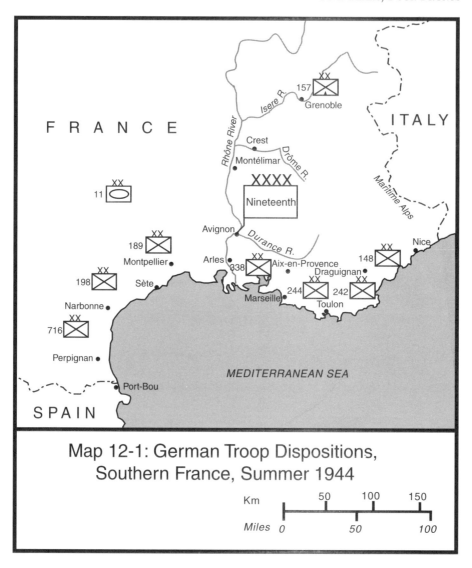

Map 12-1: German Troop Dispositions, Southern France, Summer 1944

Barcelona, I might have extended my trip to Spain. Because of its location at the border, Port Bou was presumably a preferred place for agents from both sides, who, after all, seemed to know each other. A young man came to my table and asked to talk to me for a moment. He stated that my companion was under observation by the Gestapo for suspicion of espionage. I considered this nonsense and a case of showing off. When he demanded that I return with the lady at once to France, I declared that I would return in the evening, as planned, but not earlier. What a pity that at that time I did not know of the existence of my cousin in Barcelona! We exchanged our vital statistics, but I never again heard from this young man. After I reported the incident to my nice Bavarian *Oberst*, he called and gave hell to the local Gestapo *Obersturmführer* in charge of this agent . . . which the *Oberst* could well afford to do, being an intimate friend of Heinrich Himmler!

My companion later mentioned that she knew the boy, and that he repeatedly tried to score with her in Perpignan. So that's how it was!

Again our division was worked into shape, for the umpteenth time. Men and arms were replenished and small exercises were undertaken. Besides this, as mentioned earlier, we enjoyed the few pleasant weeks that remained. But in some way, everything we did in those days seemed already to be more and more senseless. In early June, we received a new division commander, *Generalmajor* Otto Richter. His arrival only reinforced this idea in our minds. At this point, it may be instructive to look back on the commanding generals under whom we had served in the 198th Infantry Division during the war.

The outgoing division commander, *Generalleutnant* von Horn, was the former military *attaché* in Paris before the war (and went on to the same duty position in Switzerland after relinquishing command in 1944). *General* von Horn grew up in a family that came from a long line of civil servants; in fact, the family had been raised to the hereditary nobility for such service in the middle of the nineteenth century. His grandfather, Carl von Horn, was, for some time, *Oberpräsident* of my East Prussian home province. *Generalleutnant* von Horn's father was also a general, whose sister, Doris von Horn, had married the future *Generalfeldmarschall* von Mackensen. Von Horn came to us as an *Oberst* i. G., and after a short period at the front, was promoted to *Generalmajor.*

He did not need to procure authority, he *had* it! Cutting an elegant figure, with the cool, self-confident manners of a *Grand Seigneur*, he could, with perfect courtesy, keep anyone at a distance. He was not a charismatic leader of his men, not one who one would find at the front of his fighting units, brandishing an automatic weapon . . . but neither would he complain about a "headache." Officers, NCOs, and soldiers all naturally and implicitly respected and trusted him.

The first two combat commanders of the 198th Infantry Division were troop officers. *Generalleutnant* Otto Roettig, who commanded the Division until 10 April 1942, had been a regimental commander in Lüneburg before the war. *Generalmajor* Albert Buck, the Swabian who succeeded him, was, before the war, a battalion commander in Ulm on the Danube. Buck was killed in action on 6 September 1942 together with his Ia *Major*

Buhl. Then came *Generalmajor* Ludwig Müller, who commanded until von Horn took over on 7 February 1943. (I didn't know Müller, who commanded only while I was assigned to the reserve unit in France during my convalescence.)

The new commander, *Generalmajor* Otto Richter, originally came from the 48th Pioneer Battalion in Breslau. He assumed command on 3 June 1944, and on 29 August was taken prisoner by the Americans.

I think that, as a commander, he was decidedly inferior to his predecessors. It must have been increasingly difficult for the personnel bureau to fill positions of high command with worthy occupants. In 1944, hundreds of division commanders were needed, and in addition, the higher command positions and staffs had to be filled. The available pool was obviously more than empty.

An example of Richter's shortcomings may suffice to explain why we felt less confidence in him than in his predecessors. At the outset of his tenure in command, he gathered all commanders of his division for a party—at his personal expense—in Narbonne. In the best officer's club manner, he toasted each individual group of guests for more than an hour. The "gentlemen regimental commanders," the "gentlemen battalion commanders," the "gentlemen separate detachment commanders," the "gentlemen medical officers," the "gentlemen of the division supply train," and so forth, on and on and on! There was no opportunity for congenial conversation among the invited, who would have gladly used this opportunity to get to know one another. As dispersed as our division was, many of us barely knew the other by name. Nevertheless, Richter's lean figure stood straight as an arrow in the big room, and he was obviously enjoying himself. Of course, with every new toast, the conversation was interrupted. The persons addressed got up from their seats politely, but obviously displeased, and returned the general's toast. Had he realized what the roughly 150 participants later had to say about him and the circus he brought about, he would not have been very content with his investment. Clearly, this was a man more interested in form than in function, and in war, there is little room for that.

Other factors beyond Richter's shortcomings also contributed to the growing doubt felt by many of us. During his command, there was depressing news from all fronts. In the summer of 1944, the front in the East was disintegrating and the Allies were breaking out in Normandy. The news of 20 July 1944, however, was the outstanding event. At 12:42 PM, a powerful detonation interrupted the presentation of the war situation in the presence of Hitler at Rastenburg. Four completely uninvolved men at once fell victim to the bomb but, of course, Hitler survived practically unscathed.

Other persons were more or less seriously injured. The failed coup would have consequences reaching far into post-war era.

On the evening of 20 July, I was called to the telephone. At the other end was my usually nice Bavarian *Oberst* and regimental commander who furiously fumed to me that an attempt had been made on the *Führer*'s life in Rastenburg, yet Hitler, hardly wounded, was still alive. The assailant and his cohorts, I was told, came from a "very small clique of miserably dissatisfied, cowardly officers," and so on. By name, he only mentioned von Stauffenberg. . . .

Born in 1907, Claus *Graf* Schenk von Stauffenberg was a career officer and, until his appointment to the Staff College, was an officer of the Cavalry Regiment 17 in Bamberg. His comrades from the Staff College and close personal friends during his days at the military school, *Oberst*s Eberhardt Finckh and Mertz Von Quirnheim, were also involved on 20 July and were later executed.

As a young officer, Stauffenberg was an ardent follower of Hitler, as were his above-mentioned friends. Stauffenberg stepped on a mine in North Africa, whereby he lost an eye and suffered considerable wounds to his right arm and hand. Nevertheless, he was retained in service, and in 1943, he was promoted to *Oberstleutnant*. In 1944, he was promoted to *Oberst*. At the age of only thirty-seven, he was Chief of the General Staff to the Commander of the Reserve Army, headquartered in Berlin. I would call that a satisfactory military career. . . .

This was what I mentioned to *Oberstleutnant* Gümbel on that fateful night. I further opined that it raised my doubts that professional dissatisfaction alone could have been the motive for the attempt on Hitler's life. The *Oberstleutnant* then became quite angry and ordered me to report to him immediately! In matters of National Socialism, the bearer of the Blood Order could not take a joke.[29] By all means, he said, I could rest assured that I was not in danger due to my utterances. My commander was much too decent a character to turn me in for such a commentary. It only came to a "serious lesson"—a personal verbal admonishment—as I suspected.

After 20 July, we had barely four weeks to spend at the Mediterranean. On 14 August, we were alerted, since enemy landing forces were spotted by the *Luftwaffe* approaching the Mediterranean coast of France. On the morning of 15 August, the Allies landed between Toulon and Cannes.

Leutnant Grossjohann shortly after commissioning in 1940.

Infantrymen of *Leutnant* Grossjohann's 7th Company of the 2d Battalion, Grenadier Regiment 308 in the Mius bridgehead, spring 1942.

The highly-respected and well-liked Commander of Grenadier Regiment 308 in 1941-42, *Oberst* Paul "Papa" Schultz (here as a *General-major*, later in the war).

Leutnant Grossjohann outside the entrance to the "Fortress" position near Gribovka, in the Mius bridgehead, spring 1942. Note the slung machine pistol and enlisted man's belt.

Wearing what many believed
was "the most beautiful uniform
in the world," *Hauptmann*
Grossjohann poses for a formal
portrait while stationed in
France in 1943 with Reserve
(Training) Infantry Battalion 470.

Oberst Ludwig Gümbel,
Commander of Grenadier
Regiment 308 in Russia, dur-
ing the delaying action up the
Rhône Valley, and subsequent-
ly Commander of "Division
Group Gümbel" in the High
Vosges.

Hauptmann Grossjohann, left, confers with his regimental commander, *Oberstleutnant* Gümbel and other officers of Grenadier Regiment 308, Russia, autumn 1943.

A *Panzerkampfwagen* VI (Tiger I) heavy tank shown here with its turret reversed, supporting the 198th Infantry Division in the Ukraine, 1943.

A knocked-out Soviet T34/76, somewhere in the
Ukraine, 1943.

A Sturmgeschütz III assault gun of the type that
supported *Hauptmann* Grossjohann's battalion's counterattack near Luka in January 1944.
This photo was probably taken in late summer
1943.

Generalleutnant Hans-Joachim von Horn, Commanding
General of the 198th Infantry Division from 12 February
1943 to 2 June 1944 (left) with *Oberst* Paul Keiser,
Commander of Grenadier Regiment 326.

Hauptmann Grossjohann in Russia with his horses, Susi
(left) and Siegfried, autumn 1943.

Inspecting the flimsy defenses inherited by Grenadier Regiment 308 when it took over its sector of what the Propaganda Ministry called, "the Mediterranean Wall."

Major Grossjohann entering his requisitioned French "staff car," outside his quarters, the Maison Rouge, on the road from Perpignan to Canet-Plage.

Major Grossjohann in his Kubelwagen, southern France, summer 1944.

Major Grossjohann (left, arms folded, facing the camera), listens as a fellow officer of Grenadier Regiment 308 speaks at an informal command and staff conference, southern France, summer 1944. The regimental commander, *Oberst* Ludwig Gümbel, is at the right.

The strain of battle shows on the faces of the commander of Grenadier Regiment 308 (*Oberst* Gümbel, seated in the front passenger seat of his Kubelwagen), some of his staff, and of the commander of one of his battalions, *Major* Grossjohann, second from left. August 1944.

A surprised *Major* Grossjohann (center) whips around at the sound of an incoming shell, a fraction of a second before it impacts out of the photo, to the right. His comrades reacted a split second later. Note that Grossjohann has lost his left shoulder board. (Somewhere in the Rhône Valley, August 1944).

Oberst (later *Generalmajor*) Otto Schiel (seated in the passenger seat of his *Kubelwagen*), who assumed command of the 198th Infantry Division in early September 1944, shortly after his assumption of command.

General der Infanterie Friedrich Wiese, Commanding General of 19th Army from the withdrawal from southern France through the defense of the Vosges.

Generalleutnant Erich
Abraham, Commanding
General of LXIII Corps
in Alsace in 1944–45.
Major Grossjohann
received the Knight's
Cross from Abraham on
28 December 1944.

Generaloberst Gotthard
Heinrici, one of Georg
Grossjohann's comman-
ders during his days as an
enlisted man, replaced
Heinrich Himmler as
Commanding General of
Army Group Oberrhein in
late January 1945.

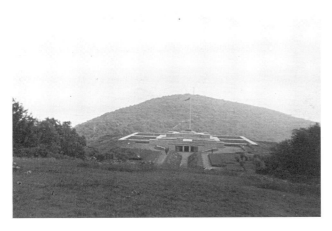

The monument on the Hartmannsweiler Kopf, the mountain top in the High Vosges that was the scene of *Major* Grossjohann's last combat in January, 1945. The monument commemorates the fierce fighting that took place there in the First World War between French and German forces, when this terrain was close by the border between *German* Alsace and France. [Photo from the an album in the collection of Lieutenant Commander Ron Wolin, USN (Ret.). It was originally taken by an unknown soldier of Artillery Regiment 32 in 1940.]

Some of the First World War fortifications on the Hartmannsweiler Kopf. (Photo from the same album in Commander Wolin's collection.)

Major Grossjohann poses for a portrait while on leave in early 1945. His Wounds Badge in Silver, German Cross in Gold, and newly-bestowed Knight's Cross are all clearly visible.

Chapter Thirteen

Retreat Through the Rhône Valley

Historical Commentary

Although the wisdom of the Allied landings in southern France had been a topic of furious debate between Churchill (who opposed them in favor of using the assets elsewhere, such as Brittany or the Bay of Biscay) and Eisenhower, the success of the Operation DRAGOON landings on the Mediterranean coast quickly exceeded even their most ardent supporters' expectations.

As a result of effective deception operations by the Allies and overextended defenses on the German side, the three full infantry divisions of the amphibious assault echelons of the US VI Corps *under Major General Lucian Truscott hit beaches defended by about two German regiments. Greatly assisted by French partisan activity and the landing of a provisional airborne division (the* 1st Allied Airborne Task Force *under Major General Robert Frederick) on the night of 14–15 August, the invading* 3d, 36th, *and* 45th Infantry Divisions *pushed quickly inland. On their heels came the French* II Corps, *commanded by General of the Army Jean-Marie de Lattre de Tassigny. While the* VI Corps *drove north up the Rhône Valley, de Lattre de Tassigny's forces were to seize Marseilles and Toulon, ports critical for the logistical support of the Allied forces landing in southern France.*

Many of the German defenses and key parts of the command structure in the invasion area quickly fell apart. The Commanding General of Field District 800 at Draguignan, Generalmajor *Ludwig Bieringer, was captured along with his staff on D+1. Two days later,* General der Infanterie *Ferdinand Neuling, Commanding General of the German LXII Corps, was captured just a few miles away. The 242d Infantry Division surrendered to the French in Toulon on 22 August, and the 244th capitulated in Marseilles on the 28th.*

Surprisingly granted permission by Hitler to withdraw, the remainder of the Nineteenth Army attempted to retreat up the narrow Rhône Valley during the second half of August and first part of September. The brunt of the fighting fell to the two best formations in Blaskowitz's force, the 11th Panzer and the 198th Infantry. Harassed by French partisans whose morale was invigorated by the success of the Allied landings, and strafed by Allied aircraft from bases in Corsica, these two divisions also had to contend with pursuit by the US VI Corps. *With the better part of three infantry divisions at their heels, they also had to deal with efforts to cut off their retreat altogether. The principle force involved in this effort was* Task Force Butler, *an* ad hoc *unit commanded by Brigadier General Frederic Butler, the Deputy VI Corps Commander. This brigade-sized unit included mechanized cavalry, tanks, tank destroyers, truck-borne infantry of the* 36th "Texas" Division, *self-propelled artillery, motorized engineers, and medics. Their mission was to cut off the Germans' route of withdrawal, thus precipitating the capture or annihilation of the Nineteenth Army. Working in concert with elements of the* 36th *and* 45th Infantry Divisions, *it managed to close* Route Nationale 7 *by 28 August, assuring the destruction of large parts of the 189th and 338th Infantry Divisions.*

Although Blaskowitz lost 88,900 of his roughly 250,000 men during his withdrawal to the Vosges, it could have been much worse had not elements of the 198th Infantry Division fought through the elements of Task Force Butler, *which tried to cut them off on* Route Nationale 7 *near Montelimar and Loriol in late August 1944.*

Georg Grossjohann Remembers . . .

On 15 August 1944, the enemy succeeded in landing three American infantry divisions and an Allied airborne task force in southern France. The weak German units didn't have much to oppose them, and they were already badly decimated by the heavy fire from the Allied naval gunfire and by air attacks. The invading Allied units pushed forward in three directions. The strongest advance went towards Toulon and Marseilles, to secure those two ports for subsequent use. The second group moved through Provence toward Grenoble, where no resistance at all was to be expected. The third finally headed for Nice, but it encountered heavy resistance near the French-Italian border and came to a halt. The American and

French were supported everywhere by the French resistance movement. Twenty-four thousand resistance fighters were said to be in action at that time.

In my experience, these guerrillas only appeared where and when they could do so without great risk to themselves. Typically, they would liquidate small German rear guards or scattered groups, and then mostly from ambush. Even then, the German OKW allowed them the status of combatants if they complied with two conditions—to come forward as an integral military unit and to wear clearly visible armbands to identify themselves. Nevertheless, the French guerrillas would always avoid open confrontation. Instead, disguised as civilians and without any distinguishing mark, they would lurk in the shadows, waiting for a chance to strike in some clandestine way. During the battles of retreat up the Rhône, German soldiers disappeared again and again without a trace. The most common victims of French "resistance" included lone messengers or communications people who were sent out in small parties to repair cables.

I remember one such case very clearly. I had sent a motorcycle messenger with a companion to the regimental command post. They had to drive through a small forest *en route*, but after a short while they returned without having reached their destination. They were fired on by civilians in the woods and one of them received a bullet wound in his thigh. Half an hour or so later, a young Frenchman walked by the isolated house that was my command post. First, we did not pay any attention to him, but then our motorcycle messenger jumped up and yelled, "Well, there is one of those 'brothers'!" Shortly after, the young man stood before me, pale as death, probably suspecting what was coming. When he was searched, we found a heavy American Colt .45 automatic pistol, a hand grenade, and finally, the white armband with the Cross of Lorraine insignia of the *Forces françaises de l'intèrieurs* (FFI). During his interrogation, he admitted shooting at Germans in the nearby wood within the last half hour. When captured, his mission had been to assess our strength here because his group wanted to finish us in the evening. Clearly, by posing as a civilian and concealing his membership in an organized military group, he forfeited the protection due a combatant. A court martial immediately awarded him the death sentence and he was executed by firing squad shortly thereafter. All in all, the French resistance was loath to expose themselves to a great amount of danger in battle and did not earn too much admiration from us.

Before the Americans and French landed in southern France, our regiment had already been moved to the area around the port city of Sète, presumably because our high command expected the Allied landings to take

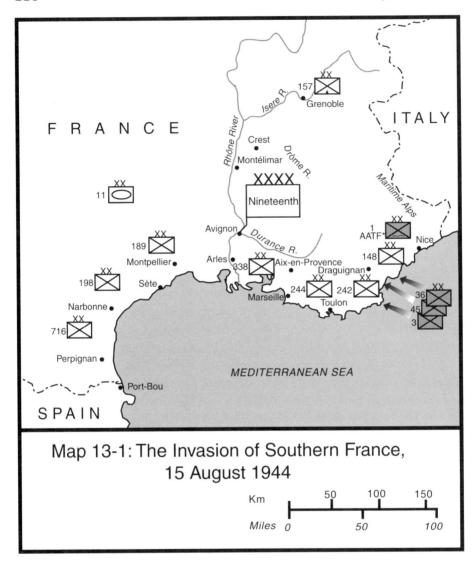

Map 13-1: The Invasion of Southern France,
15 August 1944

place in that vicinity. After the successful landing, we were pulled out and bused eastward. We crossed the Rhône near Arles at least to slow down the advance of the Americans toward Toulon and Marseilles.

The division staff moved on to Aix-en-Provence. We were deployed for now in the areas to the southeast of it. The bridges across the Rhône had already been destroyed up to the north of Avignon before the landing, mostly by Allied air raids.

The two most battleworthy German units, the 11th Panzer Division, and the 198th Infantry Division, stood *exactly* on the wrong side of the Rhône, which may show, intentionally or not, what little effect the German defense had! There existed the danger for all rear echelon units in southern France and in Army Group G to become cut off from the Burgundian Gate, due to the forthcoming collapse of Army Group B in northern France. But nothing that I knew of was done at least to move out all unnecessary dead weight before the start of the battles in the area of the Nineteenth Army. The only good road along the east bank of the Rhône was, therefore, totally blocked by retreating rear echelon units!

As commander of the Nineteenth Army, I would not have worried about the rear echelon units' activities unless they were urgently needed to bring supplies to the front. I would have ordered them to get out of the way, to allow freedom of movement to the combat troops. Trying to stop the advance of the Americans and the allied French units towards Toulon and Marseilles ended in failure. Grenadier Regiment 305 fought only one or two days against the US *3d Infantry Division*. Our Grenadier Regiment 308 and the 198th Infantry Division's *Füsilier* battalion were fighting further north in the area of the small Durance River against the US *45th Infantry Division*. Because the capacity of bridges and ferries was not sufficient, Grenadier Regiment 326 did not even cross the Rhône to get into the fight. Astonishingly, withdrawal to the Vosges was permitted by the highest Commander-in-Chief on 18 August.

During the period 20–22 August, Toulon and Marseilles were already encircled by the enemy who, on 23 August, reached Grenoble without encountering any resistance during the advance. The danger of the Nineteenth Army becoming cut off so far south was colossal. North of Montélimar, the wooded foothills of the French Alps reached directly into the Rhône valley. Here, and some twenty kilometers further north near the river Drôme, the opponent pushed forward to the Rhône.

I probably was not the only one who could not understand why the Nineteenth Army was capricious enough to move its only two valuable divisions painstakingly to the east bank of the Rhône. There was no doubt that these would not have any chance against the overwhelming opponent, and therefore, three days later, we had to be pulled back northbound in forced marches.

Toulon and Marseilles fell on 28 August, with great loss of men and materiel to our side. But by 25 August, after a tremendous forced march, the 11th Panzer Division and our 198th Infantry Division already stood in readiness east of Montélimar to force out the Americans from their commanding position at the entrance to the Rhône valley.

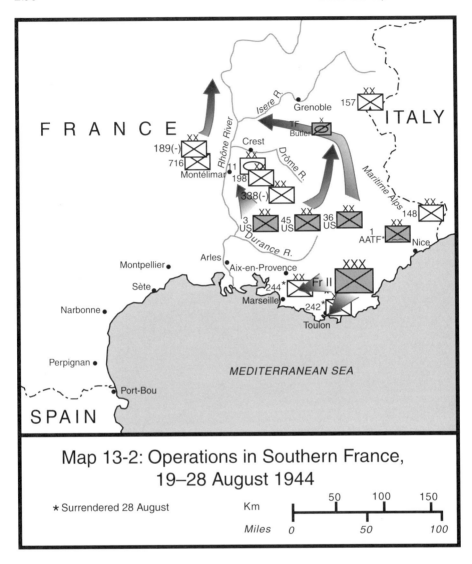

Map 13-2: Operations in Southern France, 19–28 August 1944

★ Surrendered 28 August

Km

Miles

Our attack failed, foiled by strong American artillery fire. My regiment fought near Sauzet, and our neighbor to the right, Grenadier Regiment 326, fought at Bonlieu at the Roubion River. Grenadier Regiment 305 secured the south from the enemy advancing in our direction.

It is interesting to consider an American report from this battle, cited by Graser.

The Germans attacked the lines of the *36th Division* along the Roubion at their weakest point—Bonlieu—and thrashed the combat engineers there. This attack also split the *141st* and *142d*

Infantry Regiments. Attempts by the *1st Battalion, 141st Infantry Regiment* and *Task Force Butler* to close off *Route Nationale* 7 near La Concourd, failed

Since the *141st Infantry Regiment* is under constant pressure and is not capable of achieving control of the hills north and northeast of Montélimar, reinforcements will be moved toward Crest on the Drôme. Artillery and airstrikes will support the troops in blocking the enemy's withdrawal up the Rhône.[30]

As a directly involved battalion commander and eyewitness, I must say that this announcement by the American commander remains incomprehensible to me to this day. Who could have, on 25 August, imposed such great pressure upon the *141st Infantry Regiment*, situated exactly opposite from me? Me, with my roughly one hundred men fit for combat? I agree only with the last sentence of the report: American artillery and a few dozen *Jabos*[31] inflicted indeed disastrous losses on the retreating German supply columns and rearward units.

In my opinion, all the Americans would have had to do was to climb down from their secure heights above the Rhône north of Montélimar into the valley and to fight. They could have bagged us all. Thank heaven that our opponents there were not Russians!

I do not believe that there were noteworthy enemy forces in place at the west bank of the Rhône, other than elements of the *Maquis*. Even these guerrilla forces, however, would not have been a problem for two divisions (11th Panzer and our 198th Infantry) to brush aside or move around them in an orderly manner. To this day I still don't know why we crossed over to the east bank of the Rhône. . . .

The success of the Allied landings in Normandy proved that Rommel's concept of defending at the beaches was not necessarily the most prudent. The opponent succeeded with the landing in spite of strong fortifications, large-scale laying of mines, and beach obstacles of all sorts, albeit with considerable losses. With our experiences from the Maginot Line in 1940, we should have known better about the value of fortifications, yet, the defensive conditions on the Mediterranean coast could never be realistically compared with those on the Atlantic. There was nothing set up behind the weak coastal defense at the Mediterranean. It was obvious that this line of defense would be overrun in the first attack. So why should one expose it right there to certain destruction? As things developed in northern France, the defense of southern France became meaningless in a short time anyway. After barely fourteen days, this was the result of the defensive actions of the Nineteenth Army versus the allied landing in southern France!

The coastal defense east of the Rhône was wiped out within a few hours. Tens of thousands of German soldiers were killed, wounded, or taken prisoner. Once more, tremendous amounts of irreplaceable materiel, such as arms and vehicles, were lost. Both so-called "strongholds," Toulon and Marseilles, were finished. Two good battle-capable divisions were decimated, mainly for the purpose of securing the delayed flight to the homeland for rear echelon units, which actually succeeded only with limitations in any case.

If, at the time of the advance of the Allied landing fleet, we would have pulled back from the coast every battle-worthy fighting unit, free of the dead weight of rear echelon units, and then deployed them out of reach of the devastating effect of the heavy naval artillery, we could have established a flexible posture for battle. The invading enemy would then have run into empty terrain, and could later have been made to suffer considerable losses.

But for the last years of the war, it was probably true what *General* Hans Kissel said about the potential of the German leadership in general. It seemed as if these people had completely resigned and forgotten everything they had mastered so well at the beginning of the war. Certainly, at this point in time, there were few survivors of the first, or even the second, generation of fighting soldiers of the *Wehrmacht.*

Because the bulk of the 11th Panzer Division was badly needed by the Nineteenth Army to keep the *Route Nationale* 7 open north of Montélimar, on 27 August, our Division stood alone as rearguard, fighting around Montélimar. By 28 August, we were compressed into an area that became smaller and smaller.

It may be worthwhile to mention an event from the days of battle around Montélimar. Early on the morning of 27 August, my aide-de-camp, a recipient of the oakleaves to the Knight's Cross, *Oberfeldwebel* (later *Leutnant*) Christian Braun, volunteered, as always, with a few men for patrol. In Russia he had perfected his personal recipe for taking prisoners by cutting field telephone wires in the enemy's rear, and then waiting for the repair party to show up. When they arrived, all Braun and his companions had to do was to welcome them to German captivity—it worked every time! After less than an hour, he and his men came back with a whole platoon of American infantrymen, including two officers, as prisoners. He told us that they were about to freshen up in the early morning hours in an isolated house. Braun had only to fire two rounds from his submachinegun into the front door and loudly bark commands to surrender. That was enough to convince the Americans to give up. The two young officers were especially surprised when they realized the simple trick that had bested

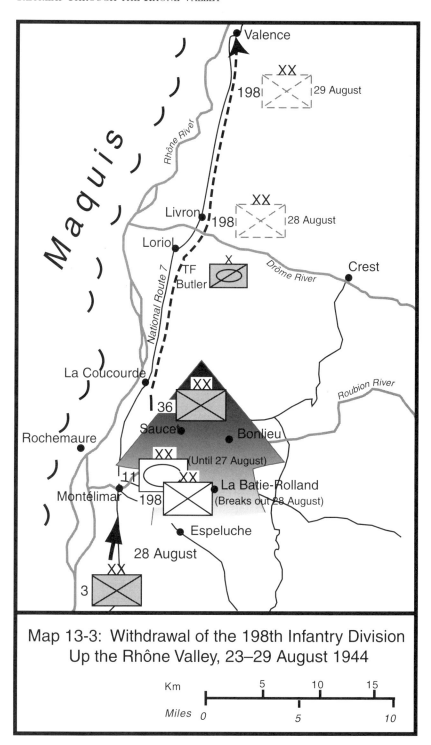

Map 13-3: Withdrawal of the 198th Infantry Division
Up the Rhône Valley, 23–29 August 1944

them. In all, more than thirty American soldiers were captured by Braun and his small patrol.

When the patrol returned with the prisoners, I offered cigarettes and a glass of wine to the two officers, which they declined, as they were probably taught during their training. They had their own cigarettes and they may have assumed that we wanted to poison them with the wine. Or they may have simply been loath to partake in something which was not available to their men. They proved to be exemplary prisoners. They never left my side when we broke through to the north the next morning. Since I simply had no use for them, I gave them the choice to march a few hundred meters up the hill and return to their own people, but they refused the offer. "No, Sir," they said, "we are prisoners now!" All they asked for was quick transportation to more tranquil domains, a wish I could by no means fulfill.

During the many attacks by their own *Jabos* they ran in all directions, but afterwards I had all of them right back on my neck!

Only a nation that, based upon its tremendous material superiority and being so sure in the end to have the war's outcome in their favor, can afford to go to war with fighters like these. Of course, there were different experiences with Americans on other occasions.[32]

In the morning of 28 August, I received the regimental order regarding the breakthrough to the north planned for the early morning of the 29th. North of the Drôme River, the Rhône valley widens again. Therefore, the most difficult part was to pass through the approximately twenty kilometers between Montélimar and that river. The order caused my battalion, with the support of some tanks, to advance through the high ground east of *Route Nationale* 7. The tanks would link up with me early in the morning. Right away, I raised concern, because in my opinion it made no sense to get involved in further fighting in the woods with the far better equipped Americans. What mattered was to reach the north bank of the Drôme, if possible, without any further losses. My *Oberst*, accustomed to similar situations from Russia, just like me, shared my opinion but stated, "Grandjean, this is an order from the General, so you can't do anything about it! He wants to march out the same way." Then I said, "Herr *Oberst*, I'll wait and see how the situation looks tomorrow morning and act accordingly." With this he agreed.

I ordered my company commanders to keep the greatest possible distance from the enemy in the early morning of the next day, and to assemble at my command post. Anyone who could not be there in time for any reason would have to get through on his own. The direction was known, and we would meet later north of the Drôme on *Route Nationale* 7. At the crack of dawn, everybody at my command post was ready to march off, hopefully without having to effect a fighting breakthrough, but waiting for the promised tanks as well as for the rest of their companies. Only part of my battalion was there at the determined time, the others were still involved in occasional skirmishes with the Americans. When the tanks still did not show up a half hour after the agreed upon time, I ordered the elements present to form up and move out. Our route of march took us not through the mountains, as I been directed to do, but directly along the bank of the Rhône, covered by high swamp grass and brush. I could imagine why the tanks did not appear. To deploy them on narrow mountain roads, through the woods with dense undergrowth on each side, where the enemy could lie in wait behind every bush, was especially dangerous for them.

In late afternoon, after we had crossed the Drôme almost untouched, I was not surprised to learn that during his attempted breakout, my Division Commander and many of his staff were captured, and right on the course that was meant for me, too!

Much later, we laid our hands on an old American newspaper in which his capture was described in detail—when a US soldier tried to get him out from behind a bush, he demanded to be taken prisoner by an officer. Of course, I could not judge if the US Army paper reported truthfully, but that he put great emphasis on good manners certainly sounded right. After all, this was the man who spent an entire evening toasting his subordinates at his own party![33]

In the days immediately following Richter's "departure," our Ia, *Oberstleutnant Freiherr* von Finck, assumed command of the Division. It was not easy for our 1st Battalion, nor for the 1st Battalion of Grenadier Regiment 326. In the course of the late morning hours, the latter took back La Coucourde in heavy fighting, and opened up the important road for our retreat. *Hauptmann* Dresel, who was killed in action later, was awarded the Knight's Cross for this. Now, the remainder of the Division could escape across the Drôme, suffering relatively small losses. The total losses for the Division during the breakthrough were estimated to be close to 1,500, including our commanding general.

On 31 August, the Division went into position in a line of resistance on the River Isere. In Valence, we procured provisions from a huge warehouse owned by the *Wehrmacht*. The food we got there was of such good quality that we were only able to remember most of the items by name! Incidentally, the French civilian population was already waiting all around the depot for the last Germans to leave, so that they could help themselves. As always, we left this building intact. . . .

On 2 September, we marched in close formation through Lyon, 140 kilometers to the north. Thousands of French people lined up along the road of our withdrawal, but I personally did not notice any hostile demonstrations.

North of Lyon, the retreat continued through the Saône valley, and after more strenuous marches we formed a new line of defense, northeast of Chalon-sur-Saône, at the Doubs, the western tributary of the Saône.

Oberst Otto Schiel, an older gentleman from the OKH, assumed command on 3 September. He was an energetic man, the sort who makes a successful businessman. On 1 October, he was, as usual, promoted to *Generalmajor. Major* i. G. Grauer became the new Ia of the division, replacing *Oberstleutnant Freiherr* von Finck, who, in the mean time, had had a bad accident.

The Americans followed us very carefully along the Rhône and in the Saône valley. To the west, between the rivers and the Swiss border, where the *Maquis* practically rolled out the red carpet for them, the Americans moved, by their standards, quite quickly ahead. During this, they occasionally attempted to push from the French Jura into the Doubs valley. My battalion marched further west, through the world-famous wine town Beaune, known to me quite well from spring 1943. There, I had a surprising encounter.

We stopped for a short break in the center of the town and, together with a few of my men, I sat down on the terrace of a restaurant for a glass of wine. When I was seen by the French waitress who was serving, she was so stunned that she almost dropped her tray. The pretty young woman had been the girlfriend of a comrade of mine in nearby Dijon in 1943, and both she and her sister had been guests in my apartment several times. I understood her terrifying situation right away. At this point, of course, nobody in her hometown could learn that she was the girlfriend of a German officer. As I was paying my bill, she whispered to me that her German friend had been killed in Russia. A former comrade of his from Dijon had recently informed her of this.

Up to this time, when the German troops had to pull out of much of France, it was my experience that there had been more "collaboration" than "resistance" on the part of the average French citizen. There were in France, as well as in our country, before and after 1945, always disgruntled informers, who often for most abject reasons, denounced their fellow citizens to their own officials, or to the German occupation forces. This was one reason for collaboration. There were also numerous Frenchmen who despised Communism, and who perhaps foresaw what could happen to them if the Germans were defeated in the east. As far as the former lot are concerned, nobody was saddened by the fact that they later sometimes were punished, and even sentenced to death. For the second category, of course, harsh punishment was more than questionable. . . .

Perhaps their judges believed in having to restore France's honor by sentencing collaborators to death or long imprisonment. Some of these people were actually guilty of little more than establishing a passable relationship with the occupying forces. They may even have, out of honest conviction, approved of enduring relations with the Germans, but still have remained French patriots. France did lose the war with the Germans in 1940, but not its national honor!

What was done to French girls was especially ugly; indeed, it was most crude and heartless how French girls, whose only crime was to fall in love with a German, were treated by the French mob. Typically, their hair was shaved or closely cropped, then they were humiliated and beaten as they were run out of their native villages or towns by a local mob, seething with hatred. For the French men who participated, this may have been an expression of primitive sexual jealousy and insulted arrogance.

Evidently, one has to put up with the fact that any major upheaval brings the lower side to the surface. We, too, had most evil denunciations, and not only after 1945.[34]

Our division moved into its next position at the Doubs River. The front line of our Corps ran from Chalon-sur-Saône to Dole and on to Besançon. By 8 September, the front had to be shortened because of numerous penetrations by American tanks. The next morning, the line of resistance lay along the Ognon, five to twenty kilometers northwest of Doubs.

On 8 or 9 September, my colleague, *Major* Dr. Majer, together with his adjutant, was wounded by tank fire and captured by the pursuing Americans. Later, when he returned to his hometown of Stuttgart, Majer told me that he was brilliantly taken care of by the American nurses. Without penicillin, which at that time was not yet available to us, he would most likely not have survived his severe injury.

During the days of fighting in the first half of September, I had three experiences that were most significant. One was quite successful, one questionable, and one a little unusual.

I had positioned a few infantrymen equipped with *panzerfausts* at a railroad underpass—it could have been on the line southwest of Dole.[35] Suddenly, a jeep with four US soldiers came rolling along toward our underpass, clearly unaware of any danger. It stopped hardly ten meters away and the occupants prepared to dismount. Two of my men had aimed their rocket launchers at the jeep already, when I whispered to them not to shoot at the vehicle, but beyond it. Seconds later, there were two terrible explosions and our four Americans froze in place. When we called on them to surrender, they came marching forward with their hands up. Later, they said they believed our lines to be much further to the north. This was why they did not expect *panzerfaust* fire from an ambush position, but rather perhaps artillery fire, at the most. We took them and their jeep to my command post.

The boss was a well-fed, redheaded major, apparently of Irish decent. He and his comrades were not as touchy as the two US lieutenants from Montélimar. Together we had a strong drink, and at that time I was even rich enough to offer a choice between whiskey or French cognac. "I prefer whiskey," the redhead said objectively. When we searched the vehicle, we found maps with the firing plans of the American artillery. Our major was no little fish, but obviously the artillery officer of the US division which opposed us. Of course, the American soldiers were allowed to keep anything that was personal property, but the maps were clearly a different story. Despite his entreaties to the contrary, I had to withhold them from him.

Years later, I met him on the street in Bad Tölz. (See Map 19-1) We exchanged a few casual words, but I had the impression that our short encounter was not especially pleasant for him. Besides, it was shortly after war's end.

The event of questionable import was this. Later on, when we took some American prisoners, one of them asked to be able to speak to the German commanding officer. My English at that time was still somewhat bumpy, but it quickly became clear what concerned the G.I. "Sir, I am Jewish!" he told me. I responded that, to me, he was just an American prisoner of war (PW). Besides, I was absolutely certain that no American PW would be sorted out in this respect. Antisemitism was not an issue for me. In my East Prussian homeland, my father did business with Jews when they showed up at our farm to buy animal pelts or scrap iron. My Aunt Helene worked for decades as a chief bookkeeper in a Danzig (Gdansk) cigarette factory. Privately, she was also involved in a friendship with the Jewish owner of their firm and his family. Presumably, part of the Christmas gifts she brought each year came from the Borg family. My first wife was an apprentice in a Jewish-owned warehouse before we were married.

The unusual experience of this time was of a different kind. I often saw how German 88mm *Flak*, tanks, self-propelled assault guns or antitank guns destroyed enemy tanks, and, of course, the other way around as well.[36] This time, I was an eyewitness to playing the game in a way that was new to me. Immediately across from the position of our heavy infantry gun section, several American tanks suddenly appeared in the dense brush. The short-barreled 150mm guns were basically used only for high-angle fire. The surprised gun crews had to find means for their own protection, so they aimed directly at two enemy tanks and fired. I don't know if anything like this had been practiced before. The distance amounted surely to not much more than fifty meters. The effect was horrible. The two tanks that were hit literally exploded, while the others behind them shifted at once into reverse, as one could clearly hear. Unfortunately, those "experiences of success" became more and more scarce.

Continuously fighting, on 15 September the division moved back to the western edge of the Vosges Mountains via Lure. To present an idea of what was left of people in the replenished division one month later, 1st Battalion of the Grenadier Regiment 308 consisted of only twenty-two men, including the two officers! One of the battalion commanders was seriously wounded and taken prisoner by the Americans, the second one was killed in action just three days later. The third battalion commander in a week, *Hauptmann* Bengel, a member of the division since the very first day of its formation, had only a few weeks left to live. On 6 October, during a counterattack, he was badly wounded and died shortly thereafter in a field hospital from an infection.

It is simply impossible to detail all that took place in the battles between Chalon-sur-Saône and our later deployment west of Gérardmer. One incident that is particularly vivid in my mind took place near Lure. My soldiers brought in a seriously wounded comrade whose abdominal wall was completely ripped open by a shell splinter. Since we had to pull back, we considered dragging him along. We emptied the rear seats of my jeep and loaded him in. The poor guy was fully conscious and suffered unbearable pain. Since the larger part of the battalion had already marched off, our physician could not be reached. The moment we started to drive, the wounded soldier continuously screamed in pain, so we carefully took him out of the car and laid him on the ground. While we stood around rather helplessly, a young French woman—I think she was the local teacher— came out of the neighboring house. She made us understand that the soldier would die within a short time, so why torture him? She promised to stay with him to the end and she would see to it that he was buried in the town's cemetery. When we left, quite distressed, she was sitting on the ground with the boy's head in her lap.

By the end of September, our division was deployed around Gérardmer. Our opponents were the US *3d* and *36th Infantry Divisions*, both of which were fully motorized and equipped with tanks. But shortly thereafter, my regiment was moved back to the area of Le Thillot, not far from where we had been just a short time before. There, my future opponent, the *3d Algerian Infantry Division*, had just crossed the Moselle and approached the Cornimont-Remiremont road.

Chapter Fourteen

Regimental Commander

Historical Commentary

The month of August 1944, was disastrous for the German Armed forces in the west. Not only did Army Group G lose over a third of its strength and retreat three hundred miles to the Vosges, but Army Group B, to the north and east, sustained 10,000 killed and about 50,000 captured, and lost most of its heavy equipment in the battle of the Falaise Pocket. This massive debacle forced them to withdraw toward the water barriers of the Low Countries in the north, the Westwall *(called the "Siegfried Line" by the Allies) in the center, and the Vosges in the south. By September, Army Group G controlled 1st Army, consisting largely of units which had been pulled back from Normandy, and Nineteenth Army, consisting mostly of rebuilt units withdrawn from the south of France.*

In late September 1944, the US Seventh and Third Armies linked up, forming a continuous front from the Swiss border south of Belfort to the English Channel. Seventh Army received a three-division corps, the XV, from Third Army, to double its fighting power, previously represented only in its VI Corps. Less than two months after the DRAGOON landings, the US Seventh and French First Armies—now collectively called Sixth Army Group—arrived at the foothills of the Vosges, in which the Germans were determined to stand until at least the spring of 1945.

Although the various elements of Army Group G had been hit hard indeed, they now had marked advantages in terrain and weather. The Sixth Army Group traced its lines of communication (that is, supply) down a single railroad line to Marseilles, and was rapidly running low on all classes of supply. The Germans, on the other hand, were on the doorstep of the Reich, closer than ever to the wellsprings of German industry—which, despite Allied strategic bombardment, actually increased their production through the remainder of 1944. Although the Luftwaffe *continued to be practically impotent in its effects on the battlefield, increasingly poor weather was frustrating the attempts of the* XII Tactical Air Command *to support the maneuver of Allied elements as well. From 15 October 1944 to 15 January 1945, there were only twenty-three flyable days, and the small number of P-47 Thunderbolt fighter bombers available (never numbering more than seventy) were employed overwhelmingly against deep targets, rather than ones near the front lines.*

The narrow, winding, easily-blocked mountain roads, already inhospitable to armor, became increasingly impractical to use as they became muddy and eventually frozen or covered with snowy slush. The Allies' mobility advantage would be nullified by the steep and slippery peaks, crags, and crevices of the Vosges.

Reconnaissance for the construction of defensive works designed to enhance the already high defensibility of the Vosges got underway in the second week of August 1944. The actual construction work, performed by Alsatian and German members of the Reichs Arbeits Dienst, *German soldiers and captured Russians who had defected to the German Army, began on 1 September. Although the fortifications were destined to never be completely finished, multiple belts of thick barbed-wire-protected trenchlines were completed, connecting strongpoints, replete with overhead cover. Extensive minefields, antitank obstacles, and roadblocks supplemented these defensive works. While the American and French attackers would be prey to the worst winter in the Vosges of the twentieth century to that time, many German defenders would enjoy the relative comfort and protection of covered defensive bastions.*

Overall, Georg Grossjohann and his Landsers *of Grenadier Regiment 308 could count on fighting in a far more advantageous* milieu *in the Vosges than they had encountered anywhere else for years. No attacker had ever succeeded in breaking through this densely-forested mountain range—ever. Romans, Huns, Swedes, French, and Germans had all tried over the two millennia of the region's recorded history, and all had failed. Over the next few months, the Americans and French would attempt to penetrate the German defenses through the few trafficable passes, and the German defenders would doggedly attempt to keep them at bay . . . for to the backs of Army Group G lay only the easily-traversed Plain of Alsace and then—the River Rhine.*

Here, in the dense forests of the seemingly impassable Vosges, the Allied superiority in men and materiel would disappear, and be replaced by entirely different factors. In the words of Gerhard Graser, chronicler of the 198th Infantry Division,

> *"In the wooded mountain terrain the formation of a contiguous front was not possible. The individual strongpoints were far apart. The intervening land could only be covered through flanking fire of heavy weapons and artillery. The fighting always consisted of small battles in the underbrush, man on man. The American infantryman, accustomed to the protection of superior airpower and artillery, and used to advancing behind tanks, suddenly found themselves robbed of their most important helpers. The persistent bad weather hindered their air force, and the terrain limited the mobility of their armor to a significant degree. here the individual soldier mattered the most. For teh German soldier, there was the courage of despair that gave rise to the utmost resistance: after many years of combat all over Europe, his back was to the wall of the homeland. On their side, the Americans believed that the banner of victory was already half-fastened to their colors and that it would take only one last energetic exertion for them to victoriously end the war. So both sides fought with unbelievable bitterness and severity."*

In mid-October 1944, OKW issued a Führer Befehl, *an order directly from Hitler, which directed that the Vosges would be held to the last man.*

Georg Grossjohann Remembers . . .

Because *Oberstleutnant* Gümbel had to take command of a "division group," or provisional division to which we were subsequently attached, the leadership of the regiment was passed on to me. This was an honor I probably would not have received if my older and honorable colleague, Dr. Majer, had not been crossing the Atlantic as a wounded prisoner.

As regimental commander, I still took a direct part in the infantry battle. While we were moving northwest through the wooded hills north of Ramonchamp to link up with another unit, I noticed a soldier who was in the bushes ahead of me, aiming his weapon at me. I immediately fired my whole magazine in his direction. With one more leap I stood next to him. He was a very young officer, not Algerian or Moroccan, but a blond Frenchman. I had hit him in his thigh, close to his torso, and I saw right away that any help would be too late. He still managed to ask me for his morphine needle, which every American—and therefore French—first-aid kit contained. I stayed with him for a few moments and tried to give him some encouragement, but then I had to go on. In more than four years of war,

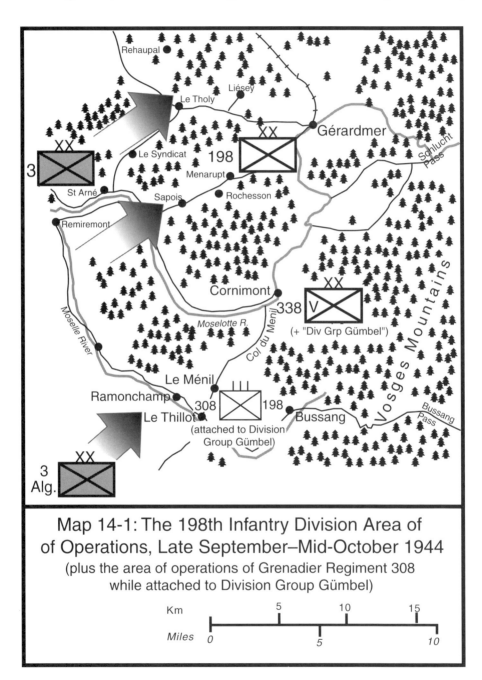

Map 14-1: The 198th Infantry Division Area of
of Operations, Late September–Mid-October 1944
(plus the area of operations of Grenadier Regiment 308
while attached to Division Group Gümbel)

our souls became callused, although without this protection, we probably could not have endured so much!

The more deeply we moved into the thick forest, the more dispersed our lines became, because we had to secure our western flank at least scantily. Yet, in the end, I had to give up. With barely 150 men, one could not mop up an extremely clever opponent, presumably superior in numbers, in five to six kilometers of thick forest. We also had an uneasy feeling that the Algerians or Moroccans had already passed us in the north, and that it was only a flank guard that we were fighting. This feeling would become an extremely unpleasant reality by the evening.

It was, therefore, not feasible to advance any further. It also appeared to me to be extremely risky to leave my thin line of defense in this dense forest during the night.

My aide-de-camp and I noticed at dusk how clever and dangerous the opponent was. For some time, there had been total silence and we had a short exchange of thoughts as we were standing in a clearing. Suddenly, a shot was fired, and a messenger who had come with us stood for a second as if frozen, then fell to the ground. Upon my rather frightened call, "Fiege, what's the matter?" he answered in clearly understandable words, "I am dead, *Herr Major*!" Seconds later, that's what he really was. One could move only with the most extreme caution. Comrades carried the dead back as usual, wrapped in his ground-sheet. During the long war I had experienced many things, but that a messenger reporting his own death was one of the more macabre.

Shortly before complete darkness, I ordered to pull back and only kept outposts on the clear hills outside the woods, facing north and northwest.

A patrol confirmed our concerns from late afternoon. The opponent had practically encircled us. Some houses were in flames in Ramonchamp, situated some five hundred to one thousand meters south of us in the valley. One could clearly hear the bustle of vehicles and voices in the clear night. We were surrounded.

After my return to the command post, I heard the rattle of shovels in the dark. When I questioned what they were doing there, they answered, "We're digging a hole for Fiege!" Exhausted and depressed as I was, I just could not control myself anymore and yelled, "This is not a hole, you idiots, this is a *grave*!" Right away, I regretted my outburst, since the poor guys were at least as depressed and worn out as I was. Their irreverent expression was only a kind of cover for their stress.

This nocturnal episode was always one of those especially deep impressions I had of the war.

Some years ago, when I was back in Le Thillot, I couldn't find exactly where my command post had been, high over Ramonchamp. The dead that we buried there had been reinterred elsewhere in Alsace long before my visit.

After my return, my adjutant of that time, *Oberleutnant* Albert, reported that we had lost telephonic contact with the task force, but I had expected that anyway. That's one of the problems with being surrounded.

Fortunately, we were located high in the hills, and we were able to maintain radio communications. I asked for permission from the commander of the 338th Infantry Division, to which Group Gümbel was attached, to take the regiment back to Le Thillot. I was allowed to do so, with the stipulation that I might take back the left wing, but had to leave the right in its current place. In reality, this would have meant that half the regiment had to stay encircled by the opponent. No further radio messages were answered by division after that. Here, I would like to quote excerpts by the often-mentioned *Herr* Graser, known for writing the history of our division,

> "Now Grenadier Regiment 308 finds itself in a very peculiar situation. It is asking permission to pull back to its old position, but the 338th Division allows only a retreat of half of the regimental wing. . . . At about 11 o'clock at night, hours after no more radio messages from the regiment were answered, the regimental commander decides to order a break out to Le Thillot, simply on his own!"[37]

It was true, too. First, I held something like a "war council" with my officers. Without any voices of opposition, we agreed that only now in the dark would we have a last chance to smuggle ourselves out of this fix so I ordered a pullout against the division commander's orders. I later discovered that I did exactly what they secretly hoped for and expected me to do.

Since we could not use any roads, we had to leave some vehicles behind, but we took all weapons and horses and got them back to Le Thillot safely. We avoided any unnecessary noise. There was absolutely no talking allowed. We marched in a long column through the brush, until we reached National Route 66, which was clear of the enemy, just short of the town. From the town's entrance, we soon heard the somewhat timid call, "Stop, who's there?" My answer "Grossjohann, 308!" was followed by a loud and clear, "Thank God, Grandjean, that you're back!"

As it turns out, *Oberstleutnant* Gümbel could not allow my breakout. He was, to a certain extent, bound by the directives of the 338th Infantry Division. Now, his relief and joy were tremendous. This illustrates a peculiar phenomenon that I believe was prevalent in the German Army during this time.

Many times before and after that, I found that superior commanders—at the Division level and above—modified clear orders or were forced to broadly interpret them. This was because while *good news*—such as the success of our advance that morning—was immediately passed with great fanfare to higher headquarters, *less encouraging* information—such as requests to withdraw—were greeted with pure hysteria. Consequently, generals usually left it to insignificant small fry, like maybe regimental commanders, to make the truly sensible decisions on the spot. Any commander who had not gotten the idea by now, and who literally interpreted his orders, was simply beyond help.

So, in this case, when he was briefed in the morning, the Commanding General of the 338th Infantry Division would learn that Grenadier Regiment 308 had withdrawn from Le Thillot. It would be a *fâit accompli*. He would, in turn, pass it up to IV Luftwaffe Field Corps headquarters, whence it would go to Nineteenth Army and finally Army Group G, all as part of a routine situation report . . . and they would do nothing about it. But if the commander of the 338th had asked permission for the withdrawal, there would have been hell to pay.

Thus, a major who, in the teeth of heavy enemy opposition, got his unit knocked out of their position would, at worst, get bawled out. But generals were subject to demotion and relief for even *asking* to withdraw. As far as I know, that never happened to a thirty-three-year-old major!

As expected, nothing happened, and everything worked out for the best. My *Oberst* was happy, the Commanding General of the 338th Infantry Division was content, and since the Chief of Staff of IV Luftwaffe Field Corps was a close friend of my *Oberst*, he was satisfied as well.

As later became obvious, the defense of Le Thillot, the approach to the Bussang Tunnel, was now secured for weeks to come. Today, the tunnel no longer exists. It was blown up in 1945. Now, there is a wide road through the pass.

Together with some other units, including Machinegun Battalion 40, we formed a light, but as we soon realized, a rather strong, front opposed to our Algerian "friends." I was named battle commander of German forces defending Le Thillot. Graser explains the situation well,

> During the whole course of October, the French tried with repeated, tenacious attacks, to break open the gate to the Bussang Pass. They could not achieve any success worth mentioning. On the contrary, after they succeeded in pushing off parts of the 338th Infantry Division from the Ménil Pass, they were again driven off this mountain in a counterattack by Grenadier Regiment 308. Ramonchamp, the village situated sharply northwest of Le Thillot,

changed ownership more than ten times in the weeks of battles, raging back and forth.[38]

Concerning the successful defense of Le Thillot, I believe Grenadier Regiment 308 contributed to it in a considerable, perhaps even decisive, way. Referring to the recapture of the Ménil Pass, the following has to be noted: The *Col du Ménil*, at 621 meters elevation, is situated northeast of the little town of the same name, on the Le Thillot-Cornimont road. What was taken by battle was not this low-lying pass road, but the heights above it. In the context of the total events, this was certainly not an important matter, but it was played up in the daily *Wehrmacht* report, mentioning names, and so on. I was personally honored with a letter from the division commander. We became quite humble, as I said before, for every little success was used to make the *Wehrmacht* report appear less distressing, to avoid provoking an attack of madness from the highest warlord.

Recently, I asked for a copy of the corresponding army news report from the German Federal Archives at Cornelimünster, but it was not available there. Therefore, I have only our Nineteenth Army newspaper article about the defense of the Ménil Pass, written in somewhat bombastic style by the Nineteenth Army Propaganda Company. The single true statement contained in it is that my adjutant and I were wounded by artillery fire. I had several small splinters pulled from my head, some others were even removed years later.

The days in Le Thillot were quite lively. My place as battle commander was in a downtown hotel, but my real command post was located in the west end of town, next to National Route 66. Both structures are still preserved without any change up to the time of this writing. A small wall against which an assault gun that was temporarily under my command got stuck, still showed the ruts from the vehicle's attempts to get off the wall, as late as 1976.

The main weapons that assured our successful defense were the twin-barreled 20mm automatic cannon of Machinegun Battalion 40. The town of Le Thillot is situated in a valley. For each attempt to advance toward it, the opponent had to climb down from the heights opposite, which fortunately were only covered with low brush. When the two double-barreled *flak* weapons opened fire with their explosive bullets against an evident attack, the offensive spirit of the attacker expired quickly!

My presence in the main battleline was almost always necessary because artillery fire on both sides of the main road often caused panic with the young soldiers of this separate automatic weapons outfit. They would jump out of their foxholes and look for cover in the houses further behind the town. They suffered especially high losses each time because the French artillery would fire extensively. Regrettably, the NCOs of this unit, which normally did not belong to our Regiment, were no special heroes. The strong leadership necessary in battle was in short supply among them. Nevertheless, the Algerians did not have any success with us until the day of our relief.

Apart from being responsible for the defense of the town, as battle commander I also felt a certain accountability for the French civilian population, which understandably had no more ardent wish than to see us disappear eastward behind the crest of the Vosges Mountains.

The mayor of Le Thillot, whose name, Georg Grosjean, coincidentally resembled mine, was a rational partner in any conversation about official issues. There were no language problems, especially since my aide-de-camp, having been chief dealer in a Baden-Baden casino, spoke excellent French.

After the war, a little book titled, *Final Battle in the Vosges Mountains*, was published by Pabel Publishers. The author, W. Borcher, mentions the efforts of my successors in Le Thillot in evacuating the civilian population. Our successors were from the 269th Infantry Division under the command of *Generalleutnant* Hans Wagner (the Ia was *Major* Schwutke). At various times during subsequent fighting in Alsace, I served under Wagner, either directly or as commander of an attached unit. The story he related to me further illustrates the command climate during the fighting in the Vosges.

By the time Wagner wanted to evacuate the town, our Nineteenth Army had passed to the command of Army Group Oberrhein . . . which was personally commanded by the *Reichsführer-SS*, Heinrich Himmler. In their efforts to spare the civilian populace in the vicinity of Le Thillot, both Wagner and Schwutke followed the unofficial rules. Upon asking *General der Flieger* Erich Petersen, Commander of IV Luftwaffe Field Corps, for permission to make contact with the French forces regarding evacuation of the civilian population, Wagner got a typical response. "I cannot and must not give my approval, Wagner," Petersen cried. "My God, don't you understand? I would have to make a written report to Himmler if I were to do this. Do you know what *that* means?"

In matters like these, front line soldiers simply had to work it out on their own. Himmler was sitting in his headquarters at Triberg. Why should one have to rub under his nose what one intends to do several hundred kilometers further west, namely to perform a simple humane act to protect endangered civilians? My division history reports that immediately after taking over my duties as battle commander, without asking anyone, I sent a French nurse on a bicycle to go and appeal to the French commander of our Algerian opponents to cease fire at certain times so that groceries could be delivered. During this time, we offered to refrain from any belligerent activity. I also offered to hand over the orphanage and the old-folks' home on the main street. The nice nurse, executing her duties in her habit, came back with a positive answer, as expected. The cease-fire intervals were observed, and all military action was halted. I am sure that the French also adhered to the agreements on this point, but I was denied the means to transport the children and the elderly, including caretakers. I could not afford to allow the French to approach with a column of trucks because word of this might have gotten all the way to Triberg.

Upon assuming command in the area, *Generalleutnant* Wagner decided to take all this a step further. Monsieur Grosjean, the mayor, gave him full support and all parties agreed to uphold the tightest discretion. The evacuation of the citizenry of Le Thillot took place during a foggy night, not into the area behind the German troops as I had suggested, but more logically, to the French side.

Exactly thirty years later, for the first time in 1974, and for the second time in 1976, I paid a visit to the mayor of Le Thillot, accompanied by my family. Both times we were received in a very friendly manner. In 1980, the old gentleman died, in his eighty-seventh year. I considered it more than a gesture of pure courtesy when his family sent me an announcement of his death.

The great majority of the French could certainly not complain about the conduct of the German soldiers in their country. One could not blame the *Wehrmacht* for the actions of certain party organizations—strongly supported by tens of thousand of collaborators. Yet, after 1945, the French not only ignored this, but also the fact that it was not us who declared war in 1939 on them, but they on us. In the spring of 1945 and after, the people of certain communities in Baden-Württemberg would have been very content had they received as much understanding and good will from some French commanders as, for example, the inhabitants of Le Thillot had enjoyed from us in the fall of 1944.

In Le Thillot, we were apprised of the news that *Generalfeldmarschall* Erwin Rommel had succumbed to the serious wounds he had suffered from being strafed in Normandy the previous summer. The real circumstances were only made known after the war. This news report fit right in to the depressing general situation of these days and weeks.

Rommel was an unusually brave battlefield leader, full of surprises and determination. Considering the special conditions of the theater of operations in Africa, he understood how to outmaneuver the apparently methodical and quite uninventive British generals. In his military undertakings, as well as in his private life, he had always been immensely lucky. Yet, even he failed to prevent the Allied invasion on the Atlantic coast.

Rommel had his shortcomings, though, and many of us did not share the cult of adulation to which many subscribed. He was not only inconsiderate of himself, being rather reckless on the battlefield, but also toward his subordinates. Without demonstrating any scruples, he was even known to take credit for his subordinates' successes—few things endear a commander to his men less than this. During the 1940 campaign in France, his 7th Light Division took the highest losses of all divisions involved in the western campaign, including infantry divisions! In view of some of these characteristics, it had to be difficult to see him as a sympathetic human being.

His rocket-like ascent from *Oberst* to *Generalfeldmarschall*—in less than three years' time!—was not only the result of the relentless dedication of his troops and himself, but also of a wisely-crafted program of self-promotion. It was certainly no accident that he finagled the assignment of several prominent members of the Propaganda Ministry to serve as (reserve) officers for his division in France, and later for the Afrika Korps.

As a person, Rommel was in many ways a typical Swabian, demonstrating the great spectrum of positive and negative cultural characteristics by which they are distinguished. It was not for no reason that Rommel had more enemies than friends, and being the *Führer*'s "favorite general" made many envious. So, when it became a matter of life or death for him, he found no friends. The five generals from the court of honor decided for his Swabian *Landsman* Speidel, and therefore against him.

In spite of his shortcomings, Rommel was nevertheless an absolutely exceptional field commander. The news of his death at that time was very bad for us, like so much other bad news.

Beginning in November, after almost six weeks, my regiment was withdrawn from Le Thillot and reassigned to the control of the 198th Infantry Division. I was informed that the IV Luftwaffe Corps Commander, who was my superior during the time in Le Thillot, wanted me to sign out in person before I left his area of command. It was already past midnight, after our relief, when I arrived at Corps headquarters. I was told that the General had gone to sleep, but wanted to be awakened as soon as I got there. Shortly thereafter, he appeared fully dressed in his *Luftwaffe* uniform, not in his bathrobe, as I had expected. For almost fifteen minutes, *General der Flieger* Petersen conversed with me and expressed his appreciation of our firm defense at Le Thillot. He had also arranged that I would receive a few hundred of those much craved front line ration packages for the soldiers of my parting regiment.

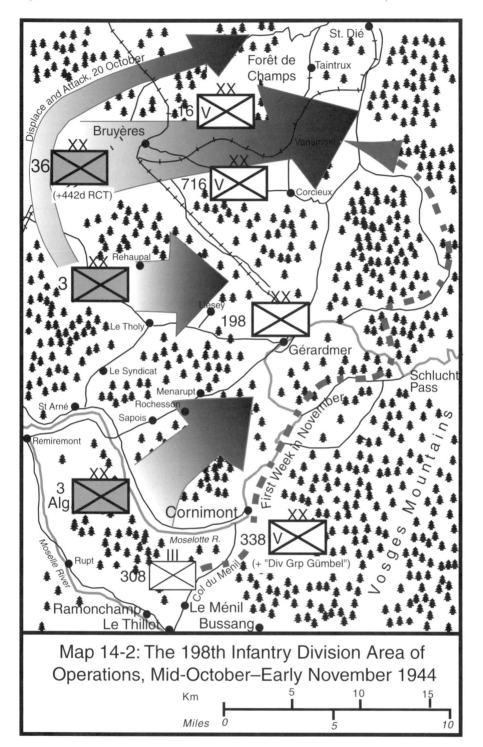

Map 14-2: The 198th Infantry Division Area of Operations, Mid-October–Early November 1944

Our new sector was in the *Forêt de Champ*, southwest of St. Dié. Our mission was to prevent American access to the road junction in Corcieux. In the area of the nearby small town of Vanémont, there was very heavy fighting with Japanese, who tenaciously attacked over and over again. Our *Landsers* were rather shocked and bitter. "The Japanese are our allies, aren't they?" they asked. "Are they, too, fighting us now?"

In a narrow valley German units had encircled a battalion that came from Texas. The Hawaiian-Japanese of the *442d Infantry Regiment* had been ordered to get them out of there, at any cost. It meant bad business for the Americans! To get about three hundred Texans freed, some eight hundred Japanese were killed or wounded. A report about this fighting, in which mostly our division was involved, appeared in *Reader's Digest* in 1960.[39]

Chapter Fifteen

Farewell to My Regiment

Historical Commentary

On 12 November 1944, the US Seventh Army *began a major offensive designed to penetrate the Vosges passes, from the most important pass at Saverne to the more minor passes to the south, namely those at Saales, St. Marie-aux-Mines, and Bonhomme. A week later, further south, the French* First Army *opened a complementary offensive, designed to break through the Schlucht Pass and, more importantly, the Belfort Gap.*

The American effort yielded success surprisingly swiftly. By 22 November, elements of XV Corps *had broken out past Saverne onto the Alsatian Plain; by the next day, the Saales pass was in the hands of the VI Corps' 3d Infantry Division; within a week, all the passes in the American zone had been seized. Whole German divisions, such as the fresh, but inexperienced 708th Volks-Grenadier and the tenacious 553d Volks-Grenadier, practically ceased to exist. Strasbourg, a city of great cultural—and political—importance to both the French and the Germans, fell to the US* XV Corps *23–25 November.*

The German defense of the Vosges passes in the French zone—including the Belfort Gap—was much more successful. Elements of Nineteenth Army held out in these positions, which represented the southern half of the so-called "Colmar Pocket," until late January. After 6 December, Nineteenth Army came under the personal command of Reichsführer-SS *Heinrich Himmler in his role as Commander of Army Group Oberrhein.*

Although the Germans had possessed many advantages in their defense of the Vosges—advantages they continued to press in the sectors where they faced the French—their commanders were faced with several problems as well. At this point in the war, many units were manned by soldiers—even Luftwaffe *airmen and* Kriegsmarine *sailors—not originally trained as infantrymen, or who had been recently called up due to the reclassification of their conscription status. Also, many units suffered various difficulties from being manned by* Volksdeutschen *(ethnic Germans from occupied countries) or even non-Germans, such as soldiers from various parts of the Soviet Empire. Although still a far cry from the* Volksturm *militia of old men and boys that would eventually defend the towns and cities of the* Reich, *the personnel situation of many German units at this stage of the war was far from ideal.*

The situation on the Allied side of the Vosges was also less than perfect. Most of the American infantry units committed in the Vosges were comprised in large part of soldiers who had been reclassified from other military occupational specialties. Thousands of former antiaircraft gunners, medium bomber crewmen, radio technicians, and men from other decidedly non-infantry backgrounds had been pressed into service as riflemen, machinegunners, and mortarmen in the units fighting in the Vosges Mountains. Former members of the Army Specialized Training Program (ASTP), men who by virtue of their high IQs had been originally selected to perform duties in some of the more esoteric non-combat specialties, filled the ranks of the American infantry units in the Vosges by the thousands.

In some ways, the situation in the French units was even more difficult. Many of the soldiers battling through the snow and mud were actually colonial troops, from Algeria, Tunisia, and even Senegal. Although their officers were mostly French, these men were completely unaccustomed to the hardships of a northern European winter, and were fighting far from home for a cause that was obscure to their interests— at best. Motivating these otherwise often savage warriors to fight against the entrenched German foe was sometimes a great challenge to the French leaders of these colonial units. Within a few short years, in fact, some of these spahis *and* tirailleurs *would be on the other side of the lines from the French in the wars of independence in North Africa.*

For the remainder of the war, it was against these French colonial troops that Georg Grossjohann would lead his men.

Georg Grossjohann Remembers . . .

After these battles, I was informed that the personnel office had named a new commander for Grenadier Regiment 308. My *Oberst*, the previous regimental commander, was named commander of the Salzburg-

Berchtesgaden security district. Before he departed, he informed me that I had been recommended for the Knight's Cross by *General der Flieger* Petersen. I could only think of how "Papa" Schultz had been recommended for the Oakleaves to his Knight's Cross before he was replaced in Russia. . . .

Maybe I had contributed to this relief by my sometimes quite unorthodox behavior. If the division commander had insisted on retaining me as a regimental commander, he would have succeeded. *Generalmajor* Schiel was fairly new, though, and did not know me very well; besides, I had spent much of the last two months actually under the command of another division. Additionally, his official expert for personnel was not my special friend, which I would understand only much later.

The appearance of a successor, who was senior to me and had also completed a course for regimental commanders, was probably a special grace of fate for me. Once, in 1943, I had interfered with my fate, and then made up my mind never to do it again!

One of the battalion commanders, whom I personally knew well and valued a lot, became successor to *Oberst* Keiser in Grenadier Regiment 326, but only lasted a few weeks before being killed in action. My successor, too, led the regiment only for a few weeks before being interned in Switzerland.

After I relinquished command, the division considered giving me command of the Division Füsilier Battalion. This was a fairly elite unit, which was used for reconnaissance, screening, and other light infantry duties. I assume that some gentlemen higher up did not agree with my assignment to command this unit.[40] *General* Petersen, as well as the Commanding General of Nineteenth Army, *General der Infanterie* Wiese, had not forgotten my six weeks of defending Le Thillot, the gateway to the Bussang Tunnel. I was destined for further regimental commands.

In position on the Schlucht Pass, an equally important location, was a mixed unit the size of a regiment, made up of volunteers including Azerbaijanis and Germans. The incumbent regimental commander was an older *Oberstleutnant* who was obviously tired of the war. I was ordered to take over his command. Thus began my last combatant assignment of WWII.

I inherited a regimental staff consisting of men mostly older than I. One of the messengers had been an actor before the war, another was an opera singer, and so forth. As a driver and orderly, I got a Bavarian freight hauler—my loyal Joseph—with whom I enjoyed thirty years of dear friendship after the war. I visited him and his family quite often in his lower Bavarian homeland. He had a kind-hearted Austrian wife, who was his genuine life partner, staying by his side through better and worse, until his death. Nevertheless, from a military point of view, over the next three weeks, I experienced confusion and disorganization that was unbelievable.

Only a few days after assuming responsibility for the defense of the Col de la Schlucht, my staff and I were ordered to the southern edge of the Vosges Mountains. The *1st French Armored Division* and the *9th Colonial Division* had broken through south of Belfort and reached the Rhine along the Swiss border. I assumed command of Grenadier Regiment 490, which together with other units, was deployed southeast of Belfort to protect the southern flank of the Nineteenth Army.

The local commander was *Generalmajor* Rudolf von Oppen, a quite courageous gentleman, who was especially candid when expressing his opinion. "You know, my dear Grossjohann," he said during our short orientation talk, "Some time ago, I was invited to meet *Herr* Himmler. Actually, he is quite a nice guy. It's unimaginable how much blood is stuck on his fins!" He really said fins!

My command post was in Brebotte, about eleven kilometers southeast of Belfort, just on the south/east bank of the Rhine-Rhône Canal. Late on the afternoon of 19 November, French tanks attacked in great numbers from the woods to the south, and we had nothing with which to oppose them.

The only chance of saving the soldiers of Grenadier Regiment 490—who were entrusted to me for a short time—from the tanks was to use the canal a few hundred meters behind us as an obstacle. I ordered a withdrawal behind this natural tank barrier during nightfall. Naturally, I asked no one for permission—this time, there really was no opportunity to do so. The mission to protect the southern flank of the Nineteenth Army could be accomplished from behind the canal as well as, or even better than, from before it. The next morning, *General* von Oppen called to tell me that two gentlemen from the staff of Army headquarters wanted to interrogate me at noon because of my "evasion" behind the canal! But personally, the general agreed fully with my decision.

Towards noon I appeared, as ordered, at the general's command post, where the two gentlemen were already expecting me. One was an *Oberstleutnant* i. G., the other a judge advocate. I described the previous evening's situation to them and explained that the enemy attacked with about the same number of tanks as I had infantrymen; besides that, we had no any armor-piercing weapons at our disposal. Then I told them quite briefly about my experiences during the first weeks in Le Thillot, where I was also left alone with my fate. I explained that I had been in the business long enough to have learned that these days, one could rely on one's own

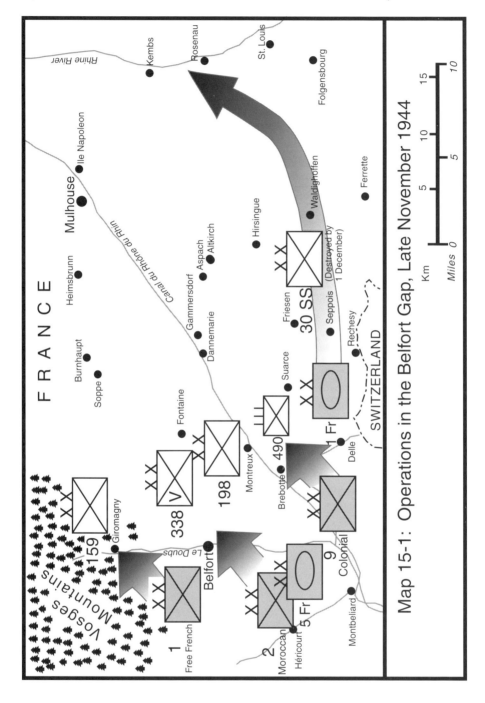

Map 15-1: Operations in the Belfort Gap, Late November 1944

judgment as a soldier. The two gentlemen were quickly convinced and assured me that, based on statements by the general, they would not raise any complaints against me. With this, the case was dismissed.

The same day, Grenadier Regiment 490 was attached to the 198th Infantry Division, which had been moved here to the south, to defend against a French penetration of the Belfort Gap, and subsequent breakout onto the Plain of Alsace. This would not have been possible had I not brought it to safety behind the canal the night before. As mentioned, it was again almost the same situation as in Le Thillot, which also could only be defended because I did not execute a senseless order.

Graser captured the situation well in his history,

> As part of a quickly established defense line, Grenadier Regiment 490, under the command of *Major* Grossjohann (formerly of Grenadier Regiment 308), was placed under command of the division. In addition, a battalion of '*Jagdpanther*' tank destroyers from the SS were brought in, too. . . . At dawn on November 21 an attack by Gren. Reg. 490 expelled the enemy from the town of Suarce. Parts of this regiment advanced via Lepuix-Delle to the road junction 1500 m south of the town."[41]

The regiments of the 198th Infantry Division on my eastern and western flanks lagged behind, but my old bunch in Grenadier Regiment 308 followed me as my regiment advanced until we reached the Swiss border in the foggy darkness.

Of course I did have a great advantage with the support of the *Jagdpanther* battalion,[42] but my leading infantry battalion, attacking along the road, nevertheless sustained considerable losses at the hands of the French, who tenaciously defended the cemetery in Suarce.

Ultimately, in the course of the next few days of battle, my old regiment, to which I had belonged for almost four years, became more and more compressed into a small area near the Swiss border. They were finally faced with two choices—internment in Switzerland, or being taken prisoner by the French. Understandably, they preferred the former option. *General* von Horn, our former division commander from Russia, who by now was the German military attaché in Switzerland, of course, took special care of his former regiment, as far as it was possible.

In the evening hours of 21 November, I was wounded in my left hand by a small shell fragment. The splinter penetrated my thumb, causing such severe pain that, together with great fatigue, I became quite sick. Early the next morning, I was operated on at a dressing station and then returned to my outfit. Grenadier Regiment 490, which I was leading until then, left the control of the 198th Division the same night and returned to its 269th Division.

For me, it meant the final departure from my old division. Thereafter, I took again charge of my job at the Schlucht Pass.

The next two to three weeks went by relatively calmly, at least for us in the pass. The early start of winter, most of all the heavy snowfall, created a situation in the High Vosges Mountains—Schlucht Pass is 1,150

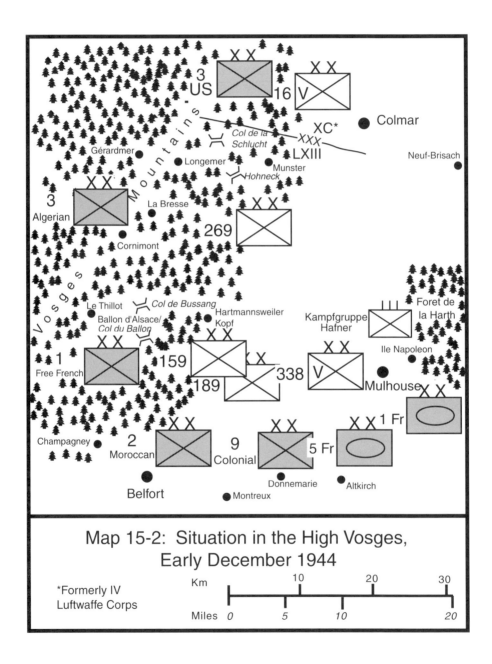

Map 15-2: Situation in the High Vosges, Early December 1944

*Formerly IV
Luftwaffe Corps

meters above sea level—which made any fighting seem almost impossible. Nevertheless, the French succeeded, after hours of difficult marching through drifting snow and dense fog, to surprise and defeat the weak German position on the 1,360-meter-high Hohneck, the highest peak of the Vosges Mountains. The peak was not in my sector, but in that of our neighbor to the south, the 269th Division, to which I was actually subordinate. *Herr* Borcher reported about this event in his booklet, *Final Battle in the Vosges Mountains*, very explicitly and quite dramatically, "The German infantry on the Hohneck could only have been surprised because they rather thoughtlessly relied on the belief that in this weather they did not have to expect an attack. Unfortunately, they were wrong."

The loss of Hohneck, which in good weather provided an excellent view into the Rhine valley, not only hit the 269th Infantry Division, the LXIII Corps, and the Nineteenth Army like a bomb . . . it also deeply disturbed *Herr* Himmler in Triberg.

Himmler, highly excited, demanded an immediate restoration of the position, as it was called so nicely in such cases! This was not without reason, as it soon became clear. What the enemy achieved at Hohneck, he tried again a few days later at the 1300-meter-high Rainkopf, five kilometers further southwest, and was only denied a similar success with heavy sacrifices on the part of the German forces there.

My unit was put on highest alert. Pioneers of the 269th Division succeeded little by little, to lay and tighten up a belt of mines between the French at Hohneck and their command post, which was established about one kilometer west of Hohneck, in a chalet off the mountain road.

Chapter Sixteen

Intermediary

Historical Commentary

With American elements on the Rhine and Strasbourg in Allied hands, the battered elements of the German 1st Army skillfully conducted delaying operations to the French-German frontier. Pressed back by most of the US Seventh Army, which had pivoted to drive northward through the Low Vosges in the west, and over the Alsatian Plain in the east, the German defenders gave ground grudgingly. In the Low Vosges (which the Germans call the Hardt*), the Germans even counterattacked when they could, using elements of the 21st Panzer Division and 106th Panzer Brigade to slow the American advance. Nevertheless, the US XV and VI Corps divisions pursuing them gradually forced them back onto the Maginot and* Westwall *fortifications which paralleled the border. By 16 December, elements of the* 45th Infantry Division *were on German soil, attacking the labyrinth of* Westwall *pillboxes near Niederschlettenbach and Reisdorf.*

The Germans' Nineteenth Army continued to doggedly defend in the south. The French First Army's II Corps continued to attack eastward through the southern High Vosges, while I Corps attempted to drive northward through the Belfort Gap. II Corps' 3d Algerian Infantry Division (3ᵉ Division d'Infanterie algerienne) of Général de Division Guillaume led the attack through the High Vosges, and seized the dominating heights at Hohneck. It was an element of this division that stubbornly defended this key terrain against German efforts to recapture it.

Within Sixth Army Group, all American and most French offensive operations came to a halt in mid-December as the Germans unleashed a great offensive in the Ardennes. Generalfeldmarschall *Model's Army*

Group B swept out of the snow-decked forests on the Belgian-German border with twenty-five divisions organized into three field armies. Initially, they seemed on their way to their geographical objective of Antwerp, which would split the US 12th Army Group *from the Anglo-Canadian-American* 21st Army Group *in the north. Operating under low cloud ceilings which obviated both German and American tactical air support, the armored spearheads of the Fifth and (later dubbed Sixth SS) Panzer Armies surprised the overconfident Americans in the Schnee Eifel sector, and wiped out two-thirds of the completely green US* 106th Infantry Division. *Stunned by an enemy many American planners thought to be practically defeated, outfits like the US* 28th Infantry Division, *still smarting from the beating they sustained in the Hürtgen Forest in the autumn, buckled and, in some places, broke. The US units on the "shoulders," or flanks, of the rapidly-forming salient held on stubbornly, however, and within a few days, American resolve strengthened as the Germans were stopped at places like Manhay, Celles, and Bastogne.*

Stopping the drive was one thing; forcing it back was another. Amidst the grim fight in the wintry darkness of the Ardennes, General Eisenhower, Supreme Commander Allied Expeditionary Forces, optimistically saw an opportunity to cut off and destroy significant parts of the German Army in the west. To this end, he ordered Lieutenant General George Patton's Third Army *to cease its operations in the Saar and turn northward to attack into the left, or southern, shoulder of the Army Group B salient. Patton needed to use two of his three corps for this operation, and so accordingly required a shortening of his lines.*

To cover the sectors vacated by Third Army, *Patch's* Seventh Army *suspended its pursuit of the 1st Army and "gave left," that is, they thinned out their own lines in the Low Vosges and on the Alsatian Plain to take over the defense of much of the Saar. Hitler decided to capitalize on this new "weak point" in the Allied positions, and directed Army Group G to attack through the brittle American defenses into the Low Vosges. He and his planners at OKW hoped that seizing the Saverne Gap would cause an Allied withdrawal from the Alsatian Plain, and thus cause a geographical and political rift between the French and Americans . . . just as he hoped to split the Americans and Anglo-Canadians in the north. In this way, reasoned the* Führer, *it might be possible to achieve a separate peace in the West which would allow the Germans to focus all remaining energy and resources against the onrushing Soviets in the east.*

This offensive, codenamed Operation NORDWIND, became the last German offensive in the West. Although it ultimately failed, it came very near to causing an American withdrawal to the High Vosges; such a withdrawal would, of necessity, require the abandonment of Strasbourg, which was absolutely unacceptable to DeGaulle. After much internecine arguing, it was agreed that the American VI Corps would withdraw no further than the Moder River, thus protecting French prestige—and citizenry—in Strasbourg.

Indirectly, all of this had a great effect on the fortunes of Georg Grossjohann. On one hand, the French cessation of major offensive activities allowed him and his men to remain longer in the fastness of their Vosges positions. On the other hand, the commitment of the last German reserves to two major offensives deprived the Nineteenth Army of reinforcements which might otherwise have allowed them to reinforce their positions, or even conduct more counterattacks to regain lost ground.

Georg Grossjohann Remembers . . .

On the evening of 11 December, I had a conversation with *General* Wagner, who expressed great concern about the fact that until now all attempts to regain Hohneck had failed, including an attack just that day. German troops had surrounded the enemy, but they would not budge. In a mood swing, I declared, "*Herr* General, I'll go to the Hohneck and try to talk the French into a pullout!" After that, my officers and I celebrated this somewhat insane decision so extensively, that the next morning we were not exactly in great shape. But we still upheld our decision, which by now could not be reversed anyway.

Remarkably, though Himmler was usually strictly against any contact with the enemy (as earlier in Le Thillot), he was at once willing to give me his strongest encouragement. My companions and I had to take appropriate credentials with us to Hohneck to establish ourselves as negotiators. *Capitaine* Lartigau, Commander of the 1st Company of the *3d Algerian Infantry Division*'s *4th Regiment of Tunisian Tirailleurs (4e Régiment de tirailleurs tunisiens)*, and also on-site commander at Hohneck, turned us down. He declared that he couldn't even make such a decision. We then marched to his battalion's command post to see if we could reason with them.

Regrettably, I only learned of the earlier mentioned minefield at this time. During the march through knee-deep snow to the French battalion's command post, several French soldiers who accompanied us unfortunately lost legs. I was afraid that these fanatic North Africans would hold us responsible and kill us right there! It may have been the presence of a French officer that stopped them from doing it.

As expected, despite my entreaties to recognize the hopelessness of their situation, the officers of the battalion staff rejected our offer also. One French major, born in Lorraine, proved himself to be especially spiteful. Perhaps the major, coming as he did from a province that had belonged to Germany from 1870 to 1918, felt he had to affect ardent patriotism in front of his comrades. What impressed me more than the obstinate attitude of the French, however, was their equipment and weapons. The build-up of arms just to protect the immediate vicinity of their command post was of a scale that for us at this stage of the war was only a dream They also had superior winter clothing, rations, and so forth. All was of the best quality and in abundance. The rich brother-in-arms from overseas was, by God, not stingy.

When I returned, I could at least give *Hauptmann* Köck, the battalion commander charged with the mission of pushing the French off the Hohneck, quite an accurate description of the place, because the French had not blindfolded us *en route*. After all, it may hardly have been possible to lead us through knee-deep snow over a distance of 1,000 meters while wearing blindfolds.

After I reported the failure of my mission to *Generalleutnant* Wagner on the phone, I returned to my command post via Route 417. There were two German 88mm *Flak*-guns placed on one of those narrow hairpin turns off the pass road. When I passed them, the weather had changed, and Hohneck was sharply silhouetted against the sky. I asked the section commander to take advantage of this opportunity, and both guns opened fire against the hotel on top of that fiercely fought-over mountain, less than four kilometers away.

The next day, 12 December, a mixed assault unit, made up from infantry and pioneers led by *Hauptmann* Köck, attacked Hohneck again, and this time they were lucky. The hotel, already badly damaged by continuous fire, was now completely flattened by sticky bombs and bazookas. The French lost forty killed, twenty-three wounded, and about 120 prisoners. *Hauptmann* Köck's task force wound up with four killed and thirty wounded.

I had tried everything to induce the French to evacuate Hohneck. In vain! The price they paid for their inflexible attitude was too high in view of the whole situation. A few weeks later, Hohneck would have fallen into their hands without a fight! There were praise and decorations for the brave assault force. *Hauptmann* Köck received the Knight's Cross. My adjutant and I had a chance to speak with the French prisoners the same day. Regrettably, they had not believed me when I told them that we would level the place the next day, and assumed that my visit with them was only bluff. *C'est la guerre.* . . .

A few items, mentioned in the booklet about the final battle in the Vosges Mountains, need to be corrected. The author writes that I was the chief commander of the assault team. This would have been flattering for me, but it simply does not conform to the facts. I had nothing to do with the successful assault in the end. The commander of this difficult undertaking, which resulted in heavy loss for both sides, was solely *Hauptmann* Köck.

On 28 December I had to report to the commanding general of the LXIII Corps, *Generalleutnant* Erich Abraham, to receive, from him the Knight's Cross. He carried this out in a very humorous manner, with the words, "Now the young man has the proper suit." Afterwards, the general accompanied me to my command post, where we spent a very pleasant half hour together. After the war, *Generalleutnant* Abraham lived in Wiesbaden, where the obviously multitalented soldier first earned his bread as "violinist in a cafe." Unfortunately, I did not have the chance to see him after the war. He died in 1971 in Wiesbaden.

Incidentally, the wording for the proposal for my Knight's Cross originated from the pen of a (reserve) officer, who in civilian life was an attorney. He concluded his proposal with the words "Under any circumstance, with his humor, his harshness toward himself, and his overpowering energy, he was always on top of the situation." (!) From this language, one could almost come to the conclusion that this Bavarian barrister must also have been a successful defense counsel!

During Christmas, I was with my provisional unit at the Schlucht Pass in the High Vosges. At that time, I had a brief encounter with our Army Group Commander, Heinrich Himmler. He was not the radiant person that Hitler was. He acted like a petty bourgeois, just as *General* von Oppen once described. After the war, incidentally, I also got to know Himmler's brother, a school master in Munich, who was a quiet, amiable fellow.

My last action on the front was January 1945, at the legendary Hartmannsweiler Kopf, whose soil was literally soaked with blood from German and French soldiers in 1914 during WWI. By about the middle of the month, I received news that the new Commanding General of the Nineteenth Army, *General der Infanterie* Siegfried Rasp, had granted me a twenty-one-day furlough for bravery. The night before my departure, I was invited by him for dinner. The next morning I was relieved and my loyal Joseph drove me to Nineteenth Army headquarters. I reported to the commander of the staff quarters, an older cavalry *Hauptmann*, who in civilian life was the owner of a freight hauling company known throughout the *Reich*.

During a conversation with this entrepreneur, I learned, regrettably, not too many positive stories about our new Army commander. For a minute reason he once yelled at the *Hauptmann*, "You white-haired rear-echelon staff pigs belong at the front!" The adjutant, *Oberstleutnant* von Amsberg, formerly of Cavalry Regiment 14 in Ludwigslust, consoled the enraged officer by advising him to consider this unjustified outburst as the rantings of a drunkard, and not as a remark of his chief commander.

In the evening, when I marched to the station of the staff quarters, I was not quite sober anymore. When I therefore apologized to *Herr* von Amsberg, he uttered quickly and dryly, "This isn't noticeable here, the Commanding General is full every night." (He actually expressed himself yet a bit more drastically than that!)

The dinner took less than half an hour, then I could return to my quarters, supplied with a pass for leave.

The new Army Commander had replaced *General der Infanterie* Friedrich Wiese, a Schleswiger who had served in the Hamburg police after combat in WWI. Himmler had him fired in the manner of his lord and master, as a scapegoat was needed for the forthcoming end of the Nineteenth Army in the Vosges Mountains. *General der Infanterie* Rasp was chosen as the replacement. He had commanded the 335th Infantry Division in East, and also the 78th Infantry Division. One always expects true miracles of people who at sometime had previously enjoyed success. *General* Rasp was an officer of the general staff and of the same age group as Jodl, Speidel, and Heusinger. Of course, he couldn't change anything regarding the situation in the Vosges Mountains either.

Chapter Seventeen

Farewell to the Front

Historical Commentary

By the time Georg Grossjohann was leaving his command in Alsace in mid-January, the days of the Nineteenth Army bridgehead on the west bank of the Rhine were numbered. He was leaving behind a calamitous situation, indeed: With the concurrence of Generalfeldmarschall *von Rundstedt, Commander-in-Chief in the West, a report made by a National Socialist Guidance Officer who had been sent by Hitler to evaluate the situation in Nineteenth Army in December described it this way,*

> *The longer one observes the Nineteenth Army in their hard battles in Alsace, the more one's esteem grows for a fighting community that, after all, is not really a trained army, but actually a thrown-together heap. It is fantastic that in spite of this, a cohesive organization has grown out of that heap. To be sure, however, it is now an exhausted organization. Even the strongest will is broken through uninterrupted combat. Many individuals are at the end of their rope. If one could give them just two days' sleep, it might be different. As a result of attrition, there are regiments with a strength of 80–150 men; that such units can actually continue to attack is doubly impressive.[43] Everywhere, the decisive difference comes down to the performance of individuals. Many officers are resigned that their lives are over, and they wanted to sell them dearly.[44]*

While Georg Grossjohann could clearly count himself among the individuals who had made a "decisive difference," there was another officer who was leaving about the same time who clearly could not.

Heinrich Himmler, Reichsführer-SS and Commander of Army Group Oberrhein, relinquished command on 24 January 1945, just before the end for the Nineteenth Army on the west bank of the Rhine, whereupon the command returned to the control of Army Group G.

By mid-January, the Ardennes salient was all but wiped out in the north. The Americans had lost about 81,000 men there, but the Germans of Army Group B had lost over 100,000. Even more importantly, they had spent their last significant armored resources in the gambit, and literally could not conduct any sort of offensive activity beyond those of the most minor tactical character for the rest of the war in the West. By the time of Georg Grossjohann's departure from Alsace, Operation NORDWIND had been stopped in the Low Vosges, and although sharp fighting continued for another two weeks on the northern end of the Plain of Alsace, it was almost pointless.

Just days before Grossjohann crossed the Rhine for the last time in the war, the Soviets opened their final offensive in the East. Four million Soviet troops in sixty-eight field armies, supported by thirteen air armies, smashed into the defenses of Army Groups Center, A, and South on 12 January. Coming in the wakes of the huge losses sustained in the Ardennes and in NORDWIND, this development absolutely sealed the fate of the Germans in the so-called Colmar Pocket—there would be no reinforcements, no replacements . . . and no way that the men there ould get even the "two days' rest" recommended by Hitler's emissary.

On 20 January, only a few days after Georg Grossjohann arrived in Berlin on leave, the French First Army, with eight French and one US division (the 3d Infantry) attacked the Nineteenth Army units remaining in Alsace. Although on paper it looked like a tough prospect, the ravages of the fighting in the Vosges since mid-October had left the seven German divisions there with no more than 50,000 men, including support troops. Even so, the first several days of the attack did not go well for the Allies, and Eisenhower decided to commit a full US corps, the XXI, with two additional American infantry divisions (28th and 75th Infantry). This was finally enough to break down the last resistance of the Nineteenth Army. Fortunately for the Germans, Hitler allowed a withdrawal to the east bank of the Rhine, but at least 22,000 German soldiers were lost in the last fighting in southern Alsace by 9 February 1945.

Georg Grossjohann's beloved 198th Infantry Division escaped across the Rhine with a total of about five hundred men.

Georg Grossjohann Remembers . . .

The next morning, my faithful Joseph took me to Freiburg-im-Breisgau, from whence I started my trip eastward. At this point in time, it was already clear that I could not travel home to East Prussia. I took a long break in Berlin, though. A nurse I knew from Russia managed to get a room for me for an overnight stay near the Friedrichstrasse railroad station. In 1943, when I went to the East for the second time, she and I were in the same train compartment, and from then on I had her home address. She was a young woman who didn't really fit into the scene of those days.

As a seventeen-year-old, she, the daughter of a Prussian government official, became pregnant. The father of the child was a *Zwölfender* in the Navy. It all happened when she and the family's maid secretly visited a dance party for servicemen. Her mother, who I got to know in Berlin, was a very resolute, realistic, and practical lady, as one often meets in those circles. She energetically discouraged her daughter's plans to marry the Navy man. The mother led her daughter through the elegant family home, explaining to her, "This is the ambiance in which you grew up. Do you want to spend the rest of your life in a two-room apartment among the petty bourgeois?" The daughter realized that she probably would not want to put up with this, and abandoned the idea of marriage. Her child, a little girl, had been evacuated from Berlin to Silesia, but everybody was now quite worried if they would see her again in good health. The Russians were almost there.

On the same day, I received a lesson about how good manners among officers had changed in those days. I had just sat down at the table in a coffee house near the Friedrichstrasse railroad station when an army patrol, commanded by a *Hauptmann*, appeared to inspect the papers of all the soldiers present. The demeanor with which this officer requested my paybook was extremely close to the line between brevity and insubordination. One could really sense the gratification this armchair warrior enjoyed by bothering a bearer of the Knight's Cross. Unfortunately for me, he even found a reason to further harass me, because my paybook did not include the entry confirming the award of Knight's Cross. Since I knew that a certain *Generalleutnant* Viktor Linnarz from the personnel office signed my temporary proof of ownership, I suggested that the inquisitor call that office. When I asked him if he would believe that a soldier wearing the German Cross in gold, and with a leave-pass in his pocket personally signed by his Army commander, would feel the necessity to decorate himself with the Knight's Cross, he simply shrugged his shoulders. He demanded that I come with him to his guard post, which I declined to do. I explained that I had to drive out to Dahlem anyway, where I left my luggage, and in which there would be the certificate of award. So, the *whole Army patrol* accompanied me to Dahlem, which, as a two-way trip, certainly took more than two hours. In the presence of my rather apprehensive acquaintance, I dug the certificate out of my rucksack and held it under the nose of the "chain-dog," who was evidently disappointed. He muttered an apology, combined with the reproach, that I should not have failed to get the appropriate entry in the paybook. At the end of my rope with this nonsense, I reminded him that barely seventy-two hours before, at Hartmannsweiler Kopf, I had problems of quite a different kind than checking to ensure all the necessary entries in my paybook had been made!

Since I assumed that my family succeeded in their escape from East Prussia, I supposed that they found refuge with some friends in Königsberg in Neumark. As it happened, I was right. Only one day later, I took my family to Ludwigslust, where at least I knew a few people. The local mayor arranged for them to be moved into the beautiful home of Countess Voss. Later, when the Russians had moved into Ludwigslust, my family went on towards the west and then lived in the vicinity of Hamm in Westphalia. Soon enough, I returned to the Western front.

During my leave, the Nineteenth Army had, after heavy fighting, abandoned the bridgehead in Alsace. My former division commander in the 198th, *Generalmajor* Schiel, was meanwhile also sent "into the desert" as a scapegoat. He obviously did not succeed in working miracles. In his place, *Oberst* Barde took command of the what was left of the Division. As a *Generalmajor*, he was killed in action a few days before the war's end.

Himmler, too, had disappeared, leaving Army Group Oberrhein on 24 January. After his failure on the Upper Rhine, he tried to earn his spurs on the Eastern front, as commander of Army Group Vistula. A short time later, supposedly because of work-related overstrain, Himmler was replaced in that position by one of my former East Prussian commanders, the now *Generaloberst* Gotthard Heinrici.

During my return trip from Ludwigslust to Freiburg-im-Breisgau, I contracted a cold with a high fever and was taken to the army hospital in Freiburg. I had asked to inform *Oberstleutnant* von Amsberg that I had finished my leave, but that at this time I was in the hospital.

In the meantime, the Nineteenth Army had moved their headquarters to Waldkirch, northeast of Freiburg. A few days later, a few members of my regimental staff from the Schlucht Pass appeared. Their fate was up in the air and they were hoping that with a new position for me, we would all be able to stay together. Despite some concerns, my physician let me go, and my men could take me with them. They were quartered in a small hamlet in the Clotter Valley for the time being. On one of the following days, I drove to Waldkirch to report back to the army from my little enjoyable leave. Since I had been selected for a course for regimental commanders, and had to react on short notice for my enrollment, *Oberstleutnant* von Amsberg suggested sending me in the meantime to the military school in Furtwangen.

I was allowed a few days of rest, but then had to leave my staff, which had grown so dear to me. For these men it meant being split up and, according to their capabilities, to be used in different units.

At least I was able to keep one man with me—my trusty Joseph. Ultimately, I kept him until the end of the war. Technically, still being a regimental commander, I could bring about the necessary transfer, which was signed by my adjutant.

The commander of the military school, *Oberst* Müller-Melahn, was an old acquaintance. In 1940, he was a major and battalion commander in Regiment Newiger in Ludwigslust! Another long-time acquaintance was my former *Oberfeldwebel* Braun from 198th Division. He had been promoted to *Leutnant* for outstanding bravery and was awarded the Oak Leaf Cluster to the Knight's Cross.

Together, we trained future company commanders. The practical part, like the handling of machineguns, assault rifles, and *panzerfausts*, for example, was *Leutnant* Braun's assignment, while I was put in charge of tactical training. The instructions, which had to be limited to studies of terrain and tactical/doctrinal instruction, seemed to me, and probably also to the participants, already so senseless that we used instruction hours in class mainly for exchanging ideas on tactics, and time outdoors in the training area as "field trips."

In Furtwangen, I got to know a girl who took care of Westphalian children who had been evacuated from the big cities there to Furtwangen. Had I then only suspected what would develop from this for me, I would certainly have avoided meeting her again after the war.

I married that girl in 1947, only to be separated in 1953 and divorced in 1955, in Munich. She turned to another man, even while I did everything I could for her. Maybe it's indeed true that fate has planned a certain amount of positive, but also negative, experiences for every person and we have little choice but to live through it all!

From Furtwangen, *Leutnant* Braun and I visited our old regiment and the division, which was now awaiting the unavoidable end behind the Rhine at the so-called *Westwall*. From Furtwangen, I also went to visit my Bavarian *Oberst* in Berchtesgaden. He had gathered several former members of the 198th Infantry Division around him, or more precisely, they had come and gathered around him. There was our former division adjutant, now wearing the uniform of a *Sturmbannführer* of the *Waffen SS*. (I hope he still had his army uniform ready for himself when the Americans came!) Then there was the smart *Oberleutnant* E. who, in his earlier days, was swiftly promoted to *Hauptmann* and who, in 1942, in his first heavy battle, suffered a nervous breakdown with such lasting effect that he never again showed up at the front. The third one was that older *Hauptmann* who we found near Uman, completely exhausted, at night in a Russian village. They all led quite a comfortable life. They had sent for their wives and lived until war's end in a fine hotel. The Americans probably then put a quick end to this idyll.

My trip to Berchtesgaden took me through Konstanz. When I got off the ferry, I was very surprised to find my strapping *Oberstleutnant* of the reserve training regiment from Dijon and Auxerre standing on the pier. I had left him a little over a year ago as an *Oberleutnant*, and now I stood before him, a *Major*, decorated with the Knight's Cross! He feigned his delight about us meeting again so well that I expected an embrace in the Russian or French manner any moment!

He stated that he and my former comrades from the training regiment had been very proud of me. I thanked him befittingly and departed, without exhibiting anger, just as I had after my unexpected reunion with the Brazilian Coffee Bean.

The so-called fight-to-the-end for our homeland was a disgraceful, macabre, creeping sickness for the German *Wehrmacht*, whose bravery, hardiness, and unselfishness can never be surpassed by any other army! We should have been spared such an ending. But the military courts threatened with the most dire consequences anyone daring to escape the certain downfall. Parts of my old division were chased all the way into Alpine valleys until finally the end came on 8 May 1945.

Chapter Eighteen

The Last Days of the War

Historical Commentary

Even with the Soviets at Küstrin, just ninety kilometers east of Berlin, and the Western Allies across the Rhine at Remagen and in the process of destroying the German First and Seventh Armies in the Saar, incredibly, the German Army continued to function administratively. As Georg Grossjohann got his orders to report to a course for infantry regimental commanders, the end was near indeed.

Throughout March, the Soviets' Second and Third Belorussian Fronts overwhelmed and eradicated German pockets of resistance on the Baltic: Kolberg fell on 18 March, and Danzig followed twelve days later The same fate had befallen Georg Grossjohann's home town, Kagenau, in late February. Although German Landsers *put up unflagging resistance in the East, and the 1st and 2d SS Panzer Corps even put together one last offensive in Hungary, the only questions that remained by the end of March were who would take Berlin, and exactly when Germany would capitulate.*

In April, the situation unraveled quickly. Army Group H was attacked savagely by the Canadian First and British Second Armies as they stormed through the northern Netherlands and into the north German Plain, while after some fierce but pointless fighting, the greatest part of Army Group B was encircled and destroyed by the US First and Ninth Armies in the Ruhr. About 317,000 German soldiers surrendered in the process. The exhausted and depleted forces of Army Group G were brushed aside in most places by attacking elements of the US Third and Seventh Armies as they drove across southern Germany and into Austria and Czechoslovakia. German forces in the Black Forest succumbed to the advances of the mostly-colonial French First Army, in the course of which Eisenhower had to restrain the French from wreaking too many excesses on the German population in places like Stuttgart. Some US divisions were rerouted to take over otherwise French zones of attack and occupation. Army Group Southwest was trapped against the Alps by the US Fifth and British Eighth Armies in northern Italy. The long-feared "Alpine Redoubt," the possible existence of which had deeply concerned American commanders for months, failed to materialize, and very few Germans embraced the "Werwolf" German partisan movement ordered by Himmler.

With one last enormous push from the East, the Soviets completed the encirclement of Berlin on 25 April, and elements of the 58th Guards Division linked up with a unit of the US 69th Infantry Division at Torgau on the Elbe on the same day. German forces in Italy surrendered on 2 May. German forces in Denmark laid down their arms on 5 May, and the last German resistance in coastal Netherlands ended on the next day. Although most of Schleswig-Holstein and parts of Austria were not yet taken by the Allies, Großadmiral Dönitz, who took over upon Hitler's death, ordered the German armed forces to surrender as of 8 May. Incredibly, Generalfeldmarschall Schörner ordered the men of Army Group Center to fight on in Austria, even though Dönitz specifically ordered a breakout to the West on 5 May. As a result, the last German forces in Austria did not surrender to the Soviets until 11 May— although Schörner himself flew out to the west just before the capitulation, and surrendered to the Americans. On 12 May, the last significant German armed units ceased resistance on islands in the Aegean and Mediterranean, including the garrisons in the Dodecanese and on Crete.

Georg Grossjohann Remembers . . .

At the end of March 1945, I was finally transferred to the course for regimental commanders. Just two years before this writing, the Federal German archives in Cornelimünster discovered that there were two copies of my orders for the course from March 1945 in the their records, so they were kind enough to relinquish one for me to keep. Unbeknownst to me, the orders included an order of merit list drawn up by Army Group G headquarters, which indicated that I had been slated to command a grenadier regiment.

Even in March 1945, I took care that my Joseph was allowed to accompany me to the course. Once there, Joseph was highly welcomed, because soldiers of his rank were in perilously short supply. Now, however, he worked not only for me, but also for a major from the general staff.

Originally, the course was planned to begin at the Army Communication School #1, in Halle-on-the-Saale, but that was quickly canceled. Next, I was to proceed to the tactical training facility at Grafenwöhr. Upon my arrival there, a huge Allied bomber squadron was just flattening the last walls of the camp. In spite of the now hopeless situation, the course was continued, though quite sporadically, until the end of the war. Somehow, I was still impressed by this unperturbed muddle.

Among other things in the orders to report to the course was a directive that "Army Group G is to provide a final evaluation of *Major* Grossjohann no later than 1 May 1945! I am almost sure that it was sent out, but got stuck somewhere at the war's end.

The last stop for the course was the garrison for mountain infantry in Mittenwald, and Krün and Wallgau, two quaint mountain villages that were nearby.

The news announced on 30 April that Hitler had been killed during the defense of Berlin was received in different ways by the participants in the course. Astonishingly, the numerous *SS* officers working in this area reacted especially coolly, a phenomenon which *Bundeswehr-General* Gerd Schmückle later mentioned in his book *Ohne Pauken und Trompeten*.[45] We all understood that this was the beginning of a very difficult time for the German people. After Hitler's death became known, the course director, Generalmajor von Larisch, assembled the attendees one more time in the schoolhouse of Krün. "What you have learned in the past weeks was certainly not in vain, for just a few years from now, there will be a new German army!" These were the general's words of farewell.

In my reveries, I thought of the statement of my little *Oberst* after the victorious French campaign. He, too, was correct then by portraying the end of that campaign only as the end of outpost skirmishing. . . .

Only a few years later, of course, the words of *General* von Larisch also became reality. As early as 1948–49, the Western allies are said to have debated a military contribution by Germany and to have inquired under what conditions the Germans would be willing to establish a new army. . . .

In any case, after his speech, *General* von Larisch declared the course dissolved. Every participant received several weeks' pay and, if they desired, a rucksack, clothes, and heavy mountain boots from the stock of the mountain infantry.

A few days earlier, I asked that my Joseph be discharged with his papers completely in order. Without difficulties, he reached his hometown and his especially friendly and big family. His old mother became a dear friend to me in the difficult post-war period. "If it wasn't for the *Major*, our

Joseph might not be alive anymore," she said. Being the owner of a farm in Lower Bavaria, she supported me occasionally with plenty of food.

Shortly before the Americans moved into Krün, I withdrew to a comfortable ski lodge in the Karwendel Mountains, accompanied by two *SS* officers and a major i. G. The lodge was owned by Christian Weber, a well-placed Party member, and president of the Bavarian Motor Racing Club. In the higher mountains, well hidden by the deep snow, the *SS* men stashed away large stocks of food. Thus we didn't suffer, but actually enjoyed the beautiful start of springtime. Soon, we learned that some female *SS* auxiliaries had "fraternized" with the Americans right after their arrival. I tried in vain to stop one of the *SS* officers from visiting his girlfriend in Krün. He left anyway, but he was expected! In the darkness of night, the well-informed victors shot him on sight, in a meadow in front of the farmhouse in which his girlfriend had found shelter. With certainty, one of her colleagues gave him away to the Americans and, in turn, received considerable stocks of groceries and luxury items that had been in storage.

The girlfriend of the *SS* officer was sentenced to a long prison term by an American military court for abetting a fugitive. She served her term in the women's prison in Aichach. I later once paid her a visit in prison.

I don't have to talk about the attitude of a large part of German people, specifically in my case, the Bavarian population, towards soldiers just before and after the war. Everybody must have had his own experiences. It happened that when soldiers wanted to take a rest with the farmers, those would cry out "the Americans are coming," which would cause the soldiers to flee into the mountains. Then, the farmers would loot the luggage that was left behind. Regarding the willingness of our population to collaborate with the victors, we don't, by God, have to look down on the French in their days past.

One day at breakfast in our lodge, we were discovered by some armed foreigners and they took us away. Fortunately, one of us had gone up to where the butter was kept in the ice and observed our capture. Armed with an automatic pistol, he followed us through thick brush, fired a few rounds into the blue sky, and our paths and the paths of our escorts separated surprisingly quickly. After this, we went back to our hut. It seemed now, however, appropriate to abandon our comfortable shelter at once. We separated and left the lodge by different routes. I had all unnecessary ballast removed from my rucksack and, except for a couple of pairs of socks, filled it to the top with thousands of cigarettes from the *SS* depot. Later on this proved exceedingly useful.

In the beginning, I hiked along lonely mountain trails until I arrived at Kochel am See, where I deposited all my medals, as well as pertinent documents, with a home owner whom I trusted.

Afterwards, I crossed much of southern Germany, where I could easily evade the Americans, whose checkpoints were only on major roads. I had no problems with food. All I needed to do was to take a pack of cigarettes from my rucksack, which I guarded with my life, and soon I could enjoy a healthy meal at a farmhouse of my choice. Then, I arrived in Betzgau near Kempten im Allgäu at the house of the mayor, who was until now also the local farmers' leader. (See Map 19-1) I offered my help with harvesting hay, which had already begun. Since I grew up out in the country in my East Prussian homeland, I still had profound knowledge of all types of work related to agriculture. Therefore, I was soon entrusted with activities requiring higher qualifications. Together with the two nice daughters of the house, I took care of the milk cows, including my part of the milking.

As eventually happened with all leaders, great and small, from any Nazi Party organization, my mayor and ex-farmers' leader was one day arrested and imprisoned. What his crime may have been, I don't know. Maybe one could suppose that he indoctrinated National Socialism into the cattle of Betzgau—and I don't mean just the bovine ones!

General George S. Patton, Jr. opened the camp doors soon after the war's end, and sent all the little fish home, and in many cases, back to work. He paid for that by losing his post as Commanding General of the US *Third Army.*

The mayor's nice wife asked me if I could not at least stay until her husband would come home. In view of subsequent events, maybe this is what I should have done.

One late afternoon I went for a swim at a nearby pond. There, I was approached by an American officer, who assumed I had been a soldier. He asked for my papers. A German-speaking Dutch woman, probably a souvenir the American got in the Netherlands, translated. He was quite a nice young man and said I must be very exhausted after wandering around so much without sufficient food and shelter for such a long time. Of course I did not tell him that I had been quite well cared for by a local farmer. The American called his driver and ordered him to take me to the Army hospital in Kempten. As always, I took my well-stocked rucksack with me, sort of like a beach bag. I picked up my ski-pants and the good hiking boots from Mittenwald from my mayor's lady a few days later. In all truth, I could inform her that I now had been "taken prisoner."

The hospital, under American supervision but German management, served first-rate food from American stocks. After a long time, I could again sleep in an army bed, and with the help of a pass by the German chief physician, everybody could move around freely.

Chapter Nineteen

Discharge from the Army

Historical Commentary

For the first two weeks after the official capitulation, the Allies governed Germany through the offices of a provisional government, headed by Dönitz. On 23 May, this government was disbanded, and by 5 June, the Allied Control Commission, presided over jointly by Marshal Zhukov, Field Marshal Montgomery, and General of the Army Eisenhower, took over the responsibilities of governing all territory that had been Germany as of the end of 1937.

The 1938 Anschluß (that is, the union of Germany with Austria) was declared null and void on 14 May. Germany and Austria were divided into zones of occupation, each under the jurisdiction of one of the four major victorious powers, namely the United States, Great Britain, the Soviet Union, and France. Germany was thus not only occupied and governed as a conquered nation, but was also quickly dismembered. Under the agreements reached at Yalta in February 1945, the new Polish state had to cede its eastern provinces to the USSR, essentially all the territory taken by the Soviets in September 1939. In turn, Germany lost Danzig, East Prussia, Pomerania, and Silesia.

Georg Grossjohann's ancestral home disappeared into Poland, whence it remains to this day; he had no home to which to return. In this unfortunate regard, he had ample company. Due to these vast territorial changes, millions of Germans were homeless, displaced to—or even in—what remained of Germany. Just before the Soviet annexation of the Baltic nations in 1939—allowed by a secret protocol to the German-Soviet 1939 Non-Aggression Pact—tens of thousands of ethnic Germans left the land to which their ancestors had come as early as the thirteenth century, and fled to Germany. Fleeing first from the Soviet juggernaut in the last days of the War, and later being expelled by Poland and Czechoslovakia, ten million Germans reached the German rump state after losing probably three million more in the process en route. *Ethnic Germans, from their centuries-old settlements in southeastern Europe (primarily in Rumania, Yugoslavia, and Hungary) were also expelled, and flooded into the prostrate homeland of their distant ancestors, some of whom had emigrated as many as seven hundred years before.*

Germany was also awash in refugees other than ethnic Germans. Some 200,000 Balts fled to Germany to avoid the ravages of the Soviet Army. They, too, could not return. Millions of civilians from the German-occupied countries of eastern Europe who had come to serve in German war industries—some voluntarily, most not—also added to the legions of displaced persons. In short, the era that began in 1939 with the exodus of ethnic Germans from Latvia, Lithuania, and Estonia ended after World War II in the chaotic, grossly overcrowded, rubbled, and burned-out shell of western Germany. It was by far the largest migration in Europe in recorded history.

This swollen population inhabited a land that lay largely devastated. German cities and towns laid buried under an estimated four hundred million cubic meters of rubble. In the fiery whirlwind of the last spring of the War, many fields were untended, and livestock had dwindled. Thousands of Germans literally starved to death, and many more barely subsisted on Allied handouts. Beyond the simplest of bartering and black market activities, there was practically no economy.

The De-Nazification Program, designed to eradicate all vestiges of National Socialism and to punish former members of Nazi organizations, got underway quickly. In the American zone, all adults were obliged to respond to a comprehensive questionnaire, intended to establish their links to the Party. Between the information gathered in this way and through extensive interrogations of known Party officials, millions of Germans became ineligible for public employment. This, in turn, added to the confusion, as in many areas, there were few or even no experienced public administrators left to conduct the day-to-day business of government.

Such was the environment into which Georg Grossjohann was released after the war. To the victorious Allies who now ran Germany, he was a former conqueror who had himself been conquered. To some Germans, he was just another ex-member of an officer elite whose failure lay in abundant evidence everywhere one looked. In fact, he was a lifelong soldier in a country without an army and a refugee in his own nation.

Georg Grossjohann Remembers . . .

Two weeks later, I was declared healthy and shipped to a prison camp in Biessenhofen near Kaufbeuren. There, too, I was very lucky because, as a whole, the American troops in that region behaved in a way occupation forces should—that is, according to international law.

I had already had a typical experience in Kempten which was just north of theFrench sector. One day I had company in my room—a reserved older gentleman. Later I learned that he was a high Party official and secretary of state in some kind of *Reich* ministry. Apparently, he had been warned in time and had moved from the French sector into the nearby American zone of occupation. When the French wanted to pick him up from his hideaway in a farmhouse, he escaped to Kempten.

Furious about their failure, the French went to the farmer's wife and threatened to burn down the farmstead if the Party official did not immediately return to their zone of occupation. Evidently, he had told his hostess that he had to go to Kempten to the hospital. Unlike me, he really needed medical help. So the scared woman showed up in the hospital and fervently begged her guest to return to the French sector, something he did not show the slightest inclination to do.

Being a professional soldier, I did not expect to have problems with anyone, so I accompanied the woman to the American command post and explained to a young officer, who spoke German fluently, what the French were planning to do. Already by this time, one could notice the tension building between the French and the Americans. The Americans, for example, had already had to pressure the French to pull out of Stuttgart by temporarily discontinuing their supplies.

The *Hauptmann* drove with the fearful woman to her farmhouse at once and, as I learned a little later, energetically discouraged the French from their plan. Incidentally, I later saw the Party official—at a distance—in the camp at Biessenhofen. He was already segregated from the ordinary military prisoners, in a separate compound cordoned by barbed wire. In this camp, fortunately, quite orderly conditions prevailed, unlike many other prison camps (for example, Bad Kreuznach). In our camp, we had tents with straw to sleep on and simple, but adequate food.

I met many old acquaintances, even some from my East Prussian peacetime unit, all older by some years and higher ranking than when I saw them last.

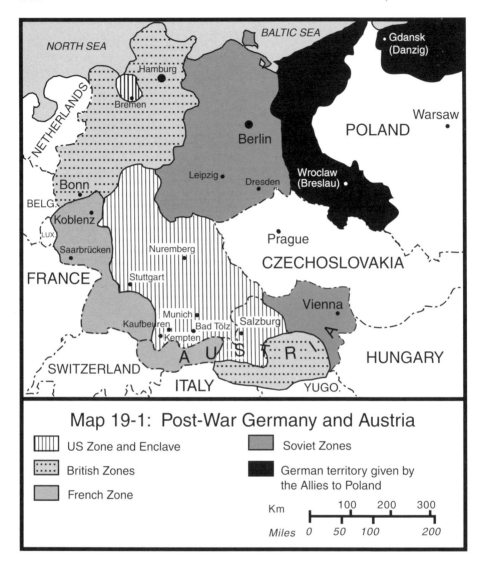

Map 19-1: Post-War Germany and Austria

[||||] US Zone and Enclave   [▓] Soviet Zones

[:::::] British Zones   [■] German territory given by
                                        the Allies to Poland
[▓] French Zone

Km |—————|—————|—————|
           100   200   300

Miles 0   50   100   200

The day I arrived, the Americans were just in the process of segregating the high-Party officials from the regular prisoners. Generals and general staff officers were moved the same day into a newly prepared camp across the street. Later on, they were kept in special camps for many months.

An officer of the American guard unit wanted to name me leader of a company of officers. I explained to him that perhaps one of the many administration officials with equal or higher rank would be more suitable, and to my great relief, he agreed. A few days later, I was called into the tent where, after a brief interrogation, if there were no charges against them, everybody was discharged from the *Wehrmacht*.

The Americans were especially suspicious of people who couldn't present their soldier's paybook. At Biessenhofen, almost everyone who had the book and was a soldier in the Army or the *Luftwaffe*, was discharged at once. The American who questioned me wanted to know if the German cross in gold on my passport photo was not the golden Party pin! In good conscience and faith, I answered negatively, and I was certain that he knew that anyway. Then he asked me about my attitude towards Hitler. My answer, that I hadn't yet had time to think about it and that it would probably take too long to do it here and now, seemed to satisfy him. He even responded to my request to give me the pages of my paybook, containing the entries of promotions and awards, rather than throwing them into an almost-full carton . . . and, in this informal manner, thereby put an end to my seventeen years as a soldier.

My years as a professional had left me little time for introspection or reflection. Now, on the precipice of the end of that phase of my life, it occurred to me that soldierly life has two faces: the pompous/pathetic and the mystical/glorious. I had met many officers who wore the first face, but I had also known so many soldiers and officers who treasured the second.

My first experience with that mystical and glorious face of military existence had been as a recruit at Marienburg, in West Prussia, in 1928. On the occasion of the visit of Wilhelm Groener, the Weimar Republic's Minister of Defense, I participated in a *Grosser Zapfenstreich*, or Grand Tattoo. This ceremony is one of the most impressive in a German soldier's life, and is reserved for occasions of great import. To have one conducted in one's personal honor is one of the highest tributes to which one can aspire.

In all garrisons, the *Locken*[46] was played each night to signal soldiers that it was time to return to their barracks. Fifteen minutes later, the tattoo was performed. It was routinely played each night by buglers or staff trumpeters as a signal that all soldiers not on pass or furlough must be in their barracks by the time the last note was played.

The Grand Tattoo, however, was something very different. It is practically impossible for anyone who witnesses, much less participates in, a Grand Tattoo to fail to be profoundly moved. It was played by the regimental band, augmented by kettle drums, fifes, and even carillons, and featured an honor company whose flanking files carried flaming torches.

Each Grand Tattoo began with a crescendo of rolling drums, then the shrill shriek of fifes, which denoted the *Locken*. This was followed by the call to evening prayer, signified by the playing of *Deutschland Über Alles*, the national anthem, which was, after all, originally a hymn by Haydn. Next, a selection of the some of the most stirring German martial tunes were played.

I always liked *Der Fehrbelliner Reitermarsch* the best, and it was nearly always part of the band's repertoire for a Grand Tattoo. This tune combined the very emotive elements of soldierly pride and melancholy sorrow. Count Moltke (the Elder), its creator, must have been a very intuitive and sensitive man to be able to so effectively reflect these fundamental emotions of every soldier's life through the media of rolling drums, skirling fifes, and trumpet fanfares.

Behind the ranks of Prussian grenadiers marched the drummers and buglers, and not just to help them keep in step; they would also signal the beginning of an assault. Many a grenadier was sent headlong into hand-to-hand combat by the electrifying bugle and drum call to "Lower Rifle—Prepare to Attack!"[47] This, too, was part of the Grand Tattoo.

"Gentleman, this is a festive moment," one of my East Prussian aristocrat regimental commanders once orated on the occasion of a Grand Tattoo. "The terms associated with this event, such as 'the oath on the colors', 'a hero's death', 'field of honor', . . . all these may, out of context, sound like empty phrases, but through centuries, they have helped many men in times of strife—and not just on our side—to more easily give their lives for their people and their country." True enough. Yet, in this spring of 1945, there would be no Grand Tattoos conducted in honor of the millions of German soldiers who had given their lives during the last six years. . . .

I received my discharge papers and some money (I think it was eighty *Reichsmarks*), and was allowed to leave the camp. At that time, the Americans generally behaved extremely arrogantly, but I did not encounter any hateful US soldiers in Biessenhofen. Before one could finally leave the camp, everybody received a checkmark of white oil paint on both pant legs. So I stitched a patch of fabric on each leg of my new ski pants and the GI giving out the paint marks placed them right there, in accordance with my wishes.

The purpose of those marks was hard to understand, but maybe the American commander was a rancher at home, and was used to branding cattle before they were let go. After 8 May, our market value to the

Americans was probably not higher than their livestock at home! That only came to an end when, in 1948, the Russians started to make it clear to the Americans that they intended to be the future "King of the Hill."

Before the discharge "ceremony"—a pathetically far cry from a Grand Tattoo—I had bundled up my humble belongings and left the camp as an orderly, released civilian. Outside the barbed wire I took several deep breaths. I survived. I was healthy. I was free. Everything else would fall into place. Never again in my life did I experience independence and freedom as something so beautiful as at that moment.

As a *Zwölfender*, I had extended my military service by some unpleasant years but, as of now, it was finally finished . . . quite differently from anything I could have imagined in 1928!

Epilogue

"Der Jörg wird Schaschke." ("*Georg will be a soldier.*") With this apodictic phrase—words that were probably more simply built on a foundation of the old East Prussian sense of reality—my grandfather described the future path through life of his youngest son. Of course, he was proven to be correct. As we have learned, when he was hardly seventeen years old, this son enlisted in the *Reichswehr* for twelve years: A new "*Zwölfender*" entered this world. That the reader could relive this time from the preceding pages is a credit to my father's abilities as an inspired—and inspiring—raconteur. I gave him much practice, for in my childhood and youth, I was his grateful audience.

He very reliably answered my almost unceasing questions about his own childhood or his experiences as a professional soldier, with an abundant flow of mostly comical, but sometimes also reflective, episodes from his nearly inexhaustible repertoire. He was, by God, *not* one of those ridiculed by Gryphius, the famous poet of the seventeenth century:

> A man in his sixties recently passed;
> He came into the world, ate, drank, slept, and
> died at last.

No, Georg Grossjohann had something to tell. The idea of writing down all his memories was always vaguely floating around his consciousness. Only my mother's persistent encouragement made the deed follow the idea. In retrospect, I am very, very grateful for these writings. Unlike many people's recollections, which are irretrievably lost with death, his will stay alive with us, his family.

I think this is quite significant in our time, which presses forward with ever more restlessness and frenzy; many of us do not often glance back to our forebears for inspiration, or even with due reverence.

My father died in 1992, after the effects of a stroke tied him to a wheelchair for five years and unfortunately almost completely robbed him of his ability to speak. He would forget what happened a few minutes ago, but events and people which affected his life forty or more years before remained forever present. To a medical professional this may be natural, but to me this is proof of how much the confrontation with his own past meant to him. This is not to be taken in the context of narcissistic reflection, but to better comprehend him and others. "Where do I come from? Where do I go?" were not empty musings to him, but living realities.

To publish the story of this "little cog" as part of the huge, historical clockwork, and to make it available to a larger audience, means to keep his memory, as well as that of other ordinary people and soldiers of his generation, alive; it also allows us to give my father that for which he perhaps hoped.

In my opinion, preference for knowledge of the lives of prominent people in study of history has often been a mistake. Testimonies from the so-called plain folk have often been no less informative, but have been allowed to "fall between the cracks." This book will, in that respect, make some small contribution. We have limited ourselves to the events of which my father had personal knowledge, and have avoided most of the great political or strategic issues, although the reader should be aware that Georg Grossjohann had some very strong opinions on those subjects, which may not have been always congruent with those of more senior leaders!

Even so, should the reader come to the conclusion that my father was a militarist, I want to clearly emphasize that he was *not*. There were many things he didn't even like very much about being a soldier. It was simply the case that there were few promising alternatives available for the youngest son of a farm family during times of economic crises like the 1920s. This is what my grandfather was thinking about when he spoke the terse words mentioned above.

For a seventeen-year-old, it was a momentous decision to join the *Reichswehr* and commit oneself for so many years. It consequently limited one's ability to plan for an individual future life. This outlook by itself may have dampened the patriotic enthusiasm of the young defenders of the Fatherland.

One must never expect that a man of such a young age understands all of the potentially bitter implications of what it means to be a soldier, or that one could predict later developments. Young men leave such things to others and first try to make the best of their own difficult situations. When WWII started, my father shared the tepid enthusiasm for the war's prospects that typified the attitude of most German soldiers of his rank and station. The "final-victory" zealots were, in any case, seldom at the front for long, and limited their actions to making the lives of these men as unpleasant as possible.

Since the War, it has become a convenient custom for many to judge the German soldiers of WWII generally as war-mongering aggressors. Look around modern culture, however, and consider: the individual has no chance but to be absorbed by the masses. The recollections contained in this book can help bring into our minds that our soldier forebears were all common people, each with a history of their own, each perhaps equally worthy of relating.

I very much hope that my father has succeeded in telling his.

Andreas Grossjohann, M.A.
Bad Soden-Altenhain
December 1993

Now that you have read the story of Georg Grossjohann and his men during their combat on four fronts during the Second World War, perhaps you would be interested in knowing more about the military origins of the author.

Five Years, Four Fronts is actually only the last part of Georg Grossjohann's military memoirs. In fact, readers will have noticed that this book is seasoned with some flashbacks to the author's earlier years as a soldier in the Reichswehr, the Army of the Weimar Republic. These were taken from the earlier years of the author's German-language memoir of the full seventeen years of his military service to Germany. Aegis is considering translating and publishing this "prequel" to *Five Years, Four Fronts*, and readers who would be interested in procuring this book in the English language should contact the Editor-in-Chief, Aegis Consulting Group, PO Box 629, Bedford, PA 15522.

Appendix A

The Military Curriculum Vitae of Georg Grossjohann

Born in Kagenau, East Prussia (today Kagenovo, Poland) 26 April 1911.

Enlisted in the *Reichswehr* on 1 June 1928.

9th and 10th Companies of Infantry Regiment 3 at Osterode, East Prussia, 1 June 1928–30 April 1931.
> Promoted to *Oberschütze* 1 September 1930.

Regimental signal platoon, Infantry Regiment 3 at Osterode, 1 May 1931–31 March 1933.
> Promoted to *Gefreiter* 1 June 1932.

9th Company, Infantry Regiment 3 at Osterode, 1 April 1933–22 August 1939.
> Promoted to *Obergefreiter* 1 June 1934.
> Promoted to *Unteroffizier* 1 October 1934.
> Promoted to *Feldwebel* 1 May 1937.

Platoon Leader, 1st Company, Field Replacement Battalion 21, 21st Infantry Division, 23 August 1939–29 December 1939. Combat in Polish Campaign.

Platoon Leader, 9th and 12th Company, Infantry Regiment 371, 161st Infantry Division in East Prussia, 29 December 1939–3 February 1940.

Platoon Leader, Regimental Pioneer Platoon, Infantry Regiment 371, 161st Infantry Division, 4 February 1940–10 November 1940. Combat in French Campaign.
> Promoted to *Stabsfeldwebel* 1 June 1940.
> Awarded the Iron Cross, 2d Class, 25 June 1940.
> Designated an *Offizier Anwärter* (Officer Aspirant) 1 August 1940.

Platoon Leader, Regimental Pioneer Platoon, Infantry Regiment 677, 332d Infantry Division, Mecklenburg and Deauville/Normandy, 11 November 1940–14 June 1941.

Commissioned as *Leutnant* 11 November 1940.

Deputy Company Commander, Infantry Regiment 677, 332d Infantry Division, Deauville/Normandy, 15 June 1941–6 October 1941.

Platoon Leader, then Deputy Commander, 7th Company, Grenadier Regiment 308, 198th Infantry Division, 7 October 1941–24 December 1941. Combat in the USSR.
> Promoted to *Oberleutnant* 1 November 1941.

Commander, 7th Company, Grenadier Regiment 308, 198th Infantry Division, 25 December 1941–13 July 1942. Combat in the USSR.
> Iron Cross 1st Class (authorized 14 July 1942)
> Eastern Front Medal (authorized 1 August 1942)
> Wounds Badge in Black (authorized 7 August 1942)

Convalescence, assigned to Infantry Reserve Battalion 56, Vienna, 14 July 1942–15 November 1942.

Deputy Company Commander and Company Commander, Reserve Infantry Battalion 470, Dijon, 16 November 1942–24 September 1943.
> Promoted to *Hauptmann* 1 July 1943.

Commander, 2d Battalion, Grenadier Regiment 308, 198th Infantry Division, 25 September 1943–12 March 1944. Combat in the USSR.
> German Cross in Gold (authorized 4 October 1944)

Special Staff Officer/Directed Duties, Headquarters, 198th Infantry Division and Headquarters, Eighth Army, the USSR and Rumania, 13 March 1944–11 May 1944. Combat in the USSR and liaison duties with Rumanian units.
> Promoted to Major, 1 April 1944.

Commander, 2d Battalion, Grenadier Regiment 308, 198th Infantry Division, from the Mediterranean Coast to the High Vosges Mountains, May 1944–late September 1944. Combat against the Americans.

Commander, Grenadier Regiment 308, 198th Infantry Division, late September 1944–mid-November 1944, in the High Vosges Mountains. Combat against the Americans and the French.
> Wounds Badge in Silver (authorized 8 December 1944)
> Knight's Cross of the Iron Cross (authorized 26 December 1944)

Commander, Provisional Regiment assigned to the 19th Army, and Commander, Grenadier Regiment 490, in the High Vosges and the Belfort Gap, mid-November 1944–late January 1945. Combat against French and French colonial troops.

Attended regimental commanders' course in Germany, March–April 1945.

Entered US Army captivity near Kempten im Allgäu, Germany May 1945.

Some of the fragments of his *Soldbuch* that *Major* Grossjohann managed to retain after his release from American captivity. Among other things, these entries indicate the award of the Iron Cross, 2d and 1st Class, the German Cross in Gold, and the Knight's Cross.

The preliminary certificate for then-*Hauptmann* Grossjohann's German Cross in Gold. The more elaborate certificate that was to follow never caught up to him.

The certificate for *Major* Grossjohann's Wounds Badge in Silver. German military awards were generally cumulative in nature; this one indicates that the silver badge is being awarded for *Major* Grossjohann's third combat wound, suffered while participating in the defense of the Belfort Gap. "Regiments Gruppe Grossjohann" was the provisional unit he commanded under the control of the 269th Infantry Division.

The preliminary certificate for *Major* Grossjohann's Knight's Cross. The formal final document—which was much larger, more ornate, and heavily embossed in gold—did not reach *Major* Grossjohann before war's end.

Major Grossjohann's Knight's Cross of the Iron Cross, presented to him by his corps commander, *Generalleutnant* Erich Abraham, on 28 December 1944.

Appendix B

The Divisions in Which Georg Grossjohann Served During WWII

The actions/activities in which Georg Grossjohann participated are depicted in bold face.

21st Infantry Division

Formed and trained in and around Mohrungen, East Prussia, in 1934–35, from units of the Reichswehr. Participated in the Polish Campaign in 1939, attacking from East Prussia as part of Third Army. The Division seized the fortress at Graudenz, and subsequntly attacked across the Narew River toward Bialystok. During the 1940 campaign in the West, the Division took part in the invasion of Belgium in May, and subsequently participated in the assault river crossing of the Aisne River in France, finishing up the campaign at Châlons-sur-Saone. During Operation BARBAROSSA in 1941, as part of Army Group North, the Division drove through Lithuania and Latvia, later fighting at Novgorod, Chudovo, and Volkov. After distinguishing itself in the withdrawal from Leningrad, the Division was transferred to Army Group Center in East Prussia in the autumn of 1944. It remained with Army Group Center until it was encircled near Heiligenbeil and destroyed in March 1945.

161st Infantry Division

Formed in November 1939 in East Prussia from recruits and a cadre drawn from other divisions. Trained in East Prussia and the Saarland before participating in the invasion of Luxembourg and France in May and June 1940. Transferred to occupied Poland for further training in preparation for the invasion of the USSR. During the initial phases of Operation BARBAROSSA, the Division was assigned to Army Group Center and participated in the some of the most important battles of the 1941–42 campaign, including Smolensk, Kalinin, and Rzhev. The Division was withdrawn in the September 1942 and was rehabilitated while performing coastal defense duties in Normandy. The Division was redeployed to the USSR in September 1943 and assigned to Army Group South. Again, it fought in some of the most momentous battles of the war on the Eastern Front, including Kharkov, Kremenchug, and Krivoi Rog. It took part in the delaying action back toward Moldavia and Rumania, and was encircled and destroyed in Rumania in the early autumn of 1944.

332d Infantry Division

Formed in November of 1940 from recruits and a cadre drawn from other divisions. Trained in Mecklenburg and deployed in April 1941 to the Atlantic coast in Normandy and the Pas de Calais regions. Initially, it prepared for the invasion of Great Britain, but after Operation SEELÖWE (SEALION) was cancelled, the Division remained in coastal France and performed defensive/occupation roles. Transferred to the Eastern Front in February 1943. As part of Army Group South's Second Army, the Division took part in the battle of Gadyach and other defensive operations in the Psel River sector. From March until June, the Division took part in numerous battles, including Trotyanets, Tarasovka, Dorogosch, Krasnyy Kutok, Proletarskiy, Bolshoy Basov, Borisovka, Novo Berezovka, and Graivoron-Krasnopolya. In June of 1943, the Division participated in Operation ZITADELLE (CITADEL) near Sybino-Gertsovka, and subsequently fought delaying and defensive actions near Butovo, Tomarovka, and Borisovka. After being encircled near Belgorod, the Division participated in break-out operations in the vicinity of Bogoduchov. After sustaining enormous casualties, the Division was dissolved in September, 1943, and its remnants were incorporated into the 57th, 112th, and 255th Infantry Divisions.

198th Infantry Division

Formed 1 December 1939 near Prague with two infantry regiments (Grenadier Regiments 305 and 308). With personnel mostly from the states of Baden and Württemberg, these units trained in the Czechoslovak "Protectorate" during early 1940. In early January, they were joined by two other major units, which basically brought the 198th to division strength. The infantry regiment, Landwehr Infantry Regiment 3, consisted of mostly WWI veterans from Baden, but was filled out with younger men (all men over forty-one years old being reassigned) by February 1940. It was soon thereafter redesignated as Grenadier Regiment 326. The artillery regiment, Artillery Regiment 235, was manned by Saxons, formerly of the 223d Infantry Division. Other divisional organizations were quickly added, also manned mostly by Swabians. Training continued throughout the particularly brutal winter of 1940. In March, as the Division prepared for a parade in Prague to mark the second anniversary of the Protectorate, it was suddenly directed to cease drilling and prepare for displacement by rail to northern Germany.

On 8 April 1940, the Division invaded Denmark, and split up to occupy the Danish islands of Sjaelland, Fyn, Lolland, Falster, and Bornholm. A task force centered around 1st/GR 308 was landed by a German merchant vessel and seized the Citadel at Copenhagen by *coup de main*. The rest of the Division seized their geographically diverse objectives under similarly tense, but practically non-violent circumstances. By the second day of operations, all objectives were secure and the operation was completed with total success.

In late May 1940—well after the beginning of the campaign in France and the Low Countries—the Division was transported by rail to the vicinity of Völklingen in the Saarland, just west of Saarbrücken. The Division marched into France on 14 June behind the units of XII Corps which penetrated the Maginot Line south of Forbach. After this, the Division pressed forward to its baptism of fire on 20 June, during the assault crossing of the River Meurthe near Flin. It continued driving south against crumbling

French resistance, and ultimately took part in the encirclement of the better part of a French corps near Rambervillers. The Division continued on to Vesoul before the armistice went into effect on 25 June. This victory in France was followed by occupation duty in the Vosges Mountains, as well as civic action to move civilians who had been evacuated from Alsace back to their homes.

The Division was transported to Rumania in April 1941, and attacked into Soviet Bessarabia as part of Army Group South in late June. Here, in some areas, the fighting initially took the form of something of a "liberation," given the large numbers of ethnic Germans (Danube Swabians, or *Donauschwaben*) who resided in this formerly Rumanian province. Penetrating the "Stalin Line," the Division next took part in the battles of Krivoi Rog, Dnepropetrovsk, and **Pavlograd. After this heavy fighting, the Division moved to the Mius River near Yanovka, and engaged in a series of offensive and defensive missions throughout the winter, spring, and early summer. In mid-July, the Division broke out of the "Mius Bridgehead,"** and attacked across the Don River.

Throughout the remainder of the summer of 1942, the 198th Infantry Division fought a series of battles as it attacked ever more deeply into the Caucasus Mountains. On 6 September, the Commanding General of the 198th , *Generalmajor* Albert Buck, was killed along with his Ia, *Major* Buhl, and his driver in a Russian ambush in the Chrebet Ingayav Mountains. Further attacks in the western Caucasus alternated with brief defensive and retrograde operations throughout the autumn, as the Seventeenth Army (to which the Division was assigned) drove toward the Turkish border.

The great strategic penetration which would have allowed the Germans to not only control the Caucasus oilfields, but also to threaten the rear of the Allied forces in North Africa, never came to be, as the 198th began its long withdrawal from the Caucasus in December 1942. After conducting a fighting withdrawal to the Crimea, the 198th was pulled out of the line for rest, rehabilitation, and reconstitution in the vicinity of Zaporozhe from early April to early May 1943. After sharp offensive action near Lyubitski and Shebelinka, the Division took part in the great, multi-army group offensive, Operation ZITADELLE ("CITADEL"), which resulted in nearly complete defeat for the last concentration of German forces capable of launching a strategic offensive in the East.

In the late summer of 1943, the Division fought a series of defensive and retrograde actions between positions on the Donets and Dniepr Rivers, including the battles of Kharkov and Krementchug. **By late August, the 198th was desperately defending the Dniepr River line**.

From September through January, the Division took part in back-and-forth fighting in and around Fastov and Byelaya Zerkov. Further withdrawals ultimately resulted, and the German XI and XLII Corps were encircled near Cherkassy; as part of the III Panzer Corps' attempt to relieve the resultant pocket in mid-February, the 198th attacked briskly but ultimately to no avail. Only about 20,000 to 25,000 German soldiers (and practically no vehicles) eventually broke out of the Cherkassy pocket, and it had been at great expense to the forces trying to break through to them as well. The Division suffered severe casualties in this battle, and was almost immediately thrown into further desperate defensive combat near Risino. Shortly afterwards, much of the Division was cut off itself near Uman, and the elements which escaped were only a shadow of a division. By late March, the remnants of the Division was slated for transfer to southern France for reconstitution, and in April, the Division left the Eastern Front for good.

In the late spring and summer of 1944, the 198th Infantry Division was rebuilt and trained in areas along the southern coast of France between Perpignan and Narbonne, as part of Army Group G. It was present in its defensive positions when the Allies landed in August and, after brief defensive combat along the Mediterranean coast, the Division began the long and dangerous withdrawal up the Rhône River Valley. After a narrow escape from the American pursuit at Montélimar in late August, the 198th withdrew to the foothills of the Vosges Mountains and defended against the assaults of American *Seventh Army* and French *First Army* forces near Le Thillot and Gérardmer through most of the autumn. As the Division was shifted about in the Nineteenth Army lines, it subsequently fought mostly French colonial forces near Dammerkirch (Dannemarie), between Belfort and Mulhouse.

Throughout December, the Division helped shore up the Nineteenth Army's defenses in the "Colmar Pocket." In early January, in consonance with Panzer Brigade 106 "Feldherrnhalle," the Division was shifted to the north of the Pocket to participate in Operation SONNENWENDE ("SOLSTICE), an offensive intended to link up with the southward-attacking forces of Army Group G (Operation NORDWIND). The offensive failed, and the 198th spent the remainder of January defending a slim slice of territory on the west bank of the Rhine, around Benfeld and Erstein.

Despite a major effort by the French and Americans to wipe out the Colmar Pocket in late January and early February, the Division escaped across the Rhine. After defending in sector near Kehl, it was shuttled into new defensive positions in the Palatinate, in an attempt to stem the US *Seventh Army*'s mid-March offensive, Operation UNDERTONE.   The remnants of the Division then gradually conducted delaying actions back into what was, for some of the remaining veterans, their Swabian homeland. Battles against the advancing U*S VI Corps* near Heilbronn and Backnang were followed by an ultimate retreat to the area southwest of Ulm where, at the end of April, the Division dissolved.

Notes

1. In the German military parlance of the period, "X-Hour" and "X-Day" correspond to the Allied expressions "H-Hour" and "D-Day," or the hour or day on which a planned operation would commence.
2. The Ia was the operations officer, closely equivalent to a US Army G-3.
3. Editor's Note: Actually, while the lack of Polish aerial resistance surely seemed to indicate the effectiveness of *Luftwaffe* strikes to *Landsers* like Grossjohann and his men, the aircraft of Polish Air Force had been well dispersed. The *Luftwaffe*'s strikes of the first two days largely hit little of consequence, and the Polish Air Force continued to operate until about 16 September.
4. As cadre for the 161st Infantry Division.
5. From 1920 to 1926, *Generaloberst* Hans von Seeckt was the Chief of the *Truppenamt*, the shadow equivalent of the Great General Staff, which had been specifically forbidden to exist by the provisions of the Versailles Treaty.
6. *Editor's note:* In the terminology of the Maginot Line, there were two types of major fortifications, namely *petite* and *gros ouvrages*; in this text, the basic English equivalents of "Fort" and "Fortress" will correspond, respectively, to differentiate between the two.
7. "Der Slavin Reiz ist unerreicht!"
8. The "German Greeting" included the right arm extended at an upward angle from the body, fingers extended and joined.
9. This unusual spelling of England refers to the lyrics of a song that was popular at the time:
   > Heute wollen wir ein Liedlein singen,
   > Trinken wollen wir den kühlen Wein
   > Und die Gläser sollen da zu klingen,
   > Denn es muß geschieden sein.
   > Wir fahren gegen Engeland!
10. Armed Forces High Command, in Berlin.
11. The tank brigades were in the process of being reorganized into actual armored divisions when the Germans struck.
12. *Translator's Note:* "*Landsers*" is an expression for "Infantrymen."
13. The *Volksempfänger* was a simple radio used commonly by civilians in Germany. The government strongly suggested that no household was complete without one . . . the better to be informed by *Herr* Goebbels and his minions! Like the *Volkswagen*, it was a basic commodity which all German households were supposed to have.
14. I took these entries from an article by G. Graser in the magazine *Alte Kameraden*.
15. Graser, *Zwischen Kattegat und Kaukasus*, 159.

16. The Tin Soldier, or *Der Standhafte Zinnsoldat,* is a fairy-tale figure which was unflinchingly loyal and correct.

17. *Translator's Note:* An *Armleuchter* is a lamp attached to an arm or brace, but it is also a euphemism for *Arschloch* or "asshole."

18. *Translator's note:* "The dice have been cast."

19. *Editor's Note:* Decoration of commanders about to be relieved—or after they were relieved—was a fairly common practice by this stage of the war in the German Army. Later, in this very same sector of the Eastern Front, Generals von Manstein and von Kleist received the Swords to their Knight's Crosses with Oak Leaves from Hitler just before he sacked them. This sort of action was apparently intended to soften the blow to the individual officers concerned, and perhaps to the Army officer corps in general, with whom Hitler's relations were increasingly strained. This ironic practice not only detracted from the prestige of some of the higher German valor awards, but also induced anxiety in many officers who won them . . . once one was notified of winning the next highest award, could relief from command be far behind?

20. G. Graser, *Vom Kattegat zum Kankasus,* 283.

21. A German Army light vehicle, very similar to the Volkswagen "Thing" of the 1970s.

22. *Oberst* Paul Keiser, Commander of Grenadier Regiment 326, quoted in Graser, *Vom Kattegat zum Kankasus,* 285.

23. *Translator's Note: Hiwis* are Russian auxilliaries.

24. *Editor's Note:* Hermann Bernhard Ramcke eventually did indeed stand and fight at Brest. On 19 September 1944, after a thirty-nine-day siege by the US Army's VIII Corps, he surrendered to Colonel Chester Hirschfelder and Major William Kernan of the 9th Infantry Regiment. Altogether, Ramcke lost 38,000 men to the Americans in the process.

25. *Translator's Note: "Kettenhunde,"* so called because of the large metal gorgets suspended on a thick chain around the necks of the military police. These gorgets were emblazoned with *Feldgendarmerie* in iridescent letters, the better to recognize their authority, even at night.

26. *Editor's Note:* On 7 March 1945, Task Force Engeman, an advanced element of the US Army's 9th Armored Division, crossed the bridge and established the first Allied bridgehead across the Rhine. Within twenty-four hours, over 8,000 American combat troops and sixty tanks and tank destroyers crossed; eventually, the better part of two American corps made it over the Rhine thanks to the failure of Major Scheller's efforts.

27. A broad red stripe denoted a general officer; a narrower red stripe identified an officer *im Generalstab,* or a graduate of the Staff College.

28. Occupied Czechoslovakia.

29. Orginally, the "Blood Order" was a medal awarded only to those few hundred early members of the National Socialist German Worker's Party (Nazis) who marched with Hitler in the unscuccessful *Putsch* in Munich in 1923. (Gümbel was one of them.) Later, however, it was awarded to several

thousand others whom Hitler believed to have made some particularly highly significant contribution to the Nazi political cause.

30. From an unspecified official American operations report, quoted in Graser, *Vom Kattegat zum Kaukasus*, 312.

31. *Translator's Note: Jabos* was short for *Jagdbombers*, or fighter bombers, such as the American P-51 "Mustang" or Republic P-47 "Thunderbolt."

32. *Editor's Note:* Perhaps because the thought never crossed the author's mind, he may have failed to consider two other possible explanations for the Americans' lack of enthusiasm for release. They may have suspected a cruel ruse when offered the "chance" to run away—"shot while attempting to escape" is an explanation as old as firearms, and one which was only too common on both sides during WWII. Alternatively, the captive officers may have perceived the author's offer to include an assumption of their "parole," or a promise to not engage in further belligerent activity—an option not open to US officers since its specific abolition following the Civil War. Then again, they may have simply been lazy or even cowardly, as the author clearly implies.

33. Generalmajor Otto Richter and his staff were captured by elements of the *3d Battalion, 143d Infantry Regiment*, a federalized Texas National Guard unit, commanded by Lieutenant Colonel (later Brigadier General) Theodore H. Andrews. For this and other exceptional combat accomplishments during the period 26–29 August 1944—including the capture of more than six hundred German prisoners—the battalion was awarded the United States Presidential Unit Citation.

34. *Editor's Note:* For perspective, it should be remembered that in Germany at the time, a sexual liaison with a "racial inferior," such as a Pole or a Russian, was punishable by imprisonment for the woman, and death for the man.

35. *Editor's Note:* The *panzerfaust* was a rocket-propelled antitank grenade launcher. There were at least five different variants produced during the war, with effective ranges between 30 and 250 meters. The armor penetration capability of the various models' shaped charge warheads ranged from 140mm (5.5 inches) to 220mm (8.7 inches), all of which were more than capable of knocking out any American tank then available.

36. *Flak* was an abbreviation for *Flieger-abwehr-kanone*, or antiaircraft gun. Assault guns were antitank guns or artillery pieces mounted on tank chassis, without a turret—this made them cheaper to produce, and sometimes enabled the emplacement of a larger gun than might otherwise have been possible.

37. Graser, *Vom Kattegat zum Kaukasus*, 321.

38. Ibid., 322.

39. The battle to rescue the "Lost Battalion" of the US *36th Infantry Division (1st Battalion, 141st Infantry Regiment)* near Biffontaine is covered extensively in Orville Shirey, *Americans: The Story of the 442d Combat Team* (Washington, DC: Infantry Journal Press, 1946); Vincent Lockhart, *T-Patch to Victory: The 36th "Texas" Division in France, Germany, and Austria* (Canyon, TX: Staked Plains Press, 1981); and, most recently, in Franz

Steidl, *Lost Battalions: Going for Broke in the Vosges, Autumn 1944* (Novato, CA: Presidio, 1997). The *442d Regimental Combat Team*—a combined arms unit built around the *442d Infantry Regiment*—was composed almost exclusively of Japanese-American enlisted men, led largely by white American officers. During this phase of the war, they were attached to the US *36th Infantry Division*, which was originally a National Guard unit from Texas. (Although many "honorary" Texans from every state of the Union were serving in the *36th* as replacements by this stage of the war.) As Georg Grossjohann noted, the "Four Four Deuce" sustained heavy casualties in this battle and, in fact, had been taking heavy casualties since the attack on Bruyères had begun in mid-October. Fighting hard to prove themselves as worthy Americans, the men of the *442d* eventually garnered more individual awards for valor than any other American regiment in World War II.

40. The officer who did take command of Füsilier Battalion 198, *Oberleutnant* Huth, was killed on 27 December 1944.

41. Graser, *Vom Kattegat zum Kaukasus*, 328.

42. The *Panzerjäger V "Jagdpanther"* was a truly formidable machine. Built on the chassis of the fast and proven *Panther* tank, it mounted an 88mm high-velocity gun which outranged almost anything in the Allied inventory in the autumn of 1944—it certainly grossly outgunned the French Shermans. While the *Jagdpanther* had no turret—its gun was mounted directly in the well-sloped glacis plate of the vehicle—it was extremely well armored, and could withstand a hit from Allied guns at extremely close range.

43. *Editor's Note:* At full strength, a German infantry regiment would have 2,000–3,250 men, depending on the type of unit.

44. Letter from a National Socialist Guidance Officer—endorsed by von Rundstedt—who had been sent by Hitler to find out about the battles in the Vosges, quoted by Percy Schramm (ed.) in *Kriegstagebuch des Oberkommandos der Wehrmacht (Wehrmachtführungstab) 1 Januar 1944–22 Mai 1945, Band 4/1. Halbband* (Bonn: Bernhard & Graefe Verlag, 1961/64), 30.

45. *Translator's Note: Ohne Pauken und Trompeten* = "Without Drumroll and Fanfare."

46. *Translator's Note: Locken* = "Call to Quarters."

47. *Translator's Note: "Zum Sturm fällt das Gewehr!"*

Editor's Annotated Bibliography

Bernage, Georges, François de Lannoy, et al. *Bataille d'Alsace, 1944–45.* Bayeux, France: Editions Heimdal, 1992. One of the best sources for factual information about the fighting in the High Vosges in the autumn and winter of 1944–45.

Bonn, Keith E. *When the Odds Were Even: The Vosges Mountains Campaign, October 1944–January 1945.* Novato, CA: Presidio, 1994. An operational study of the fighting between the US Seventh Army and the elements of German Army Group G during the period specified in the title.

Bruge, Roger. *On a Livré la Ligne Maginot.* Paris: Fayard, 1984. Indispensible for learning about the little-known fighting in the Maginot Line during the 1940 campaign in France.

Clarke, Jeffrey J., and Robert Ross Smith. *Riviera to the Rhine.* Washington, DC: Center of Military History, US Army, 1993. An excellent reference for understanding the US Seventh Army's operations from the invasion of southern France through the reduction of the Colmar Pocket in February 1945.

Cooper, Matthew. *The German Army, 1933–1945.* Chelsea, MI: Scarborough House, 1990. Exceptional overview of the German Army's operations, administration, and organizational challenges throughout the Second World War.

Fellgiebel, Walther-Peer. *Die Träger des Ritterkreuzes, 1939–1945.* Wolfersheim-Berstadt, Germany: Podzun-Pallas, 1993. Definitive source on the soldiers who were awarded the Knight's Cross.

Graser, Gerhard. *Zwischen Kattegat und Kaukasus: Weg und Kämpfe der 198. Infanterie-Division.* Tübingen, Germany: Kameradenhilfwerk und Traditionsverband der ehemaligen 198. Infanterie-Division, 1961. The highly detailed account of the fighting of the 198th Infantry Division during WWII.

Griess, Thomas E., ed. *The Second World War: Europe and the Mediterranean.* Originally published by the Department of History, USMA, West Point, NY, and reprinted by the Avery Publishing Group, Wayne, NJ, 1989. Provides an excellent, large-scale perspective on the fighting on the Eastern Front during WWII.

Madej, W. Victor. *German Army Order of Battle: Field Army and Officer Corps, 1939–1945.* Allentown, PA: Game Publishing, 1985. Like its companion volume below, a compendium of factual information gained directly from sources in the US National Archives. Provides an especially useful guide to division-level units and individual general officers' wartime service.

_____. *Hitler's Elite Guards: Waffen SS, Parachutists, U-Boats.* Allentown, PA: Game Publishing, 1985.

Schmitz, Peter, and Klaus-Jürgen Thies. *Die Truppenkennzeichen der Verbände und Einheiten der deutschen Wehrmacht und Waffen-SS und ihre Einsätze im Zweiten Weltkrieg, 1939–1945.* Osnabrück, Germany: Biblio Verlag, 1987. Provides not only sketches of the insignia of each German unit in the category indicated in the title, but also excellent summaries of each division's wartime operations.

Truscott, Lucian K., Jr. *Command Missions.* New York: E. P. Dutton, 1954. Includes an important account of operations in southern France in August and September 1944 by the officer who commanded the American corps that conducted them.

US War Department. TM-E 30-451, *Handbook on German Military Forces.* Washington, DC: Government Printing Office, 1945. Essential work for understanding German organizations, weapons, tactics, techniques, and procedures during WWII.

Index

Abraham, *Generalleutnant* Erich 112, 156
Agay 95
Ahr River/Ahr River Valley 10, *11, 18,
    28,* 31
Ahrweiler 11
Aix-en-Provence *98,* 118, *120*
Alps, Maritime 95, *98, 118, 120*
von Amsberg, *Oberstleutnant* 157,
    161, 162
Angelberger, *Oberleutnant* Dr. 47
Angers *19, 34,* 38, *39*
Arles *98,* 118, *120*
von Arnim, *Generalmajor* Friedemund 29
Arys *4, 12,* 13, 96
Aubert, *Capitaine* Daniel 17, 23
Auxerre 59, 65, 163
Avignon *98, 118, 120*

Bad Mondorf 17
Bad Neuenahr 10, *11,* 12, *18*
Barde, *Generalmajor* Konrad 161
Belfort *19,* 131, 147, *148, 150*
Belfort Gap 144, 149, 152
Betzgau 168
Bialystok *4,* 9, *12*
von Bock, *Generaloberst* Fedor 2, 9, 15,
    37, 50
Bonlieu 120
Braun, *Leutnant* Christian 122, 124, 162
Brebotte 147, *148*
Breslau *4, 28,* 100, *172*
Buck, *Generalmajor* Albert 14
Bug, River *80,* 84
Bussang Pass *134,* 137, *150*
Bussang Tunnel 137, 146
Byelaya Zerkov 67, 68, 96

Canet-Plage 97, 108
Chemeriskoye *75,* 79, 96
Cherkassy *67,* 73, 74, 77, 78
Chishintzy *69, 75, 76,* 77
Corcieux *142,* 143
Côte d'Azur 95
Crest *98, 118, 120,* 121, *123*

Danzig 2, *4, 12, 28,* 128, 164, 169, *172*
Davidovka *46, 52,* 53
Deauville *19,* 33, *34,* 35, *39,* 65
Dijon *19,* 57, 59, 126, 163
Dniepr River 62, 65-66, *67,* 68, 77

Draguignan *98,* 115, *118, 120*
Dresden *28,* 92
Drôme River *98, 118,* 119, *120,* 121, *123,*
    124–25
Durance River *98, 118,* 119, *120*

Esch *11,* 17, *18*

Fastov *67,* 68
Fermont, Fortress 17, 20, *22,* 23
*FFI (Forces françaises de
    l'intèrieurs)* 117
Finckh, *Oberst* Eberhardt 101
Freiburg-im-Breisgau 160–61

Galatz 89
Gérardmer 129, *134, 142*
Götz von Berlichingen 59
Grand Tattoo (*Grosser Zapfenstreich*)
    173–75
Graudenz *4,* 5, 8, *12*
Gribovka 45, *46,* 47, 51–53, 56
Groener, Wilhelm 173
Grosjean, M. (Wartime Mayor of Le
    Thillot) 139–40
Gümbel, *Oberst* Ludwig 66, 101, 104–5,
    109–10, 133, 136

Hartmannsweiler Kopf 113, *150,* 156, 161
Heinrici, *Generaloberst* Gotthard 112, 161
Himmler, *Reichsführer* Heinrich 99, 112,
    139, 144, 147, 151, 154, 156–58,
    161, 165
Hiwis 81
Hohneck *150,* 151–52, 154–55
von Horn, *Generalleutnant* Hans-Joachim
    83, 99–100, 107, 149
Hunsrück Mountains 17

Jagdpanthers (Jagdpanzer V tank
    destroyers) 149
Jutersonke, *Leutnant* 51, 53

Kagenau *4, 12*
Kaufbeuren 171, *172*
Keiser, *Oberst* Paul 79, 107, 146
Kempten-im-Allgäu 168, 171, *172*
Kiev *44, 67,* 68, *91*
Kirovograd 40, *44, 91*
Kissel, *Generalmajor* Hans 28, 122

Köck, *Hauptmann* 155–56
Königsberg *4*, *12*, 161
Konrad, *General der Gebirgstruppen*
 Rudolf 47
Kremenchug 65
von Küchler, *General der Artillerie* Georg
 2, 3, 5, 15

La Coucourd *123*, 125
von Larisch, *Generalmajor* Heribert 166
Lartigau, *Capitaine* 154
Leitner, *Oberleutnant* 54
Le Mans *19*, *34*, 38, *39*
Le Thillot 130, *134*, 135–41, *142*, 146–47,
 149, *150*, 154
Lissyanka *75*, *76*, 77
Lomsha *4*, 9, *12*
Loire River/Loire River Valley *34*, 38, *39*
Ludwigslust *28*–29, 33, 65, 157, 161–62
Luka 68, *69*, 74, 96, 106
Luxembourg 15
Luxembourg City *11*, 17, *18*, *19*

Maginot Line 5, *11*, 12–14, 16–17, *18*,
 19–20, 22, 121, 150
Majer, *Major* Dr. 72, 96, 97, 127, 133
von Manstein, *General der Infanterie*
 Fritz-Erich 61, 77, 92
Marienburg (West Prussia) 173
Marienwerder *4*, 8, *12*, 64
Marseilles 95, *98*, 115–16, 118–19, *120*,
 122, 131
Mecklenburg *28*, 29, 31–32
Ménil Pass (*Col du Ménil*) *134*, 137,
 138, *142*
Mius River 45, *46*, 49, 51, *52*, 53, 55, 92,
 102–3
Mohrungen 5, *12*
Montélimar *98*, *118*, 119, *120*, 121–22,
 123, 124, 128
Moselle River/Moselle River Valley *11*, 17,
 18, *19*, *28*, 128
Müller, *Generalmajor* Ludwig 100
Müller-Melahn, *Oberst* Erich 162

Narbonne 96, *98*, 100, *118*, *120*
Narev River *4*, 9, *12*
Newiger, *Generalmajor* Albert 26–27,
 29–30, 32–33, 45, 97, 162
Nice 94–95, *98*, 116, *118*, *120*

Oktyabr *69*, *75*, 77
Operation SEALION 24, 35

Operation ZITADELLE (CITADEL) 61
von Oppen, *Generalmajor* Rudolf 147, 156
Osterode 5–7, *12*, 57
Ostrolenka *4*, 9, *12*

Panthers (*Panzerkampfwagen V*
 tanks) 74
Paris 11, 15–16, *19*, *34*, 38, *39*, 65, 95, 99
Pas de Calais *19*, *34*, *39*, 94
Patton, General George S., Jr. 153, 168
Pelakeyevka 45, *46*, *52*
Perpignan 97, *98*, 99, 108, *118*, *120*
Pervomaisk *80*, 84
Petersen, *General der Fliegertruppen*
 Erich 139, 141, 146
Port-Bou (Spain) 97, 98, *118*, *120*
Pruth River 89–90, 97

von Quirnheim, *Oberst* Mertz 101

Raeder, *Grossadmiral* Erich 35
le Rainkopf 151
Ramcke, *Generalleutnant* Hermann
 Bernhard 84
Ramonchamp 133, *134*, 135, 137, *142*
Rasp, *General der Infanterie* Siegfried
 156–57
Reiff, *Feldwebel* 41
Repki *69*, 71–72, *75*, *76*
Rhine River/Rhine River Valley *11*, *18*, 132,
 147, *148*, 150, 156, 159, 161–62, 164
Rhine-Rhône Canal 147, *148*
Rhône River/Rhône River Valley 94–95, 97,
 98, 104, 110, 115–19, *120*, 121–22,
 124–26
Richter, *Generalmajor* Otto 99–100, 125
Risino 74, *75*, *80*
Rittmannsberger, *Oberleutnant* Dr. 54,
 65–66
Roettig, *Generalmajor* Otto 99
Roman (Rumanian city) *44*, 90 , *91*
Rommel, *Generalfeldmarschall* Erwin 25,
 94, 121, 140–41
Roubion River 120, *123*
Rouen *19*, 38
Rydz-Smigly, Marshal Edward 8

Savran *80*, 84
Schiel, *Generalmajor* Otto 111, 126,
 146, 161
Schlaga-Krug 13
Schlucht Pass *134*, *142*, 144, 146–47, *150*,
 156, 161

Schultz, *Generalmajor* Paul 41, 66, 103, 146
Schwerin *28*, 32
Sète *98*, 117, *118*, *120*
Sickerle, *Oberfeldwebel* 45
von Stauffenberg, *Oberst* Claus *Graf* 101
"Susi" 81–82, 107
Suwalki *4*, *12*, 26, 28

Tichonovka 74, *76*, 94
Toulon *98*, 101, 115–16, 118, *120*, 122
Tours *19*, *34*, 38, *39*
Triberg 139–40, 151
Trier *11*, 17, *18*, *19*, *28*
Trouville-sur-Mer *19*, *34*, 35, *39*

Uman 68, 78–79, *80*, 81–82, 96, 163

Vienna 56–57, 92, *172*
Vinnitza *67*, 68
Vinograd *67*, 74, *75*, *76*, *80*
Vosges Mountains 81, 104, 112, 116, 119, 129, 131–33, *134*, 139, *142*, 144–45, 147, *148*, 150–54, 156–57, 159
Votylevka *69*, 70–72, *75*, *76*, 79, 96

Wagener, *Generalmajor* Karl 92
Warsaw 2, *4*, *12*, *44*, *91*, *150*
Weber, Christian 167
Wiese, *General der Infanterie* Friedrich 94, 111, 146, 157
Wöhler, *General der Infanterie* Otto 90

Yablonovka 74, *75*, *76*

Zhitomir *67*, 68
Zhubenny Stav 74, *75*, *76*
Zinten *4*, *12*, 13, 23
Zoppot *4*, *12*, 92

Allied
   1st Allied Airborne Task Force 118, 120

French Army Units
Corps
   II 120
Divisions, Infantry
   1st Free French 148, 150
   2d Moroccan 148, 150
   3d Algerian 130, 134, 142, 150, 152, 154
   9th Colonial Division 147, 148, 150

Divisions, Armored
   1st 147, *148*, *150*
   5th 148, 150
Regiments, Infantry
   4th Regiment of Tunisian Tirailleurs 154

German Units
Army Groups
   A 15, *19*, *21*, 50–51, 53, *91*
   B 15, *19*, 50–51, 55–56, 94, 119, 131, 152–53, 159, 164
   C *19*, *21*
   G 94–95, 119, 131–32, 137, 153, 159, 164–66
   Center *44*, *91*
   North 2, *4*, 9, 37, *44*, 50, 78, *91*
   Oberrhein 112, 139, 144, 158, 161
   South 2, *4*, 37–38, 40, *44*, 50, 61–62, 73, 78, *91*, 92–93, 165
   Vistula 161
Field Armies
   First *21*
   Third 3, *4*, 5
   Fourth 4
   Sixth 15, 55–56, 92–93, 97
   Eighth *4*, 89–90, 97
   Tenth *4*, 5
   Fourteenth *4*
   Sixteenth *21*
   Eighteenth *19*
   Nineteenth 94, *98*, 116, *118*, 119, *120*, 122, 131, 137–39, 144, 146–47, 150, 152, 154, 156–59, 161
Corps
   III Panzer 74–75, *76*
   IV Luftwaffe Field 137, 139, 141, *150*
   XLII 73
   XLVIII Panzer 68
   XLIX Mountain *46*, 47, *52*
   LXIII 112, *150*, 151, 156
   XC *150*
Divisions, Infantry
   21st 3, *4*, 5, 10, 186
   30th SS *148*
   34th *69*, 70–71, 83
   78th 157
   88th *69*, 70, 74, *75*
   148th *98*, *118*, *120*
   159th *148*
   161st 10, 12–13, 17–18, *21*, 26–28, 187
   189th *98*, *118*, *120*, *150*

198th 38, 40, *46*, 49–50, *52*, 55–56, 62, 65, *67*, 68, *69*, 70, 74, *75*, 78–79, *80*, 89–90, 95, 97, *98*, 99, 105, 107, 110, 116, *118*, 119–20, *123*, 133, *134*, 141, *142*, *148*, 149, *150*, 159, 162, 188–90
215th *21*
242d *98*, *118*, *120*
244th *98*, *118*, *120*
269th 139, *150*, 151
332d 29, 32, 33
335th 157
338th 95, *98*, 116, *118*, *120*, *134*, 136–37, *148*
716th *98*, *118*, *120*
Divisions, Mountain
    4th *46*, *52*, 83
    157th *98*, *118*, *120*
Divisions, Panzer
    2d SS "Das Reich" 68, 164
    11th 96, *98*, 116, *118*, 119, 120, 122, *123*
Divisions, Volks-Grenadier
    16th *142*, *150*
    338th *150*
    716th *142*
Kampfgruppen (Combat Groups)
    Hafner *150*
    Keiser *80*
Regiments, Artillery
    235 72
Regiments, Infantry
    3 3
    305 *46*, *52*, *69*, *75*, *76*, *80*, 119–20, 189
    308 40–41, 45, *46*, 51–53, 66–67, *69*, 72, 74, *75*, *76*, *80*, 102–3, 105, 108, 110, 119, 129, 132, *134*, 137–38, *142*, 145, 149, 189
    326 *69*, 74, *75*, *76*, 79, *80*, 119–20, 125, 144, 189
    371 12, 18, 20, 23, 29
    490 147, *148*, 149
    677 29
Training Units
    Field Replacement Battalion 21 5
    Reserve Grenadier Battalion 470 57

Italian Army Units
Infantry Divisions
    Celere 50, *52*, 53

Polish Army
Field Armies
    Carpathian 4
    Cracow 4
    Lodz 4
    Modlin 4
    Pomorze 4
    Poznan 4
Corps
    Group Narev 4

Soviet Army Units
Fronts (Army Groups)
    First Baltic 91
    Second Baltic 91
    First Belorussian 91
    Second Belorussian 91
    Third Belorussian 91
    First Ukrainian 91
    Second Ukrainian 91
    Third Ukrainian 91
    Fourth Ukrainian 91
    Leningrad 91
Armies
    5th Guards Tank 69
Regiments, Rifle
    197th 47
    694th 51

US Army Units
Army Groups
    Sixth 131, 152
Field Armies
    Third 131, 153, 168
    Seventh 60, 131, 142, 150, 153
Corps
    VI 115–16, 131, 144, 152, 154
    XV 144
Divisions, Infantry
    3d *118*, 119, *120*, *123*, *134*, *142*, 144, *150*, 159
    36th *118*, *120*, *123*, 129, *142*
    45th *118*, *120*, *123*
Task Forces
    Butler *120*, *123*
Regiments, Infantry
    141st 120–21
    142d 120
    442d 143